GW00499938

FRE
LOVE
OF GOD

Wise Sayings from Marcel

Christian Marcel

ISBN 978-1-63814-109-9 (Paperback)
ISBN 978-1-63814-110-5 (Digital)

Copyright © 2021 Christian Marcel
All rights reserved
First Edition

All rights reserved. No part of this publication may be reproduced, distributed, or transmitted in any form or by any means, including photocopying, recording, or other electronic or mechanical methods without the prior written permission of the publisher. For permission requests, solicit the publisher via the address below.

Covenant Books, Inc.
11661 Hwy 707
Murrells Inlet, SC 29576
www.covenantbooks.com

Contents

Preface

My claims are based upon reasonable results relative to our day/age. We cannot live a past historical life (Romans 15:4) nor the lifestyles of those lived before. God has blessed us in our generation from which we live according to his grace and mercy, in which he has established peace in our minds. The love of the Word of God has not lost its savor but extended our grace in him, for God has given us better understanding to serve man in our commonality.

This is our understanding of his Word—not to subtract or add from it but to reason within our mind by what is said by him. Jesus is the author of his Word—directed from heaven, given to his holy people.

Acknowledge God

> The breath of our nostrils, the anointed of
> the LORD, was taken in their pits, of whom we
> said, under his shadow we shall live among the
> heathen. (Lamentations 4:20)

It will not be very long that those who fight against themselves will fight God's anointed (Psalm 2:1–3).

But God will laugh because he sees and knows all things concerning his earth.

> Nothing in all creation is hidden from
> God's sight. Everything is uncovered and laid
> bare before the eyes of him to whom we must
> give account. (Hebrews 4:13)

When a generation fails to acknowledge God in sincerity and prayers, well, you are in trouble.

Life is not a platform for playing around and forgetting God or not acknowledging his presence both in worship and in prayers (Revelation 4:11).

> Cut off your hair and throw it away; take up
> a lament on the barren heights, for the LORD
> has rejected and abandoned this generation that
> is under his wrath. (Jeremiah 7:29)

Angels Rejoice

Every time you serve God, your Creator, the angels in heaven shout with joy, over one sinner who repents—just one sinner.

Can you grasp that? One sinner who gives himself over to God (Romans 8:1).

> Jesus said, "I tell you, there is rejoicing in the presence of the angels of God over one sinner who repents." (Luke 15:10)

> I tell you that in the same way there will be more rejoicing in heaven over one sinner who repents than over ninety-nine righteous persons who do not need to repent. (Luke 15:7)

Does this mean that angels are partial? No, we all rejoice in the presence of God daily.

> Rejoice in the Lord always. I will say it again: Rejoice! (Philippians 4:4)

The Bible says, "Everyone who calls on the name of the Lord will be saved" (Romans 10:13).

> Solomon said, "I was a skilled craftsman at His side, and His delight day by day, rejoicing always in His presence."

I was rejoicing in His whole world, delighting together in the sons of men. (Proverbs 8:30–31)

My friends, stay saved (Romans 10:17).

Anxiety

Anxiety in a man's heart weighs him down, but a good word makes him glad. (Proverbs 12:25)

Cast all your anxiety on him because he cares for you. (1 Peter 5:7)

Do not be anxious about anything, but in everything by prayer and supplication with thanksgiving let your requests be made known to God. (Philippians 4:6–7)

Armor of God

Do not let others take your Christian beliefs, behaviors, and practices for weakness.

Some who know that you are a Christian may impose their strength against you and think you are too weak to fight; let them know how weak they are, by being strong enough, but not too critical.

Protect your integrity.

Keep on your whole armor of God.

Stand up, defend yourselves.

Listen to your Bible.

> Stand firm then, with the belt of truth buckled around your waist, with the breastplate of righteousness in place, and with your feet fitted with the readiness that comes from the gospel of peace. In addition to all this, take up the shield of faith, with which you can extinguish all the flaming arrows of the evil one. Take the helmet of salvation and the sword of the Spirit, which is the word of God. And pray in the Spirit on all occasions with all kinds of prayers and requests. With this in mind, be alert and always keep on praying for all the Lord's people. (Ephesians 6:14–18)

Now go back and read verses 10–13.

Salvation is in the army of the Lord.

It's not about what you feel that you think you're right about, but after you receive the Word, steadfastness fills with emotions, an excitement without being tempestuous.

We march together with God, a victory to win.

You feel right when you belong to Christ, excited and full of joy.

But here's the point. You have to know him to be happy and excited from the storms of life.

A lasting impression of your faith and practices.

Without Christ, you will fall for anything, and there's no hope of eternal life (Matthew 24:36).

We wait in our hope and assure of our faith practices (Romans 8:1).

Attributes of God

Did Christ at any time give up his entire attributes to sin?

Christ is all-powerful (omnipotent).

One of the attributes of God is that he is all-powerful or omnipotent.

Jesus did not give up this attribute when he became human.

Jesus said about his authority, "All power is given to me."

> Who, being in very nature God, did not consider equality with God something to be used to his own advantage? but emptied Himself, taking the form of a servant, being made in human likeness. (Philippians 2:6–7)

Question: How did he empty himself?

The Bible does not say that God changed into a human being but rather that God became a human being without ceasing to be God.

Jesus took upon a form of a man, made like us (Numbers 23:19, John 4:24).

The Bible says that Jesus does not change.

Jesus Christ is the same yesterday and today and forever (Hebrews 13:8).

Scripture says that Jesus was completely aware of who he was and what he could do.

When arrested in the Garden of Gethsemane, Jesus stated that He could summon legions of angels and stop those taking Him. The word of God doing the talking (John 1:1ff).

The New Testament teaches that Jesus did exercise the use of his divine attributes while he was here upon the earth.

Jesus did miracles and healing, raising Lazarus from the grave. Many other things Jesus did in the presence of many witnesses (John 20:30).

Furthermore, self-humbling of Christ was not against his will. He willingly took on the limitations of humanity.

He never used any of his divine attributes to relieve himself of the limitations of being a human being (Matthew 4, John 10:30–33, etc.).

Jesus suffered as any other man on earth, to better serve our needs, as to how divine needs are met (Hebrews 2:18).

Jesus tells his father, "I have glorified you on the earth. I have finished the work which you have given me to do. And now, O Father, glorify me together with yourself, with the glory which I had with you before the world was" (John 17:4–5). This was coming.

Notice: The glory of Jesus was hidden from humanity during his time on the earth—although it was revealed at certain times.

The glory of God was such that no human could look at it and live.

> He alone can never die, and he lives in light so brilliant that no human can approach him. No human eye has ever seen him, nor ever will. All honor and power to him forever! Amen. (1 Timothy 6:16)

This glory that belongs to Jesus was veiled. At the end of his life, as a human being, he prayed to his Father to restore his former glory.

After his ascension, his glory was no longer veiled (concealed). We read in the book of Revelation:

> John said, "When I saw him, I fell at his feet like a dead man. And he placed his right hand on me, saying, 'Do not be afraid; I am the first and the last.'" (Revelation 1:17)

The totality of his glory was veiled until his completed work on earth.

Jesus had to veil his glory in order to accomplish his mission on earth. But while on earth, this planet, Jesus chose rather to live the life of a servant who put his trust in his heavenly Father.

The following statements from Jesus illustrate this truth:

> Therefore Jesus answered and was saying to them, "Truly, truly, I say to you, the Son can do nothing of himself, unless it is something he sees the Father doing; for whatever the Father does, these things the Son also does in like manner." (John 5:19)

The God, his word became like us in human form to teach us how to live in our human bodies until a changeable moment.

> In a moment, in the twinkling of an eye, at the last trump: for the trumpet shall sound, and the dead shall be raised incorruptible, and we shall be changed. For this corruptible must put on incorruption, and this mortal must put on immortality. So, when this corruptible shall have put on incorruption, and this mortal shall have put on immortality, then shall be brought to pass the saying that is written, Death is swallowed up in victory. (1 Corinthians 15:52–54)

Sin brought forth death no more. No more sin, no more death.

Listen, on earth, the devil fears no one, not even the word of God. Not even his servants fear God.

Authority

It is so sad that mankind cannot see the work in government from one man. Who isn't afraid of taking giant gainful steps to put things back to order where thieves have taken advantage of, yet they act as if God stumbled in providential care for our country?

Sad.

Let everyone be subject ("let you go on then" is amid exhortation where rulers are in authority) to the governing authorities, for there is no authority except that which God has established (Romans 13:1–2). Now if you have not believed that God is in control of things, where is your faith?

Listen: The authorities that exist have been established by God.

Consequently, whoever rebels against the authority is rebelling against what God has instituted, and those who do so will bring judgment on themselves.

For rulers hold no terror for those who do right, but for those who do wrong.

> God is not a man, that he should lie; neither
> the son of man, that he should repent: hath he
> said, and shall he not do it? Or hath he spoken,
> and shall he not make it good? (Numbers 23:19)

One of the hardest scriptures that mankind cannot come to decisions or terms with is one they should obey, yet some (where they are separated by political party) Christian homes, as well those who have not obeyed the gospel, are having trouble with it.

Romans chapter 13, the first few verses, except, it be by tax purposes only, then they fully obey.

This is one chapter that mankind just doesn't get: ordained by God, not by men.

Listen to Romans 13:1–3: "Let everyone be subject to the governing authorities, for there is no authority except that which God has established."

So listen, those who keep havoc, seek God and keep his commandments (Romans 13:1ff).

When being taught, if one understands the core of the language (the heart of it) rather than the details, understanding then brings about your challenge to change. Everything surrounded by the core is its fruit, and only then determines its central values.

Have you said, "Hallelujah, praise Jehovah," today, then raised your arms, reached toward the heavens, and said within your own will, "Lord, I love you and give you praise. All my life, I shall speak of your name" (Daniel 2:20)?

Listen, my friends, if you don't say anything now, I think you will say it when Jesus is established in your heart.

The angels already give him praise, night and day.

I like it when our teachers are strong in the church, then its growth is remarkable.

By creating extraordinary and developing dynamic leaders for a foundation for sustainable growth.

Now, we go to work, show strength and skills to succeed in the work of God (Luke 6:40).

Remember this, we are workers together with God (2 Corinthians 6:1).

What does authority mean?

It is my sincere understanding that it means divine reasoning according to Scripture.

Reasoning from the standpoint of divine logic enables us to arrive at correct conclusions and therefore to distinguish accurately the unreal from the real.

There are some who may say *rule, management, leader.*

But here we are speaking about God.

> And this is what we speak, not in words taught us by human wisdom, but in words taught by the Spirit, expressing spiritual truths in spiritual words. (1 Corinthians 2:13)

The term *biblical authority* refers to the extent to which commandments and doctrines within the Old and New Testament scriptures are authoritative over human belief and conduct.

Remember the state is God's *servant* and God's *agent* for bringing judgment (Romans 13:4).

Yes, the state possesses the "sword," but it does so only at God's behest.

To be a Christian is to know this: Jesus is where the buck ultimately stops.

Jesus is the authority to which all other authorities must answer.

Jesus will judge the nations and their governments.

He is the one with final power over life and death.

The state exists by Jesus's permission, not the other way around.

States typically don't acknowledge this fact, of course.

But churches know it's true (John 19:11; Revelation 1:5, 6:15–17).

Make a change in your life, allow Christ to rule. Don't be a U-Haul Christian. Stay where you're at; trouble doesn't last. The message of truth belongs for all. Stay saved (2 Timothy 4:2).

Preach the Word of God. Be prepared, whether the time is favorable or not. Patiently correct, rebuke, and encourage your people with good teaching.

Baptism

Faith carries the weight of baptism (Romans 10:17). First, there has to be a conviction on the mind before having a seal of actual faith (Ephesians 1:13). The meaning of being baptized is followed by faith (Matthew 3:14–15). Jesus being the author of faith and of baptism, the thought was in the mind of God; it was the right thing to do.

First faith, then comes baptism: one plus one equals two; there is not two without one.

Notice an example given to Nicodemus by Jesus (the Word of God, John 3:1ff).

We should concern ourselves how we live twice and are born twice rather than being born once and dying twice (John 3:3).

Man is physically born and live on earth; in order to be saved, one must be born of God by the washing of water by the Word (spiritual). For him to live again, one must be born again. Water baptism is very important to our common salvation.

Watch the conversation of Jesus to John who baptized people.

> But John tried to prevent Him, saying, "I need to be baptized by You, and do You come to me?" "Let it be so now," Jesus replied. "It is fitting for us to fulfill all righteousness in this way." Then John permitted Him. As soon as Jesus was baptized, He went up out of the water. Suddenly the heavens were opened, and He saw the Spirit of God descending like a dove and resting on Him. (Matthew 3:14–16)

Here's is what we get.

> Peter replied, "Repent and be baptized,
> every one of you, in the name of Jesus Christ for
> the forgiveness of your sins. And you will receive
> the gift of the Holy Spirit." (Acts 2:38)

Notice you cannot be once born and live twice as of physical nature alone. After your life is physically lived on earth, you will die (either way).

But if you have not prepared yourself to live again in heaven (i.e., born again), then you have not been born again while you live (Hebrews 9:27).

The gospel is our godparent, our life again, our hope of eternal life with God (Revelation 21).

You cannot live wrong and die right. Righteousness exalts a nation, but sin condemns any people (Proverbs 14:34).

An independent thinker will not be permitted to override the Word of God by conditions you make up.

Read again John 12:48.

Be Converted

> And said, Verily I say unto you, except ye be converted, and become as little children, ye shall not enter into the kingdom of heaven. (Matthew 18:3)

There are many who do not have a humble spirit.

There are a few who can take criticisms in the raw, but many cannot. There are some who will become intimidated by actions or just a few words someone said, and instead of thinking about it, they snap and go off and damage minds. Gossip sets in, ugly words come out, people hurt, etc. Then you lost a friend or relationship you once had. Children can see light at the end and quickly forget about their madness. Adults who are not taught the ways of God tend to hate and get even, get mad quickly when attacked.

I say, first, reason with that person then say your peace; turn away from foolish men.

> A joyful heart is good medicine, but a crushed spirit dries up the bones. (Proverbs 17:22)

> And you became imitators of us and of the Lord, for you received the word in much affliction, with the joy of the Holy Spirit. (1 Thessalonians 1:6)

Be Proactive

Sometimes we can't help feeling hesitant in some way if we believe a reason exists for us to be so, yet we sometimes confuse hesitancy with unnecessary cautiousness.

There are times, of course, when we are right to be wary, but there are also times when we refuse to take necessary action because we believe we have found a reason that might protect us from failure or disappointment.

Make every effort to look more closely at how valid your reason really is and what it is not.

Grab a hold of it proactively; its hands are extended for you to take.

God is with you.

Take the hand of God.

A need to look: What does the church need to look like these days?

The reason I'm minding my own business: the church needs to look like it does inside out.

It seems as if the church is caught up to be a social meeting place on Sundays and Wednesdays. Then it is counted upon a preacher to fulfill our own obligation to God. Not so—quit thinking such.

The church is supposed to be a sanctified people whereas many shall flow into it.

And you are supposed to teach in the world as well as others who are sanctified.

Listen to your Bible.

> In the last days the mountain of the LORD'S
> temple will be established as the highest of the

mountains; it will be exalted above the hills, and
all nations will stream to it. (Isaiah 2:2)

Now if anything changes within; the church, belonging to Christ, is not doing what it should. It shall fall into the examples of Asia Minor (Revelation 2).

If not, then change the weather in your environment.

We all are workers together with God. Believers in his body; a heart filled with passion to work, as Isaiah, Paul, Peter, John, Trophimus, Timothy, Erastus, and others.

Are you with me?

There is much to do in such little time we have on earth.

If you, my friend, have been attending church for a few months, and you haven't been involved, you are not sanctified, because you have not submitted to the Word of God (John 17:17, 12:48).

There are drifters all over the world, squatters all over the world, but none in the house of God

That He might sanctify and cleanse her with the washing of water by the word, that He might present her to Himself a glorious church, not having spot or wrinkle or any such thing, but that she should be holy and without blemish. (Ephesians 5:26–27)

Be Watchful

My friends, watch out daily. Always be careful of your walk in life. Be sober.

> Be sober, be vigilant; because your adversary the devil, as a roaring lion, walketh about, seeking whom he may devour (swallow up or catch in a trap). (1 Peter 5:8)

When you see him, must you turn away? And if you cannot recognize him, be careful who you associate with, because the devil changes his appearance and attitude to capture people and make them his own.

> When an impure spirit comes out of a person, it (a thing) goes through arid places seeking rest and does not find it. Then it (he) says, "I will return to the house I left."
>
> On its return, it finds the house swept clean and put in order, (looks fake, but you can't fool the devil)
>
> Then it (this thing, whatever it becomes) goes and brings seven other spirits more wicked than itself, and they go in and dwell there, (in the fake choices one makes in life)
>
> And the final plight of that man is worse than the first. (Luke 11:24–26; see also 2 Peter 2:20)

Do not be yoked together with unbelievers.
For what do righteousness and wickedness have
in common? Or what fellowship can light have
with darkness? (2 Corinthians 6:14)

And no wonder, for Satan himself masquer-
ades as an angel of light. (2 Corinthians 11:14)

Anything he wants to become, that's his angle. And then he goes back to be a roaring lion.

Watch your step, watch your story (1 Peter 3:10).

Are you with me?

Stay alert.

Keep sober.

Watch and pray.

There are some who cannot digest or process the truth in such fashion as I have written (Hebrews 4:12). The Bible is written for our instruction (Romans 15:4). Amen.

One cannot say, "God will charge sins in the body alone while the spirit is pure. So one goes on sinning." No sir.

Listen, whatever is done in this body, whether good or bad, is going to be judged.

So if you have not the spirit of God but of divination, you will be lost.

Belief

W e tend to accept a belief that we've invested as much effort as we're prepared to in some way.

It's interesting how, once we reach this stage, we then discover a reason to invest a tiny bit more combined with a modicum of faith.

Even if you feel as if you've reached the end of your tether or patience limits, try to pay attention to the voice inside of you that urges you to try a little bit more. That voice's faith in you is justified!

> Are not all angels ministering spirits sent to serve those who will inherit salvation? (Hebrews 1:14)

I love Jesus.

> But God shows his love for us in that while we were still sinners, Christ died for us. (Romans 5:8)

I met Jesus when I was twelve years old, and never let go of his hands.

How about you?

> But when they believed Philip as he preached the good news of the kingdom of God and the name of Jesus Christ, they were baptized, both men and women. (Acts 8:12)

After one repents in faith, one's next step is water baptism, a primary principle of Jesus Christ (Hebrews 6:1–2).

You are made whole by doing all Jesus requires in faith obedience.

> For all of you who were baptized into Christ have clothed yourselves with Christ. (Galatians 3:27)

How about you? Have you been obedient?
Faith comes by hearing the word of God.
Repentance is calling up Jesus's forgiveness of sins.

> How then shall they call on him in whom they have not believed? And how shall they believe in him of whom they have not heard? And how shall they hear without a preacher? (Romans 10:14)

This is astounding, but baptism first began in the Old Testament (1 Corinthians 10:2).

John the baptizer and Jesus used it both under the law, approved by God himself, to be used in the new covenant relationship again with his followers (Luke 20:40, Matthew 3:14–15).

Bible Classes

Bible classes are used for discussions and learning (Acts 17:11).

Question: Can you teach from the seat and not be put to death in the spirit? Will educating yourself be a bad thing while educating others from your seat?

One of the saddest but probable things one can do if you go to your church, and you get involved in class, and the teacher doesn't like your answer or waves you off as if you are not wanted and continues to do this each time you are in class. Here's what you do—or I would do:

Number one: No church is owned by its people. The church I read about in the Bible books belong to Christ. You have the option to leave that discussion.

Number two: When Jesus was teaching, he realized that a prophet is without honor in his own town. Jesus went about teaching always elsewhere his message of truths.

Number three: Go to a denominational church and teach the Bible by being in class, the Word of God. Having your obedience ready to impart understanding. Hopefully you might get others to see really what the Bible says.

Number four: Never give up teaching the Word of God. Fight the good fight of faith. Take hold of eternal life. When your obedience is fulfilled, others will receive your good work.

Number five: Jesus went about teaching everywhere. Teaching in synagogues and temples, asking and answering questions, eating with sinners, teaching the foundation of basic truths.

Number six: If you are not experiencing wave-offs in your class, be a class participant.

Never be afraid to open your mind, giving examples to facts in class. And if teachers find it a good thing, you have a wonderful opportunity to teach in the future. If not, well, find a different location to teach from the seat, while adding to your education (John 6:66–68).

Blasphemy

J esus himself said in Matthew 12:31, "Therefore, I say to you, every sin and blasphemy will be forgiven men, but the blasphemy against the Spirit will not be forgiven men."

If a person truly listens to the Holy Spirit and asks for pardon and forgiveness, that person is not guilty of blasphemy against the Holy Spirit.

Any sin mankind wants pardon for is forgivable. However, if we turn our backs on the voice of the Holy Spirit, we begin to silence his convictions, and eventually we cannot hear his convicting power.

This effectively blocks the working of God in our lives because we have reached a point where we are unable to respond to the promptings of the Holy Spirit.

Allow no man to believe that there are certain sins God will not forgive.

God forgives if you change.

Change is to repent.

Blessings

Don't let the devil trick you into believing you have a blessing from God, when you know better than to accept something that looks good just because it's there and you never had it before.

Listen, when God gives you a blessing, it comes natural and not by any other means. I think many can identify with this, like, for example, credit cards, free trips, free money, free houses, cars, etc., and the list goes on.

Listen, leave that stuff alone, it's not a blessing, it's a bill that you don't have the money to pay back. You will wake up one day, and someone will take all your stuff that you thought was a blessing.

No. Don't make bad decisions. Know what a blessing is.

God's blessing doesn't lie; the devil is a liar and so is his stuff (Matthew 4).

And when you fail to take responsibility for yourself, you rob God. Money wasted in a moment as in Luke 15:11–32, the parable of the lost son.

Name one blessing.

Money doesn't make you great, it's your love in the natural sense that makes you great. Be real.

What can wash away my sins?

If there is a worm in your apple, don't eat it; good fruit is much healthier than a sneaky worm eating at the core. Get rid of it.

Sin will destroy any people, when not sober minded.

Recover yourselves by asking God for deliverance today. Amen.

There is nothing beautiful about sins.

If you are living sinful, and you think it's okay to sin, either two things, especially one.

Go see a psychiatrist and your preacher.

Because what you are doing is devilish.

No fun in sin; it damages the soul.

Spiritual leaders can help to deliver you *if* you allow yourself to listen.

Listen, there are some who fail to listen and study the Word of God.

When you fail to study your Bibles, don't run to your liberalisms (preachers) because they are ear ticklers.

People who are taught the Bible should study the Bible.

But if not, you have become an ear tickler; you fail to believe the truth and study your Bible.

Listen to the truth and not painted errors.

Let go of your comrades who talk very loudly but do nothing but please your minds (1 Corinthians 13:1).

Don't listen to noisy folks.

Why? Because they don't study. Some just have their own philosophies and not revelation, chapter, book, and verse.

> But it was to us that God revealed these things by his Spirit. For his Spirit searches out everything and shows us God's deep secrets.
>
> For God has revealed it to us through the Spirit. For the Spirit searches all things, even the depths of God. (1 Corinthians 2:10)

Blinded Minds

Nothing should be greater than our faith by showing up for Jesus (Hebrews 9:27).

How can you be awakened to righteousness when you thought that you may not be doing anything wrong? As far as the world is concerned, you may not be, but it might be because of God's concern that you have lost your first love or may not give God the love he deserves (John 3:16).

You may say to yourself, "I'm not doing anything wrong."

Here's a concern anyone may have forgotten about.

> The god of this age has blinded the minds
> of unbelievers, so that they cannot see the light
> of the gospel of the glory of Christ, who is the
> image of God. (2 Corinthians 4:4)

> Do not be deceived! "Bad company cor-
> rupts good morals." (1 Corinthians 15:33)

A list of things to think about:

Deuteronomy 31:25–29
Proverbs 15:27
Matthew 7:21–23

> So the law is paralyzed, and justice never goes
> forth. For the wicked surround the righteous; so,
> justice goes forth perverted. (Habakkuk 1:4)

Many times, it is that mankind gives about 99 percent of their time to the world and 1 percent to God.

Isn't it time you think about heavenly things (Colossians 3:1–3)?

> But as it is written: "Eye has not seen, nor ear heard, nor have entered into the heart of man. The things which God has prepared for those who love Him." (1 Corinthians 2:9)

The Body

There is only one connection factor that Jesus is coming back to get.

His people with their names belonging to the body. The called out.

It doesn't matter what you called yourselves, if you are not called by his name; it is a command of human institutions, and not of God.

The Churches of Christ are connected when the "body" is fitly joined together as one.

One Lord, one body, one faith, one baptism, and one God above and *in* you all. Amen.

Build Up or Tear Down

What is backbiting?

There are known persons who have no spiritual knowledge of the Word of God, and don't care.

So, what they do is violate the Word of God by being friends with the devil.

Such attacks, attitudes of "don't care what the Word says."

They feed off others' ignorance and sins.

Both men and women alike have lack of respect for Jesus (2 Peter 1:3, James 3:5–12).

Backbiting is the stealth bomber of the unholy armed forces because the attack always comes when your back is turned.

Many unfortunate things happen in many churches around the world, simply because people are people.

There are the unattractive things Christians do, which ultimately result in the dismembering of the body of Christ.

They are the sins we commit that drive people away from the church, where people are supposed to encounter God and be healed.

Many unfortunate things happen in many churches, but among the ugliest and most destructive of these are the three unfortunate events we've focused on in the past few weeks:

Hypocrisy: the practice of professing beliefs, feelings, or virtues that we don't really have.

Mediocrity: the state of being moderate to inferior in quality in our spiritual lives—ordinary, powerless, religious people. Satisfied with the status quo's Christian lifestyle. It's not meant to be.

And finally, today's unfortunate event: the third of the uglies, which is called backbiting. If Satan has an arsenal of weapons, backbiting is among the weapons in his secret artillery. It's the stealth bomber of the unholy armed forces because the attack always comes when your back is turned.

Backbiting is the coward's approach to problem-solving.

In a church, I know a woman who seemed so sweet to everyone in their faces, but as soon as they turned their back, she had something nasty to say about them.

She was so good at making everyone think she liked them, but I was surprised by some of the remarks she had for them when they weren't listening, and you know, it made me wonder what she was saying about me when I wasn't around.

This person has no godly attributes or speaks well of her own family and friends.

Such ignorance is devilish and demonic yet sits in the building where the saints meet, scrutinizing and criticizing, finding fault, leaving unsatisfied with anyone she comes in contact within the body.

Here's the exact definition of such character: Backbiting occurs when somebody goes behind another person's back and says bad things or spreads rumors about them to destroy their character.

Backbiters are good at pretending they love everyone, but deep inside, they are vicious toward other people.

They tear people apart with their words, behind their backs. They lie to ensnare, trap, destroy.

Nowhere is this truer than in the mouth of a backbiter.

They are ruthless with their words, and they have not learned to tame their tongues, and the result of their words is destruction.

You people need to wake up and stop ignoring it.

In such cases. the leaders of the church must act.

Otherwise, they are in contempt of God.

Are you building up the body of Christ with your words or tearing it down?

> He who is not with me is against me, and he
> who does not gather with me scatters. (Matthew
> 12:30)

We can be just as much enemies of Jesus with our mouths as we can with our actions. Words are very powerful in the building up or tearing down of the body of Christ, his church.

> The tongue has the power of life and death, and those who love it will eat its fruit. (Proverbs 18:21)

> O LORD, you have searched me and known me. You know when I sit down and when I rise up, you understand my thought from afar.
> You scrutinize my path and my lying down, and are intimately acquainted with all my ways, read more.
> Even before there is a word on my tongue, Behold, O LORD, you know it all.
> You have enclosed me behind and before and laid Your hand upon me.
> Such knowledge is too wonderful for me; It is too high; I cannot attain to it. (Psalm 139:1–6)

> The secret things belong to the LORD our God, but the things revealed belong to us and to our sons forever, that we may observe all the words of this law. (Deuteronomy 29:29)

> Who does great and unsearchable things, Wonders without number? (Job 5:9)

> Can you discover the depths of God? Can you discover the limits of the Almighty? (Job 11:7)

> The Lord is slow to anger but great in power; the Lord will not leave the guilty unpunished.

His way is in the whirlwind and the storm,
and clouds are the dust of his feet.

He rebukes the sea and dries it up; he makes
all the rivers run dry. (Nahum 1:3–4)

Remember this always: Nobody can understand what God does here on earth (Ecclesiastes 8:16–17). No matter how hard people try to understand it, they cannot. Even if wise people say they understand, they cannot; no one can really understand it.

There were and still are some groups of persons who by virtue of position or education exercise much power or influence in the world today.

How the elite treated their workers' matters had gotten worse.

What did it teach us?

The world was in disarray, the Word of God wasn't followed, men became worsened in everyday life, until God raised up a man called Martin Luther King, a peaceful man like that of Jesus, maybe a slight different because he was, as we've known him, a man.

Therefore, God has mercy on whom he
wants to have mercy, and he hardens whom he
wants to harden. (Romans 9:18)

But you know, God can raise up whomever he pleases to bring together a change in the life of man to save him from devilish acts of disobedience.

The world began to change during and after Martin Luther King. I wouldn't classify him as a hero, since he was a religious man, but a humble man who worked repentance in the hearts of believers belonging to God.

Souls were saved, and change became necessary for all mankind; the minds of reasoning serve those who love the Lord.

But some of which will not change or have not changed but have departed this life to be judged by the Lord (Hebrews 9:27).

Listen to 2 Timothy 2:26.

> (Until), they will come to their senses and escape from the devil's trap.
> For they have been held captive by him to do whatever he wants.

Today, some have viewed the troubled past, which has nothing to do with righteousness; however, things should not remind us of who these devilish people are, but make a compassion, using the Bible, and lift up Jesus.

In John 12:32, Jesus said, "And I, if I be lifted up from the earth, will draw all men unto me."

We must pay closer attention, therefore, to what we have heard so that we do not drift away.

For if the message spoken by angels was binding, and every transgression and disobedience received is just punishment, how shall we escape if we neglect such a great salvation?

This salvation was first announced by the Lord, was confirmed to us by those who heard him (Hebrews 2:1–3, Hebrews 10:35).

So do not throw away your confidence; it holds a great reward.

To make America great again means to change your mind and serve the Lord and his people; otherwise, God will judge your faith.

Nothing to do with sin, faith, as some political folks are trying to impress upon the innocent and the wise.

Listen, whatever you do, don't vote where the devil is telling lies to win over your mind.

Stand up! Stand up for Jesus. The truth shall prevail (Psalm 1:1ff). Amen.

Who will turn to God?

Husbands, love your wives, just as Christ loved the church and gave himself up for her. *Better* means "the absolute ability one can do." Wife, submit to your husband, and the both will become a doer of the Word. Without such manner, you will be unequally yoked.

Children

If a woman pulls her children away from God, they become her children; and when the father teaches God, she fails to obey (1 Corinthians 11:1ff, Ephesians 5:23).

They become God's children when they obey.

A lost child can never be regained from a lost mother. Especially when she has her roots in the world.

Then from its stem, she will convenience, convert, advise other mothers the same.

Her system of beguilements shows her genius love for the world and its behavior.

When the Bible says a thing, why are others finding a way to disobey it after reading it or hearing it?

If a father fails to teach a child the righteousness of God, how can God be glorified?

Choosing Church Leaders

Expeditiously is not a good thing when it comes to our logical approach on particulars, because most importantly, people should think things through.

Here's why: 1 Timothy 5:22–25.

Never be in a hurry about appointing a church leader.

Do not share in the sins of others. Keep yourself pure.

Stop drinking only water and use a little wine instead, because of your stomach and your frequent ailments (a message for Timothy).

Remember, the sins of some people are obvious, leading them to certain judgment.

But there are others whose sins will not be revealed until later.

Christian Soldiers

Blessed are ye, when men shall revile you, and persecute you, and shall say all manner. Of evil against you falsely, for my sake.

For all who are concerned, don't allow yourself to be taken in by untrue accusations.

The devil is a liar, accuser of men.

But you Christian soldiers.

Let your conversation be "always" full of grace, seasoned with salt, so that you may know how to answer everyone. (Colossians 4:6)

But in your hearts sanctify Christ as Lord. Always be prepared to give a defense to everyone who asks you the reason for the hope that you have. But respond with gentleness and respect. (1 Peter 3:15)

Remember, the devil has a heart of stone.

His humblest is meaningless.

He will curse you to another (Psalm 1:1ff).

In the beginning (the book called Genesis), if man and woman are married and naked in the garden, why were they ashamed to be seen with each other after the sin?

Before, it was okay (Genesis 3:7).

Was there power in the forbidden fruit?

God said no. Eve said, "I'm going to try it as the beast asked me to do. I will ask my husband to participate. Let's see what happens."

It was two humans made from dirt in Eden; no sin until later as the days went by.

But why were both ashamed?

Symbolically from that point of view, does it mean that nakedness in sin makes things shameful?

Why use this illustration to prove shameful sin?

How does it fit today?

What is a parenthetical statement?

They were ashamed before God. Now that they had sinned.

Yes, they were.

But why was it because they were naked?

Was it supposed to be an illustration for sin shamefulness?

The Church

The church belonging to Christ is the only institution written in the Bible where most denominational groups don't attend. It teaches truths whereby a man can be found saved. Why? The Bible tells us to sanctify them (any man) in truth; my word is truth (John 17:17).

Tell me, how can a man drive himself from truth and say "Holy, holy, holy" and "Hallelujah" but don't follow the road to salvation?

Listen your Bible.

> Not everyone who says to Me, "Lord, Lord," will enter the kingdom of heaven, but only he who does the will of My Father in heaven. Many will say (a lot of people will plead their case) to Jesus on that day, "Lord, Lord, did we not prophesy in Your name, and in Your name drive out demons and perform many miracles?" Then Jesus will tell them plainly, "I never knew you; (get away from my presence) depart from Me, you workers of lawlessness!" (Matthew 7:21–23)

That's your new zip code.

Yet many denominations are attacking the church of our Lord by speaking against it, and some are weak in the church but into wanting to change those denominational errors.

Look, families don't run the church. Families are in the church or into the body of Christ.

There are but a few who like to dominate and think they can call all the shots. (Subject to keep others from growing.)

No! Jesus runs the church; we leaders are responsible for making sure the church is run according to the Word of God.

And when we start listening to Jesus, rather than a great deal of opinions, we put our complete trust in Jesus.

Remember this.

No one can give you salvation but Jesus.

No one can raise you from the grave but Jesus.

No one can give you a new body after your passing but Jesus.

Hear ye him (Matthew 17).

About finding a church, what does it mean?

To define what we mean inexplicitly is to say what we think about it explicitly, by finding a church of your likening, not a church of your choice; it determines the outcome.

What I mean is, go find the right church of Christ that fits your spiritual speedometer.

Some of which have places where families can grow to be in larger groups.

Because it can accommodate what you might be looking for in growth.

These programs are protective services for all mankind.

Classes where many shall gather and participate in more proactive activities.

If it fits your needed efforts, then go to a place of your liking.

If a church I have has growth for active families, how proactive is the church?

Good question.

However, if a church is in the building process, it could encourage others to participate regularly.

I say, work it out, but if after a time, it shows no growth, you too are to be tested (2 Peter 3:18).

Growth over time adds value; it will show up to be an example for others.

Look, if any church shows no changes over time, its destiny will eventually become self-evident.

How sad.

My friends, it is hard to build such a greater focus.

Our spiritual charge should be of trustworthiness, not low quality, but going the speed God gave us to go.

Not speaking of elderly people, but any shoes that are worthy in doing a work of God.

> Dear friends, you always followed my instructions when I was with you. And now that I am away, it is even more important. Work hard to show the results of your salvation, obeying God with deep reverence and fear. (Philippians 2:12)

Many a times speakers will entertain a body of believers, but in the end, it doesn't justify the means.

Because of the character of a group, it falls, lacking the responsibility of their growth.

How can you trust any man who can't do what God says, but you trust him in the world?

Answer:

> Jesus said, "Render to Caesar the things that are Caesar's; and to God the things that are God's." (Matthew 22:21)

> Let every person be in subjection to the governing authorities. (Romans 13:1)

Two things: Stay in bed or go to church.
What is your plan?
As for me, I'd rather be in the house of the Lord.

> Better is one day in your courts than a thousand elsewhere; I would rather be a doorkeeper in the house of my God than dwell in the tents of the wicked. (Psalm 84:10)

Building the church belonging to Christ (Matthew 16:18).

The church, your work must be a fantastic stronghold, where many shall gather together to worship God as firmly glued together in Spirit and with truth (John 4:24).

It must be a remarkable place, and its atmosphere, it shall be the greatest, whereby many shall come and say, "I get to go to church where we are taught of God's commands, how we shall live, the gospel is applied daily, remembered, and its people shall rejoice by hearing it."

Be filled up with the Word of God.

Now keep your Bible open; it is written from the pen of David, out of his heart, he says.

> I will bless the Lord at all times: his praise shall continually be in my mouth. My soul shall make her boast in the Lord: the humble shall hear thereof and be glad. O magnify the Lord with me, and let us exalt his name together. (Psalm 34:1–3)

Open your Bible and let us read together these verses from Ephesians 3:16–20.

> That God would grant you, according to the riches of his glory, to be strengthened with might by his Spirit in the inner man; (let it be your will to listen and obey the word of God, by putting into practice your faithfulness to Him). That Christ may dwell in your hearts by faith; that ye, being rooted and grounded in love, (let your heart be of Christ and allow self to deeply think about the things God wants you to do) May be able to comprehend with all saints what is the breadth, and length, and depth, and height; And to know the love of Christ, which passeth knowledge, that ye might be filled with all the fulness of God.

Growth is a must to any child of his father; without growth, there is no safety.

> But grow in the grace and knowledge of our
> Lord and Savior Jesus Christ. To him be the glory
> both now and forever. Amen. (2 Peter 3:18)

(Now abides faith, hope, love—the greater is the summation of the three.)

Where no love, no faith, and no hope, whom shall you put your trust in?

Listen again. Romans 8:24, Hebrews 11:1, 2 Corinthians 4:18. "For God is love" (1 John 4:7–21).

> Now unto him that is able to do exceedingly
> abundantly above all that we ask or think, accord-
> ing to the power that worketh in us; unto him be
> glory in the church by Christ Jesus throughout
> all ages, world without end. Amen.

How dedicated are you?

Cross over to the promised land.

Get into the church.

The only one Christ is coming back for (Ephesians 5:27, 1 Corinthians 15:24).

I worry how mankind may act in the church; they are trying to right themselves with God.

You get there and get started with Jesus. Make your change.

Of all the people (adults) who left Egypt with Moses and crossed the wilderness for forty years, only two of them were permitted by God to enter the promised land, and Moses was not one of them! Only Joshua and Caleb out of that group entered the land.

Joshua 14 tells us something that's a key to Caleb, the Hebrew hero in battle.

Three times the Holy Spirit says Caleb "wholly followed the Lord God" (vv. 8, 9, 14). Every ounce of Caleb was given to the Lord.

This is the kind of heart you and I should have if we call our-selves Christians.

If you're fainthearted, the devil is going to intimidate you. And there's only one way to stand against the devil.

That is to give everything to Christ. Indeed, God does not accept a half-hearted person. One must be completely dedicated to God.

How many minutes have you invested in evangelism this week (Proverbs 11:30)?

The Bible teaches no purpose in purpose, to live by, which is in Christ.

Plan your life with God (Galatians 3:21).

A fresh look.

Jesus said "*my* church"; it indicates that at a particular time, the apostles, his body, will succeed: "I will build," Jesus said.

The church Jesus is talking about took place at Jerusalem on the Feast of Weeks, called Pentecost (AD 33). That would be his church or "called-out body of people," meaning his chosen people; by his word, they shall be saved (John 12:48).

> And you also were included in Christ when you heard the message of truth, the gospel of your salvation. When you believed, you were marked in him with a seal, the promised Holy Spirit. (Ephesians 1:13, Acts 2:38)

Apostle Peter reminds us what the saved are in Christ: "You are a chosen people, a royal priesthood, a holy nation, a people for God's own possession, to proclaim the virtues of Him who called you out of darkness into His marvelous light" (1 Peter 2:9).

Verse 10: "Once you were not a people, but now you are the people of God; once you had not received mercy, but now you have received mercy."

Now on Pentecost, that day, about three thousand people were added to the Lord; that was his church or his body of believers, beginning at Jerusalem (Acts 2:41).

Later Paul wrote to remind us that it was built upon the foundation of the apostles and prophets, Jesus being the head or cornerstone of his body.

Here's what the Bible says.

> Built on the foundation of the apostles and prophets, with Christ Jesus himself as the chief cornerstone. (Ephesians 2:20)

Then he told the Corinthian Church that "no one can lay any foundation other than the one already laid, which is Jesus Christ" (1 Corinthians 3:11).

This foundation came from God, a sure foundation, built from the mind of God.

The Bible says, "So that He might sanctify her (the body of Christ), having cleansed her by the washing of water by the word" (Ephesians 5:26, John 17:17).

Notice what the prophet Isaiah says.

> So, this is what the Lord GOD says: "See, I lay a stone in Zion, a tested stone, a precious cornerstone, a sure foundation; the one who believes will never be shaken." (Isaiah 28:16)

Then apostle Paul, writing to Timothy, says these words:

> Nevertheless, God's firm foundation stands, bearing this seal: "The Lord knows those who are His," and, "Everyone who calls on the name of the Lord must turn away from iniquity." (2 Timothy 2:19)

Then we learn that the church or the body of Christ was purchased with his blood (Acts 20:28).

> For it stands in Scripture: "See, I lay in Zion a stone, a chosen and precious cornerstone; and the one who believes in Him will never be put to shame." (1 Peter 2:6)

Jesus told his apostles these words (Matthew 28:18–20).

> Then Jesus came to them and said, "All authority in heaven and on earth has been given to me. Therefore, go and make disciples of all nations, baptizing them in the name of the Father and of the Son and of the Holy Spirit, and teaching them to obey everything I have commanded you. And surely, I am with you always, to the very end of the age."

The church is widespread (Acts 2); its beginning place was at Jerusalem, the same place Elijah, Moses, and Jesus spoke about his departure to take place (Luke 9:30).

My friends, Jesus never talked about any other church, like today's churches made from mankind word—for example, Lutheran, Catholic, Baptist, Methodist, Presbyterian, and so on.

In those days of the apostles (the Twelve), these things were unheard-of.

But God would have knowledge in the future that men would start a different kind of church other than the one named by Jesus.

Listen.

Because he knew that many denominational churches would reject him this day.

> But Jesus looked directly at them and said, "Then what is the meaning of that which is writ-

ten: 'The stone the builders rejected has become the cornerstone'?" (Luke 20:17)

Why?

Because their pursuit was not by faith, but as if it were by works.

They stumbled over the stumbling stone, as it is written in John 12:48.

The Son of God purchased the church with his own blood through his death on the cross so that people can fellowship and meet God's mandate of holiness.

It is unfortunate that the church that Jesus Christ purchased with his blood has digressed from its traditional value.

> Again, he says "See, I lay in Zion a stone of stumbling, and a rock of offense; and the one who believes in Him will never be put to shame." (Romans 9:33, Acts 4:11)

> It is just as the Scripture says: "Anyone who believes in Him will never be put to shame." (Romans 10:11)

Belief is faith, and faith is doing what God says without adding to his word.

Notice Matthew 16:18ff.

Jesus mentioned "upon this rock," indicating his word as well as those who he chose to deliver it to us.

Watch now.

> We ourselves heard this voice that came from heaven when we were with him on the sacred mountain.

> We also have the prophetic message as something completely reliable, and you will do well to pay attention to it, as to a light shining in

a dark place, until the day dawns and the morning star rises in your hearts.

Above all, you must understand that no prophecy of Scripture came about by the prophet's own interpretation of things.

For the prophecy came not in old time by the will of man: but holy men of God spake as they were moved by the Holy Ghost. (2 Peter 1:18–21)

The apostles were the carriers of his word; they were "the rock" to make a body from the words spoken by the HS, and we who obey his word are members of the body, the church.

The thing Paul talks about in Romans 12:5, "So, in Christ we, though many, form one body, and each member belongs to all the others."

For just as the body is one and has many members, and all the members of the body, though many, are one body, so it is with Christ.

For in one Spirit we were all baptized into one body—Jews or Greeks, slaves or free—and all were made to drink of one Spirit.

For the body does not consist of one member but of many. (1 Corinthians 12:12–14)

From the apostles and prophets, we are taught about one house (body), a spiritual body guided by the word of God (John 17:17, John 4:24).

Jesus never fought other churches; he fought religious leaders concerning the law of Moses, in that Jesus wrote that law.

In the beginning was the Word, and the Word was with God, and the Word was God.

The same was in the beginning with God.

All things were made by him; and without him was not anything made that was made.
(John 1:1–3)

Remember this: "And from Jesus Christ, who is the faithful witness, and the first begotten of the dead, and the prince of the kings
of the earth. Unto him that loved us and washed us from our sins in
his own blood" (Revelation 1:5).

Yes, change is necessary.

Tell your family and friends about the body belonging to Christ.

Not just any one particular thing, but the right body belonging
to the right head—Jesus Christ.

If mankind thinks of something else other than the right body
and the right head, remember the stone (Ephesians 2:20).

They are considered a thief and a robber (John 15:1ff).

Jesus is not going to present to his father a man-made body (1
Corinthians 15:24).

It has to be made just the way God commanded it to be made.

A few more things one must think about.

It is hard sometimes to teach a man with bad intentions the
rightful way to Jesus, but it is also hard to teach Jezebel rightful things
pertaining to God; similar to that of Thyatira, with some comparison, for example, gossiping, is a dividing line between what is right
and wrong—in the case of Jezebel, destroying God's people within
a body.

Jezebel—in modern usage, the name of Jezebel is sometimes
used as a synonym for "sexually promiscuous" or "controlling
women." Jezebel will have it her way or no way.

Lies implicitly encourage others to fall by her actions and her
words.

Her children have fallen; her husband lacks courage to control
his own house, with all possibility of having a dysfunctional outlook,
leading to death, defeated by Satan, yet lost its light.

This is not what Jesus wants in his body, the church.

Question: are some of you going to allow your acts of compassion to overthrow your group today?

If this is the case, listen to Jesus; he would say, "Look, here's what I'm going to do about it. I will remove your light if you decide not to hear my word."

At times, a body of believers will allow things to go too far before doing anything about removing evil, destroying a group of righteous people.

Then it seems that some concerns are…well, I'm not going to say anything, leave it for someone else to say what it is, I'm not.

Before you know it, the light is gone, seats are empty, people are gone, no more young people, no more of anything. Like it was before, loneliness, emptiness, a dead church, simply because they thought it was all together.

No.

Listen.

The church belonging to Christ is a heavenly institution, divinely ordained and appointed by Jesus, given by which he shall gather his people, who obey his word, into a place apart from worldly activities that will destroy sanctified people.

Some today will say, "Okay, now I get it," then correct it; don't allow your light to be taken away.

Listening to the spirit is most important.

The Lord hates everyone who is arrogant; he will never let them escape punishment.

> Better to eat a dry crust of bread with peace
> of mind than have a banquet in a house full of
> trouble. (Proverbs 17:1)

There are some black churches, if not other related, who have great leaders today, where love abounds, where entertainment has ceased in the minds of those who believe the Bible, and acts thereof, as defined.

But in some cases, churches or thoughts of minds have changed over time (Churches of Christ), as a group of young people who have now found new invocations and establish these ideas within minds of those who want to get away from traditional religious beliefs or values.

The fairness of this is overwhelming, and some preachers are getting frustrated and become angry at times by defending the truth or defending their position while in service.

I sincerely believe that God intends the church to move along but not run ahead of traditional values, pertaining to doctrine and practices.

Secondly, the church is not in a position to overlook ignorance but overthrow it.

Folks are implicitly asking preachers to excuse their rights to sins and to practice partiality within a body, thus bringing to others in public their sins.

After a while, the church breaks into pieces, then no one talks about why.

Or at least it comes to a withdrawal and then stops being talked about.

Answers becomes evident of your action.

Things should change.

Check your book of Revelation from chapter 2.

Life is a series of moments. What footprints have you left behind for many to remember?

Let Jesus be the center of your life.

God is the head of the church and should be the head in your life.

You have rights to live, act, and do as righteousness in an ethical way; thus, perhaps you may work for Jesus.

Begin reading Psalm 1:1ff and its following verses. When you finish, pray to God.

Not much time in reading, but make it your daily practice.

Fixing your mind (Colossians 3:1–3).

Second Corinthians 4:18 says, "So, we fix our eyes not on what is seen, but on what is unseen, since what is seen is temporary, but what is unseen is eternal."

Listen now.

> For we are saved by hope: but hope that
> is seen is not hope: for what a man seeth, why
> doth he yet hope for? But if we hope for that
> we see not, then do we with patience wait for it.
> (Romans 8:24–25)

Heaven is our hope.

Church Attendance

Why do the nations rage, and the peoples plot in vain?

The kings of the earth set themselves, and the rulers take counsel together, against the Lord and against his Anointed, saying,

"Let us burst their bonds apart and cast away their cords from us."

He who sits in the heavens laughs; the Lord holds them in derision.

Then he will speak to them in his wrath, and terrify them in his fury, saying (Psalm 2:1–12), "Laugh all you want about church, so was the rich man who laughed at Lazarus because he was a beggar" (Luke 16:19–31).

There is no doubt that Christians, followers of Jesus Christ, should attend church. It should be the desire of every Christian to worship corporately.

Ephesians 5:19–20 tells us to fellowship with and encourage other Christians and to be taught God's Word (1 Thessalonians 5:11, 2 Timothy 3:16–17).

Hearing the Word is what produces faith (Romans 10:17).

And gathering with other believers is a command (Hebrews 10:24–25); we really do need each other.

Just as God loves a cheerful giver (2 Corinthians 9:7), so He is pleased with a genuinely cheerful church attendee.

Here's what you should not do.

Watch.

Because we belong to the day, we must live decent lives for all to see (Romans 13:13).

Don't participate in the darkness of wild parties and drunkenness or in sexual promiscuity and immoral living or in quarreling and jealousy.

I assure you, the church needs you. And it needs you to be there this Sunday.

You will miss out on God's primary design for your spiritual growth and well-being.

The central aspect of corporate worship is the preaching of God's Word.

The proclamation of Scriptures is God's primary means for a disciple of Jesus to grow in spiritual maturity.

When a professing Christian misses church, they are missing God's prescribed process for spiritual growth.

When a church member misses worship service, the church drastically suffers. You don't even know why.

Why? Here's why.

If you live at home and expect other family members to be there on a regular basis, and they don't, don't you get worried or concerned?

One should, right!

The Bible is emphatic about church attendance.

The writer of Hebrews challenges us with convicting words:

> Not forsaking the assembling of ourselves together, as the manner of some is; but exhorting one another: and so much the more, as ye see the day approaching. (Hebrews 10:25)

Have you ever thought about the effect your absence has in the house of God? When you are not there, the body of the congregation is incomplete without you.

1. Your voice is not heard in the worship and singing of the saints.
2. You cannot actively serve others who may need your gifts.

3. You cannot contribute in the offering.
4. You do not receive the Word of God in a preaching format.
5. You miss out on corporate prayer.
6. You forfeit fellowship with other believers.
7. You send a message to the youth that missing church is acceptable.
8. You make it easier to miss the next week, and then the next.
9. You become susceptible to apathy and indifference.
10. You make it harder for others to bear the weight and burdens of ministry.
11. You miss opportunities to share your own struggles with the saints of God.
12. You cause unnecessary worry for your pastor, teacher, staff, and leaders.
13. You miss out on the invitation, prayers, and call to repentance.

Ask yourselves, why am I not doing what God has asked me to do? (And you still hope for eternal life.)

Not going to happen.

Jesus is coming back to get the church soon (1 Corinthians 15:24), and your end might not be his own.

Go back to Christ, listen to your brethren who cares for your soul (Galatians 6:1ff, Romans 16:16).

Go back.

Togetherness is not being scattered throughout the country.

We are fittingly joined together in one place to serve God our Creator and Savior.

Remember, not many churches but many people in the body of Christ.

Hey, get your place in the body of Christ.

When going to church, come with a goal, leave with a plan.

What are you doing with the Lord's money?

Yes, the money he has blessed you with and have.

Consider your thoughts.

Question: What do you want from God?

A very difficult question for the most?

Consider what God has given you now and what you might be doing with it.

The Bible says, "For where your treasure is—that which ye value most" (Matthew 6:21). That's were your heart is.

Lay up for yourselves treasures in heaven.

In heaven, nothing corrupts, nothing terminates—no enemies, plunder, or destruction.

To have treasure in heaven is to possess evidence that its purity and joys will be ours.

Cannot serve the master of possession.

Two masters oppose each other; no man can serve both.

He who holds to the world and loves it must despise God; he who loves God must give up the friendship of the world.

A man may do some service to two masters, but he can devote himself to the service of no more than one. God requires the whole heart and will, not share it with the world.

Make not the things of the earth your riches or portion, with reference to future time; for all the riches of the earth are perishing, contemptible things. Silver and gold are what rust will corrupt. Clothes are what moths will spoil. Any other things are subject to casualties and, amongst others, to the violence of unreasonable men, who, though they have no right to them, will ordinarily take them from you.

(I remember the days that I asked my dad to keep many books of mine; he gave me money for some of those books, but when he put them up in his laundry room, it had a leak, and water destroyed them, and mildew set up, destroying books, including mine.)

Listen now.

The reflection goes back on the negative counsel in Matthew 6:19. Do not accumulate earthly treasures, for then your heart will be there, whereas it ought to be in heaven with God and the kingdom of God. But let your riches, your treasure, be in heaven (Colossians 3:1–3).

The Body of Christ

Membership of the Church of Christ is largest in the Southern states of the United States, especially Tennessee and Texas, though there are congregations located in each of the fifty states and in over eighty foreign countries.

All else has no biblical authority to open and operate as a religious organization (John 12:48).

Respect the blood-bought church. Jesus did a lot for us and should not be taken lightly.

Respect the salvation that was once delivered to saints.

There is power in the blood.

The Churches of Christ are autonomous congregations. Meaning self-governing.

The Church of Christ follows after the design of structure found in the New Testament; Churches of Christ are no question autonomous.

Our authority of faith and practices comes from the written word of God. The Bible and its teachings are the main bonds that connect us together.

We have no primary earthly headquarters nor any organization superior to the elders of each local congregation.

Congregations are cooperatively and deliberately instructed to help orphans and widows in their time of need. We preach the gospel in places, and we do other related works. We are not to underperform in the work of God.

The mission of the church is to evangelize and bring every man to the word of God.

What does this mean to you? Read Acts 4:12.

What about Ephesians 4?

If you have answered all these questions according to the Bible correctly, you have heard the word of God (Romans 10:17).

Next, stop, attend church, and say, "What shall I do to inherit eternal life?"

Be baptized into the church belonging to the name of Jesus.

Did you ever pray, "Lord, help me please," and then you look for an immediate response?

Well, it came by other means than you expected. God works your prayer to open doors upon your behalf. Trust.

All the time, we make mistakes, daily. Decisions don't come easy. When you trust yourself to be right, it may not work in your best interests.

Ask God before any decision you make; either way, you will get his answer.

If you have ears, what are you using them for?

Make yourself a list.

Submit it to God.

Then ask yourself, what have I read from the Book of Life?

Or what have I heard from the world's mouths?

Be honest with God.

Now has God heard you?

When you ask others to pray for you.

Someone might say something that I didn't say.

Prayer is a voice to God on behalf of me.

What happens to a need that you don't follow?

If you're the one bringing people down, then surround yourself with good people, and you will be inspired by them, and you will start being a good person.

So, either way, get rid of the bad people in life.

Could one become an alien for just one day?

Life should not be wasted.

Know yourself and live in harmony with it.

Stay flexible.

Don't make stupid decisions.

If you're doing the same things, don't expect a different result.

Look. Everything done in history is the result of an action being done.

Not a thought. Not a word. Only actions are recorded by the scribes of humanity.

Do something today. Take a course, take yourself someplace, do something for yourself on a regular basis. Quitting should not be an option.

Learn how to shoot a bow and arrow. Start a book. Connect two people who can help each other. Raise a child. Build a school.

Today's generation tend to understand written instructions more so than those of past. But have they followed them?

They have much to consider and much to take in whereas those of noncomprehensive status most likely overlook languages that matter and are of importance.

Why, just live through it; and without prejudices, some fail to care.

Comprehensively according to knowledge of things from those who tend to relax and affix their minds upon finding what fits their needs.

Listen. Comprehensive study of world affairs or comprehending through thoroughly understanding with one's mind is having an extensive mental range or grasp, as in a particular subject or many subjects.

When you forget these things, you often involve yourself in a different atmosphere of liberalism rather than its intended meaning.

It happens more than once—either in written language or verbally.

Commandment

J esus matters if you don't care about any of them.
With Jesus, love for mankind is possible.

Jesus replied, "This is the most important."
(Mark 12:29–31)

Hear O Israel, the Lord our God, the Lord
is One; and you shall love the Lord your God
with all your heart and with all your soul and
with all your mind and with all your strength.
(Deuteronomy 6:4–5)

The second is this: Love your neighbor as
yourself. No other commandment is greater than
these. (Mark 12:31)

Commitment

When we understand everything, the Savior does for us. He becomes the most important person in our lives.

We then pray a lot, give thanks, and go to church.

Mark Nichols Perry.

Sermon: Commit to Commitment! Text: Romans 12:1–2.

1. The Call of Commitment (v. 1a): "I beseech you."
2. The Context of Commitment (v. 1b): "The mercies of God."
3. The Character of Commitment (v. 1c): "That you present your bodies."
4. The Commands of Commitment (v. 2a): "Be not conformed, be ye transformed."
5. The Confirmation of Commitment (v. 2b): "That you prove."

Conclusion: A Christian without commitment is incomplete; however, a committed Christian is powerful, strong, and influential.

What is Jesus trying to teach us?

What will you do when someone is begging for help? How would you treat your brother?

Let us read Matthew 15:22–28 and see what it says.

> A Canaanite woman from that vicinity came to him, crying out, "Lord, Son of David, have mercy on me! My daughter is demon-possessed and suffering terribly."

Galatians 6:1ff. Notice what Jesus is teaching here.

Will a beggar turn away from asking for help? Or have you turned away from helping your neighbor?

> Jesus did not answer a word.
>
> So, his disciples came to him and urged him, "Send her away, for she keeps crying out after us."
>
> He answered, "I was sent only to the lost sheep of Israel."
>
> The woman came and knelt before him. "Lord, help me!" she said.
>
> He replied, "It is not right to take the children's bread and toss it to the dogs."
>
> "Yes, it is, Lord," she said. "Even the dogs eat the crumbs that fall from their master's table."
>
> Then Jesus said to her, "Woman, you have great faith! Your request is granted." And her daughter was healed at that moment.

It doesn't matter what other religious leaders may see or trust; our primary treasures are in Jesus. Do it his way.

Confidence

> This is the confidence we have in approaching God: that if we ask anything according to his will, he hears us. (1 John 5:14)

Now listen. God hears you, and his answer either is manifested or unmanifested. Either way, your answer is coming in its complete form.

I have seen where some folks prayed and asked for things long ago, waiting on an answer, when in fact, they already received it long ago. Yes or no is physically seen without a doubt.

Bridges are built by engineers and not by students. Students are helpers.

You want to be a leader, don't be a heretic by trying to build a bridge without a blueprint.

Criticism

Criticism is the only reliable form of autobiography, Oscar Wilde said, "because it tells you more about the psychology of the critic than the people he or she criticizes."

Astute professionals can formulate a viable diagnostic hypothesis just from hearing someone's criticisms.

Criticism is destructive to relationships when it is

- about personality or character rather than behavior;
- filled with blame;
- not focused on improvement;
- based on only one "right way" to do things;
- belittling; to belittle, you have to be little.

Criticism in close relationships starts out on a low key, in most cases, and escalates over time, forming a downward spiral of resentment. The criticized person feels controlled, which frustrates the critical partner, who then steps up the criticism, increasing the other's sense of being controlled, and so on.

Why criticism doesn't work.

At no time in this downward spiral does an obvious fact occur to critical people: Criticism is an utter failure at getting positive behavior change. Any short-term gain you might get from it builds resentment down the line.

Criticism fails because it embodies two of the things that human beings hate the most:

It calls for submission, and we hate to submit.

It devalues, and we hate to feel devalued.

Suppose you offended someone you don't closely know; how could you handle such as to be to those whom you are closer to?

Times have changed, and everything seems like the days of old, but we only learn through intervention how to grow into much larger things that work for us.

Start with kindness and forgiveness, and with proper knowledge, develops into a much greater strength and friendship (Romans 15:4).

Godliness controls our danger anger but humbles us into the spirit of godliness.

> For this very reason, make every effort to add to your faith virtue; and to virtue, knowledge; and to knowledge, self-control; and to self-control, perseverance; and to perseverance, godliness; and to godliness, brotherly kindness; and to brotherly kindness, love. (2 Peter 1:5–7)

Lastly, critical people were often criticized in early childhood by caretakers, siblings, or peers, at an age when criticism can be especially painful.

PTSD occurs, and the mind still may carry overwhelming feelings instilled into a relationship, which causes mild problems before escalating over time into a larger problem, then deescalating again and again.

Even with church families. But we usually don't bother messing with families in the church, just people we don't dine with that often.

To discontinue or by disowning a brother or sister because one cannot find the jive in how things are done, such should be taught.

And if leaders are watching over the flock (by knowing who they are), things tend to run much more smoothly, and gossiping fails at the door.

Our family members do good when its members are communicating and are committed to one another in faith (1 Peter 5:2).

Crucifixion

A communion prayer:

> Lord Jesus, I bow before you in humility and ask you to examine my heart today. Show me anything that is not pleasing to you.
>
> Reveal any secret pride, any unconfessed sin, any rebellion or unforgiveness that may be hindering my relationship with you.
>
> I know that I am your beloved child, having received you into my heart and life and having accepted your death as penalty for my sinfulness.
>
> The price you paid covered me for all time, and my desire is to live for you.
>
> As I take the bread representing your life that was broken for me, I remember and celebrate your faithfulness to me and to all who will receive you.
>
> I can't begin to fathom the agonizing suffering of your crucifixion. Yet you took that pain for me. You died for me! Thank you, Jesus. Thank you for your extravagant love and unmerited favor.
>
> Thank you that your death gave me life—abundant life now and eternal life forever.
>
> As you instructed your disciples, I too receive this bread in remembrance of you.
>
> "This do in remembering me" (1 Corinthians 11:23ff)

Dating

Dating at times is repeatedly disturbing when a partner's participation starts to worry you.

Because your climate change in your relationship begins to take on a different temperature, relative to your normal behavior changes.

Here are some failures in dating by forcing yourself into it.

Resist the temptation to call too frequently.

If you interrupt him/her too often, you'll seem clingy, and he or she may get annoyed.

Stick to the times you agreed on for talking and hanging out together.

Don't initiate all your conversations. Give your boyfriend or girlfriend a chance to call you first sometimes too. If you ignore these tiny bits of information, it will doom to fail in a successful relationship with your partner.

Death

For then the dust will return to the earth,
and the spirit will return to God who gave it.
(Ecclesiastes 12:7)

The wind, air, spirit do not die.
Each belongs to God, a gift or our reward on earth.
I love my life with God.

Death on the Cross

The cross is not a specific kind of wood like the ark. It doesn't represent salvation, Jesus does.

Furthermore, it shows how cruel man was and is about people who try to live righteous. Doing the right things.

> As it is written: "For your sake we face death all day long; we are considered as sheep to be slaughtered." (Romans 8:36)

Men were either hung or burned, or their heads were cut off, or they were fed to the lions etc.

The cross affects us all. Thieves were on crosses.

On that day, Jesus took all shame and humiliation upon our behalf. And from his humiliation on the hill where everyone could see him, Jesus provided us with salvation from a sacrifice. He didn't cry, didn't complain, didn't show fear, but did it because that's what God wanted him to do for you and me.

> And being found in appearance as a man, he humbled himself by becoming obedient to death—even death on a cross! (Philippians 2:8)

His shout to heaven only showed his humanity; even at the point of death, we are to distance ourselves from evildoers and look to heaven. Jesus talked to the heavens.

> He was oppressed and afflicted, yet he did not open his mouth; he was led like a lamb to

the slaughter, and as a sheep before its shearers is silent, so he did not open his mouth. (Isaiah 53:7)

Yet it was the LORD'S will to crush him and cause him to suffer, and though the LORD makes his life an offering for sin, he will see his offspring and prolong his days, and the will of the LORD will prosper in his hand. (v. 10)

Today,

For everyone who calls on the name of the Lord will be saved.

But how can they call on him in whom they have not believed?

And how can they believe in him of whom they have not heard?

And how can they hear without someone to preach?

And how can people preach unless they are sent? As it is written,

How beautiful are the feet of those who bring (the) good news! (Romans 10:13–15)

When we start to hang up crosses as a symbol of shame and humiliation, we are no different than those who build idols and worship them.

God was made like us in human form. God has always been spirit throughout eternity. Not a man (Numbers 23:19). We've only seen a body-like spirit who represented man in our likeness.

You can't see the wind, you can't see a spirit, and no man can see God.

He alone can never die, and he lives in light so brilliant that no human can approach him.

> No human eye has ever seen him, nor ever
> will. All honor and power to him forever! Amen.
> (1 Timothy 6:16)

We needed a savior who was made like us.

> Therefore, since we have a great high priest
> who has passed through the heavens, Jesus the
> Son of God, let us hold firmly to what we profess.
> For we do not have a high priest who is unable
> to sympathize with our weaknesses, but we have
> one who was tempted in every way that we are
> yet was without sin. (Hebrews 4:14–15)

Jesus was made like man, who went through sufferings as we
have and are doing so that when we approach the throne of grace, we
can understand that Jesus understood our problems when he came to
earth centuries ago (John 3:16).

Theologians here define the doctrine of God, which is called
theology or significance thereof.

Lastly, Jesus could have died any way he chose, but it was by the
hands of Romans.

Jesus Christ's death by crucifixion was reserved for the worst of
criminals.

But Jesus was not a criminal; he was a just man made like us—a
savior who was sent to the world by the Father in heaven (John
3:16)—who was labeled as nothing but a blasphemer.

Jesus confirmed that He was the Messiah. But was this a blasphemer? No! The Jews were waiting for him.

Jesus confirmed that He was the Son of God.

Jesus confirmed that He was sitting right next to the father
(Hebrews 1:3).

> And when Jesus saw their faith, he said to
> the paralytic, "Son, your sins are forgiven." Now
> some of the scribes were sitting there, question-

ing in their hearts, "Why does this man speak like that? He is blaspheming! Who can forgive sins but God alone?" (Mark 2:5–7, Matthew 9:2–3, and Luke 5:20–21)

Decisions

> Though youths grow weary and tired, and vigorous young men stumble badly, yet those who wait for the LORD Will gain new strength; they will mount up with wings like eagles, they will run and not get tired, they will walk and not become weary. (Isaiah 40:30–31)

The worldly mind tends to dance in the face of Christianity without blinking an eye (1 John 2:16).

Shining words are as full of death as the result from it.

Mankind from the world tends to give Christians bad food to eat, and perhaps some Christians are still eating from the tree of good and evil. Picking bad fruit leads to spiritual separation from God eternally (i.e., the tree of decision). Stay with God.

> If you love me, keep my commands. (John 14:15)

That's the right decision.

Why? Here's why: Romans 6:1ff.

> He restores my soul; He guides me in the paths of righteousness for His name's sake. (Psalm 23:3)

What is absolute becomes our purpose decisions in life.

Have good decision-making; it is your own marketing strategy.

Everybody's decision is different depending upon their own circumstances in life and based upon principles surrounding their environment. Include God and make your life a better light; increase love and appreciation for all to enjoy.

At times, repeatedly man will come to bad decisions in worse conditions when such conditions are not warranted for better terms. Man needs to know what follows ahead or what he is headed for based upon finding of a condition and where its conclusion has final results.

Be careful how much care should be considered while our future references result in our lives.

Families, friends, church, or businesses and expectations to follow.

Be careful how we think—to rethink our own lives and not by sudden decisions that result in consequences that may follow.

Using the Book of Life, the Bible, Word of God results in our destiny (James 1:14).

The Devil

When the devil is looking for help, he then tends to run over to Christians (weak) and begs for mercy, and when you give it, he smiles. From that point, he begins using you for all purpose. Leave him alone (John 8:44).

Give no opportunity to the devil (Ephesians 4:27).

Be alert and of sober mind. Your enemy the devil prowls around like a roaring lion looking for someone to devour (1 Peter 5:8).

Don't help a devilish liar (John 8:44).

Look, leaders, tell more your group how important this is.

As for me, I am sober to all possibilities.

Devoted

One day at about the ninth hour, he had a clear vision of an angel of God who came to him and said, "Cornelius!" Cornelius stared at him in fear and asked, "What is it, Lord?" The angel answered, "Your prayers and gifts to the poor have ascended as a memorial offering before God.

Now send men to Joppa to call for a man named Simon who is called Peter. (Acts 10:4–6)

Notice here a devout man who feared God with all his house and who gave much alms to the people and prayed to God always.

Meaning, to be devout is to be deeply devoted to one's religion or to another belief, cause, or way of life.

Stop telling folks that God doesn't hear a sinner who has not obeyed the gospel yet.

"We know that God does not listen to sinners, but if anyone is a worshiper of God and does his will" (John 9:31), God listens to him.

Did God listen to Cornelius? Yes. Why? Because he was doing the right thing but needed to be baptized.

And Cornelius said, "Four days ago I was fasting until this hour; and at the ninth hour I prayed in my house, and, behold, a man stood before me in bright clothing, And said, (in other words) Cornelius, your prayer is heard, and your giving are in remembrance in the sight of God." (vv. 30–31)

God remembers your good.

What was the plan?

Listen carefully.

> Then Peter went down to the men which were sent unto him from Cornelius; and said, Behold, I am he whom ye seek: what is the cause wherefore ye are come?
>
> And they said, Cornelius the centurion, a just man, and one that feareth God, and of good report among all the nation of the Jews, was warned from God by an holy angel to send for thee into his house, (and to hear words of thee).

Words of life preach to you how to be saved.

My friends, baptism is important to our salvation (Romans 10:17).

> And he commanded them to be baptized in the name of the Lord. Then prayed they him to tarry certain days. (v. 48)

Oftentimes, folks are glad to run to the water to baptize somebody when they are neither devout nor seeking God; it's all because you want to baptize.

Nonetheless, do what is right.

If anyone hears the word of God, let them be convicted and convinced of the word of God.

Stop hurrying people to the water if they are not seriously ready to receive the word of God.

Acts of this sort is unbecoming to your own soul salvation at hand.

When anyone that has accepted faith, it came by hearing the word of God.

Now, what else? Faith leads to action, and that action is baptism.

The overall word picture of faith action is practice that's in the command. Doing all that is required gets the reward.

God is just:

> He will pay back trouble to those who trouble you and give relief to you who are troubled, and to us as well. This will happen when the Lord Jesus is revealed from heaven in blazing fire with his powerful angels.
> He will punish those who do not know God and do not obey the gospel of our Lord Jesus.
> They will be punished with everlasting destruction and shut out from the presence of the Lord and from the glory of his might on the day he comes to be glorified in his holy people and to be marveled at among all those who have believed. (2 Thessalonians 1:6–10)

Discipline

Keeping a healthy conversation and forgetting about inconsistencies that invade spaces.

Be stronger and proactive.

Changeability begins with you.

When speaking about love, it must be genuine, not wavy but serious.

Living for Jesus is to discipline the heart to serve in a holy way, against the war in the world.

Surely one can enjoy life while living in your Christian faith.

But it seems satisfying to another who loves doing wrongful things. It leads to unrepented hearts.

And it seems satisfying to tell others who are called that what they are doing is sinful or unscriptural, while it's nothing but one opinion.

Examples:

Don't tell people that a kitchen is unscriptural having in a building.

Don't tell me I can't bowl or have fun on vacation on a beach where women are present.

Don't tell me I can't discipline my kids when they are out of order in public.

Don't tell me how to live in my own house.

Enough said.

God is the judge of all foolishness in this world, and his kindness shall never cease.

When you feel a person is wrong, go to that person alone, needing no help from thy neighbor (Matthew 18:15, 5:23).

If your righteousness is fulfilled, then advise another.

Casting down imaginations, not accepting the devil's thoughts, suggestions, visions is a spiritual weapon that you must use to be victorious over the enemy (2 Corinthians 10:5–6).

You must learn to actively fight to maintain God's vision for you.

You must only accept imaginations (thoughts) that line up with the Word of God.

> If you are called, you will know it, however, to know what you haven't been called for, you won't be able to explain it to anyone. (Romans 8:28)

But fools rush in.

To know God is to totally surrender your life to him.

Otherwise, hypocrisy is nothing new.

Don't pretend you belong to God while your practice is doing evil.

Have you ever got disciplined and you said "I didn't do anything wrong"? That's not true.

No one disciplines anyone without needing it.

Jesus calls for discipline.

We are not perfect; we need our father to discipline us.

Ask God, "Lord, what is it you want me to do?" or "Lord, forgive me of me wrongdoing."

Now when you repent, don't be surprised that discipline comes. It only sharpens your saw. It requires sharpening the saw. It requires having a balanced life. Change is necessary to be in the graces of God.

Doctrine of God

A little theology explains the doctrine of God.

In fact, when God was talking about forever living in Genesis 3:22, it was before sin, but now man has to be obedient to the word of God in order to inherit eternal life through Jesus Christ the Son (John 3:16, 12:48).

Everything at the beginning had to die a physical death, including animals, plants, and man.

Before, in the beginning of time, it was from earth to heaven no sin.

Then sin. Why? Test the word of God's command?

But it didn't have to be spiritual death from man's point of view, so it was.

God fixed it by sending his only son to save his created man (John 3:16).

Therefore, to skip spiritual death, one must become obedient to the word of God (Hebrews 9:27).

Being lost is not the thing to do, as Adam and Eve experienced by forfeiting their claim on eternal life by being disobedient to the word of God (Hebrews 11:4).

Many scholars understand the first animal sacrifice, foreshadowing the eventual death of Christ on the cross for the sins of the world.

Putting these facts together, it would seem that Adam and Eve were saved and did indeed go to heaven/paradise when they died.

Sin causes spiritual death, to be apart eternally from God.

A continuous sacrifice of praise to God daily keeps us alive in the Spirit, away from sin, because of Adam (Romans 5:12–21).

Jesus taught many, including us, how to live (1 Peter 2:21).

See John 12:48.

Since Adam's sin, God put a sword in the east of the garden, drove out both man and woman.

> So, he drove out the man; and he placed at the east of the garden of Eden Cherubim's, and a flaming sword which turned every way, to keep the way of the tree of life. (Genesis 3:24)

> God presented Him as an atoning sacrifice through faith in His blood, in order to demonstrate His righteousness, because in His forbearance He had passed over the sins committed beforehand. (Romans 3:25)

Very good time at church today.
God was there.

> He has made everything beautiful in its time. He has also set eternity in the hearts of men, yet they cannot fathom the work that God has done from beginning to end. (Ecclesiastes 3:11)

Don't Give Up

Never let anyone convince you to give up your spiritual walk with Christ (John 6:66–69).

If so, you are no better off than Eve in the garden of Eden.

> "You will not certainly die," the serpent said to the woman. "For God knows that when you eat from it your eyes will be opened, and you will be like God, knowing good and evil." (Genesis 3:4–5)

God had said, "The day that you eat of [this tree] you shall surely die" (Genesis 2:17).

The serpent said, "You will not surely die" (Genesis 3:4).

That was a lie, my friends, a damnable lie to bring forth an action not intended for man; if he followed after righteousness, he would have lived, loved, and appreciated God even more.

Instead, Adam followed the words of Satan.

Satan wasn't the creator. Didn't Adam and his wife know this?

Yes. So why follow any other advice?

Listen to the rest of the lie by Satan, a non-creator.

> For God knows that when you eat of it your eyes will be opened, and you will be like God, knowing good and evil. (John 8:44)

Therefore, Jesus says of him in John 8:44 that he is both a liar and murderer.

Don't look over there at another tree that is not life, but death.

Don't follow devised tales.
Don't spit in God's face.
Don't call God a liar.
Listen to Jesus.

Doubt

And indeed, have mercy on those who
doubt; save others by snatching them from the
fire; and to still others, show mercy tempered
with fear, hating even the clothing stained by the
flesh.

Now to Him who is able, to keep you from
stumbling and to present you unblemished in His
glorious presence, with great joy. (Jude 1:22–24)

Oftentimes people don't give the people who they know love and
credit for overcoming struggles; either folks don't care or they become
accusers by living and listening to the devil. No sense of exhortation
as it is commanded by God.

Some folks seem to be hoodwinked and bamboozled and don't
even know it, because the devil has misled them at his will (Hebrews
3:13).

Being so beguiled and trapped, it is hard to get through the
thick.

Rescue others by snatching them from the flames of judgment
(Jude 1:23).

Show mercy to still others, but do so with great caution, hating
the sins that contaminate their lives.

Listen.

Then they will come to their senses and
escape the snare of the devil, who has taken them
captive to his will. (2 Timothy 2:26)

Let God be an example to others by the life you live in Christ (Job 1).

I know of some professors who are worthless, who don't care for the people.

No passion, just giving a speech on Sundays, never answering the phone, doesn't get involved in the full responsibility of the work they're called to do.

This is why we lose so many because they don't have enough money like others do or pay attention to.

Folks just don't keep up with the word of God.

Some don't get it.

> What do you think? If a man owns a hundred sheep, and one of them wanders away, will he not leave the ninety-nine on the hills and go to look for the one that wandered off? (Matthew 18:12)

Now are they quickly doing this or letting it go by—so long that it really doesn't matter?

> He that rejecteth me, and receiveth not my words, hath one that judgeth him: the word that I have spoken, the same shall judge him in the last day. (John 12:48)

Get busy, not too late; go find the strays. They are backed in the world looking for opportunities.

And give no opportunity to the devil (Ephesians 4:27).

Doubt challenges you to find answers.

Don't doubt.

Don't yield to temptation.

Why? Temptations lie and cause more doubt.

Temptation will knock on the door, just don't yield to it.

Remember 1 Corinthians 10:13.

Believe God by the highest authority in the eternal world.

Edification

We who are strong ought to bear with the failings of the weak and not to please ourselves.

Each of us should please our neighbors for their good, to build them up.

For even Christ did not please himself (Matthew 20:28), but, as it is written: "The insults of those who insult you have fallen on me."

For everything that was written in the past was written to teach us (Romans 15:4), so that through the endurance taught in the Scriptures and the encouragement they provide we might have hope. (Romans 15:1–4)

God is not a man, that he should lie; neither the son of man, that he should repent: hath he said, and shall he not do it? Or hath he spoken, and shall he not make it good? (Numbers 23:19)

Romans 13:1–4, Romans 15:1–4.

Read it again.

Applicable knowledge for all concerns today.

If then God is not a man (John 4:24), why would some treat such a mighty Creator as if he were a man?

Education

Truly, truly, I tell you, no servant is greater than his master, nor is a messenger greater than the one who sent him. (John 13:16)

Education is the thing by which another can become a student, but not in reverse; the student responsible is for learning.

The student is not above the teacher, but everyone who is fully trained will be like their teacher. (Luke 6:40)

It does not matter how long you've been a person of leadership in your body of people; everything you must learn have to come from education, and not by self-preeminence.

Get it: Jesus is the way.

Elders/Bishops

Titus 1:7, a good point given to Titus from Apostle Paul at Crete to ensure, "For a bishop must be blameless, as the steward of God; not self-willed, not soon angry, not given to wine, no striker, not given to filthy lucre."

A man must not be a faker but have genuine confidence of his responsibility.

> Unto the pure all things are pure: but unto them that are defiled, and unbelieving is nothing pure; but even their mind and conscience is defiled. (Titus 1:15)

> Be a lover of hospitality, a lover of good men, sober, just, holy, temperate; Holding fast the faithful word as he hath been taught, that he may be able by sound doctrine both to exhort and to convince the gainsayers. (Titus 1:8–9)

Oftentimes, people beg the form. They want things to be accepted by putting pieces back to its original form, but it can't.

We have a responsibility to keep Humpty-Dumpty from falling off the wall (Romans 10:17).

> Rescue others by snatching them from the flames of judgment. Show mercy to still others, but do so with great caution, hating the sins that contaminate their lives. (Jude 1:23)

Encouragement

The thing to do: pour encouragement into the hearts of others.
A flow that's rapidly in a steady stream of love.
Teaching the Word of God.

Therefore encourage one another and build
each other up, just as in fact you are doing. (1
Thessalonians 5:11)

End Times

The end of times will come so quickly that you cannot understand. God will call his resurrection (1 Corinthians 15:35–58).

Howbeit that a lot of people don't concern themselves about end times.

> For you yourselves are fully aware that the day of the Lord will come like a thief in the night.
>
> While people are saying, "There is peace and security," then sudden destruction will come upon them as labor pains come upon a pregnant woman, and they will not escape.
>
> But you are not in darkness, brothers, for that day to surprise you like a thief. (1 Thessalonians 5:2–4)

Evangelism

Evangelism can be hard when people are not listening to God, when one has preconceived notions of opinions expressed by others (John 12:48).

Listening gets you into heaven, not listening keeps you out (Isaiah 59.1–2).

Evil One

Listen, careful your mind, don't be controlled by the evil one.

> We know that we are children of God, and
> that the whole world is under the control of the
> evil one. (1 John 5:19)

When you allow your mind to wander unto what sounds good,
then you stumble into violating your own conscience.
Listen.

> If anyone, then, knows the good they ought
> to do and doesn't do it, it is sin for them. (James
> 4:17)

Don't challenge yourself to listen to what sounds good but has
a reputation of bad history.
Listen again.

> Their loyalty is divided between God and
> the world, and they are unstable in everything
> they do. (James 1:8)

No man wants to be invited to a mind of "unsubtleness."
Such table is full of troubled signs of defeat and deceit.
Here's what it all means: The action or practice of deceiving
someone by concealing or misrepresenting the truth.

When it originates in your mind, its practices become practical or easy to convince others of the same. Stay away from lures. A lure is used to bait or entice fish to attach themselves to your hook.

> So, pay attention to how you hear. To those who listen to my teaching, more understanding will be given.
> But for those who are not listening, even what they think they understand will be taken away from them. (Luke 8:18)

Eyes of God

Have you ever stuck a hairpin in a wall socket as a child?

Why?

Because your mom told you not to. And you did it anyway.

Took a lesson, didn't it? Shocking experience.

What about sin? Now how many times has God (thought the word) asked you to do something but you didn't, as if God doesn't see anything?

Watch the Word, Romans 10:17.

Examples of God's presence are everywhere (Romans 15:4).

> The eyes of the LORD are everywhere, keeping watch on the wicked and the good. (Proverbs 15:3)

> Nothing in all creation is hidden from God's sight; everything is uncovered and exposed before the eyes of Him to whom we must give account. (Hebrews 4:13)

> For the eyes of the LORD roam to and fro over all the earth, to show Himself strong on behalf of those whose heart is fully devoted to Him. (2 Chronicles 16:9)

> For He looks to the ends of the earth and sees everything under the heavens. (Job 28:24)

Does He not see my ways and count my every step? (Job 31:4)

For His eyes are on the ways of man, and He sees his every step. (Job 34:21)

For a man's ways are before the eyes of the LORD, and the Lord watches all his paths. (Proverbs 5:21)

Now all of a sudden, your life takes a dive into more of the same.

What do you do? Except you repent, you will perish (Luke 13:3).

My friends, God sees everything.

Nothing is hidden from God our Creator (Hebrews 4:13).

Either heaven or hell—your choice.

What shall it be?

There are but some leaders who have to be leaders of grown children.

Faith

Let's talk some more.

Don't float in a boat that has but one oar.

It takes two things to make a trip—oars.

> But someone will say, "You have faith, and
> I have works." Show me your faith without your
> works, and I will show you my faith by my works.
> (James 2:18)

All things are lawful unto me, but all things are not expedient; all things are lawful for me, but I will not be brought under the power of any (1 Corinthians 6:12).

There are certain weights an athlete must choose to lay aside if he's going to succeed.

They may not be bad for other people, but they are bad for an athlete. Usually happens.

In the spiritual realm, it is the same for Christians.

Paul tells us there are things that may be lawful, but "all things are not expedient."

The word *expedient* is similar to the word *expedition*. You see, Christians are going somewhere, and if something doesn't speed us along the way, then it's excess baggage, and we need to get rid of it.

It's weighing you down on your journey. It's holding you back. Let it go.

What do you know about tomorrow? (Nothing.) How can you be so sure about your life? (We can't.) (James 4:14.)

Why? Your answer is, it is nothing more than mist (a morning fog, a vapor) that appears for only a little while before it disappears.

Now, what will you do for Jesus? There are some positive things one can do to make *now* changes rather than worry about waiting until tomorrow.

Make your decisions now. Obey the commands of God. Faith comes by hearing (Romans 10:17).

Listen now, if you hear, why not believe, come to Jesus, get saved?

Acting on our power of choice provides us with more opportunity to change our lives for the better.

The more opportunities we create to change our lives, the more fulfilled and happier our lives become.

Question of concern: What is the difference between sight faith and walking by faith as it implies to your life (2 Corinthians 5:17)?

If God makes the parts inside your body work, you need to protect your outside to prevent damaging the inside.

If God has given us everything that pertains to life and godliness, why does one seek more (2 Peter 1:3)?

Question: What does your faith look like?

When you sing songs of praises, what does it look like?

Suppose now you are praying to God, how has your faith improved?

Usually when praying to God and asking forgiveness for sins, and God forgives you, why do you keep asking forgiveness from repeated sins?

God has already forgiven you; all you need to do is straighten up. Get it right.

Write about Jesus—that's the thing to evangelize (Acts 4:12).

Many people love having small talk; they do it often but pay attention to what is promised and deliver, unless you had no intention in believing it yourself.

Such people of untruths are likely; walk away next time.

They will get the message.

Learn, it takes away gossip stories.

God is always concerned "for his people."

> Though seeing many things, you do not observe.
> Though your ears are open, you hear nothing. (Isaiah 42:20)

What's going on?
Why?
The Bible reminds us to watch.

> So, you must be careful to do everything they tell you.
> (If they tell you to hate, don't do it, love instead; if they tell you to be church people instead of Christians, don't do it, be Christlike in your gatherings.)
> But do not do what they do, for they do not practice what they preach. (Matthew 23:3)

Amen, somebody.
Who are they? Those are the Pharisees and scribes who are self-identified by what they claim to be.
What will you give to God at your call of passing?
I mean, what could you take with you at your going when he comes (Hebrews 9:27)?
Listen your Bible.

> For we brought nothing into the world, and we can take nothing out of it. (1 Timothy 6:7)

Are you listening?

> Then Job stood up, tore his robe, and shaved his head. He fell to the ground and worshiped, saying: "Naked I came from my mother's womb,

and naked I shall return. The LORD gave, and the LORD has taken away. Blessed be the name of the LORD."

In all this, Job did not sin or charge God with wrongdoing. (Job 1:20–22)

Doing his will, you gain a better life.

His master said to him, "Well done, good and faithful servant. You have been faithful over a little; I will set you over much. Enter into the joy of your master." (Matthew 25:23)

Have you any souls to save (Proverbs 11:30)!

Some want to save all their money; expectations of their life have been put on hold. They who do so enjoy nothing to be proud of nor seen.

A wasted life has no gain.

Listen.

So I saw that there's nothing better for people than to be happy in their work.

That is our lot in life. And no one can bring us back to see what happens after we die. (Ecclesiastes 3:22)

Here is what I have seen to be good: it is appropriate to eat, drink, and experience good in all the labor one does under the sun during the few days of his life God has given him, because that is his reward. (Ecclesiastes 5:18)

Today, even in the church, there are some who believe "once saved, always saved" by their reason of doing nothing for their salvation.

They say to themselves, "I got saved, now I'm safe."

Not so. Read Philippians 2:2.

Therefore, my dear friends, as you have always obeyed—not only in my presence, but now much more in my absence—continue to work out your salvation with fear and trembling.

Now ask yourself this question: What am I engaged in that produces the work of God?

If it's nothing, you will get nothing.

Hebrews 9:27.

Can faith be dead in your body or alive in your body?

Let's examine (2 Corinthians 13:5).

Test yourselves to see if you are in the faith.

Examine yourselves.

Or do you yourselves not recognize that Jesus Christ is in you? Unless you fail the test.

(Watch this now: "Unless you fail the test.") For Christ cannot be in you if you are not in Christ or the Spirit in you.

> You are not in the flesh but in the Spirit, if indeed the Spirit of God dwells in you. But if anyone does not have the Spirit of Christ, he does not belong to Him. (Romans 8:9)

Now who does the testing?

You, my friends—a person tests his or her own body.

No one but you alone.

Give yourself this test today.

Be seriously committed to Jesus, without following what everyone else is doing. Do yourself a favor—test your life.

Now here's your test.

Just one simple example of a test.

> What doth it profit my brethren, though a man say he hath faith, and have not works? Can faith save him?
>
> If a brother or sister be naked, and destitute of daily food. And one of you say unto them,

depart in peace, be ye warmed and filled; not-withstanding ye give them not those things which are needful to the body; what doth it profit.

Even so faith, if it hath not works, is dead, being alone.

Yea, a man may say, thou hast faith, and I have works shew me thy faith without thy works, and I will shew thee my faith by my works.

Thou believiest that there is one God; thou doest well: the devils also believe, and tremble.

But wilt thou know, O vain man, that faith without works is dead?

Was not Abraham, our father, justified by works when he had offered Isaac, his son, upon the altar?

Seest thou how faith wrought with his works, and by works was faith made perfect?

And the scripture was fulfilled which saith, Abraham believed God, and it was imputed unto him for righteousness: and he was called the Friend of God.

Ye see then how that by works a man is jus-tified, and not by faith only. (James 2:14–26)

Test your body.

What dwells in your body that is the most important of all eternity?

Between the two, life or eternal separation from God.

By not telling others about faith is not the faith in you.

Rather you sit around talking about silly matters from one day to another.

Ask yourself, "When did I mention Jesus in my conversation today?"

Was it 1 percent or no percent? What a terrible way to expect for your hope in eternity.

Isaiah has the idea for both spiritual matters in how to present himself to God.

Listen.

> I will greatly rejoice in the Lord; my soul shall exult in my God, for he has clothed me with the garments of salvation; he has covered me with the robe of righteousness, as a bridegroom decks himself like a priest with a beautiful headdress, and as a bride adorns herself with her jewels. (Isaiah 61:10)

Dressing up in the righteousness of God, by whom you represent.

My friends, don't go to church as if you are attending a picnic or rock concert.

Present yourself, your faith to God.

There have been parents who allowed their children to put kinds of different colors in their hair, looking as if a toolbox; you don't know whatever comes next, having no respect for the reverence to God, rather giving yourself to worldly attributes is wrong.

Having a half-worldly and half-righteous mind does not reduce the word of God.

> For the righteousness of God is revealed from the beginning of old till now, the just, (that's a living you), shall or will live by faith. (Hebrews 4:12, Romans 1:16–17)

Pretending as if you have no idea of what is meant here throws you way off course in your eternity with God.

Listen, listen.

Who is faith, Jesus?

Watch.

> Dear friends, although I was very eager to write to you about the salvation we share, I felt compelled to write and urge you to contend for the faith that was once for all entrusted to God's holy people. (Jude 1:3)

Faith in fact increases your minds to understand the differences for the righteous heavenly meaning of faith in God.

Present yourself a living sacrifice, holy and acceptable to God, not to the world, going to meet with your fellow saints in a collective body of believers (Romans 12:1ff).

Listen, there's nothing to be embarrassed about making it right for a few hours, then after you get used to change, it makes you even become better.

I have seen with my own eyes how folks are encouraged to change.

How about you?

Woe to you who slip back into the world by changing your righteous mind to become cool like the world.

Do not do that.

Ephesians 4:1ff.

Church is not a picnic.

Read all of 1 Corinthians 11.

Remember this: the church that Jesus has is built upon righteous behavior and practices, not on your self-idealism.

Clean yourselves up for the righteousness of God.

Putting on your righteous suit for Jesus.

Both literal and spiritual mind.

Listen, there are different kinds of people.

One that dress like righteous behavior and one who do not.

Don't turn in your righteousness to worldly attributes.

Wasn't it God who called you out of darkness in his holiness (i.e., light)?

Yes, so who turned your hand against eternity with God?

Listen again.

Test your faith, your inner being (1 Peter 2:9).

See if your heart belongs to the everlasting God in heaven.

> Examine yourselves to see whether you are in the faith; test yourselves.
>
> Do you not realize that Christ Jesus is in you—unless, of course, you fail the test? (2 Corinthians 13:5)

> You shall not misuse the name of the Lord your God, for the Lord will not hold anyone guiltless who misuses his name. (Exodus 20:7)

> You must not swear falsely by My name and so profane the name of your God. I am the LORD. (Leviticus 19:12)

> You shall not take the name of the LORD your God in vain, for the LORD will not leave anyone unpunished who takes His name in vain. (Deuteronomy 5:11)

> Fear the LORD your God, serve Him, and take your oaths using only His name. (Deuteronomy 6:13)

> You are to fear the LORD your God and serve Him. Hold fast to Him and take your oaths in His name. (Deuteronomy 10:20)

Don't forget to fight the good fight of faith.

We're in it for the perfecting of the saints.

If the devil is busy working, how should we be busy saving souls for Jesus (Proverbs 11:30)?

Prayer is a big part of our lives. Don't let anyone tell you how to pray and when to pray.

I shall never stop feeding you the Word of God—that's my training and mission.

This battle is not yours, it's the Lord's.

God will turn your enemies against themselves and destroy them all (2 Chronicles 20:1ff).

Let God fight your battles.

> As they began to sing and praise, the Lord set ambushes against the men of Ammon and Moab and Mount Seir who were invading Judah, and they were defeated.
>
> The Ammonites and Moabites rose up against the men from Mount Seir to destroy and annihilate them. After they finished slaughtering the men from Seir, they helped to destroy one another. (vv. 22–23)

I love my family of believers and hope you have a wonderful day at services. Tell your preacher that you appreciate his work. Always give thanks.

> Be thankful in all circumstances, for this is God's will for you who belong to Christ Jesus. (1 Thessalonians 5:18)

Making your life with God his. Not yours (Romans 12:1–3).

Listen, folks, be careful of these fake, so-called Christians pretending to be righteous.

He should reconsider his decision before going to where he belongs.

To stay far away from God's people.

> Watch out for those dogs, those evildoers, those mutilators of the flesh. (Philippians 3:2)

So, the great dragon was cast out, that serpent of old, called the Devil and Satan, who deceives the whole world; he was cast to the earth, and his angels were cast out with him. (Revelation 12:9)

Therefore rejoice, O heavens, and you who dwell in them! Woe to the inhabitants of the earth and the sea! For the devil has come down to you, having great wrath, because he knows that he has a short time. (v. 12)

Someday we shall know why the devil is on the earth to tempt us to sins.

Faith for a nonchild of God cannot be defined by these principles.

He may pray in this manner: "Lord, thank you for my life, and thank you, for I give money to help the poor. Thank you for being in my life. I love you. I have faithfulness."

Listen, folks, remember Cornelius? Acts 10, read all of it.

He had to do something in order to perfect his faith.

He came by hearing, but hearing alone is not addressing your faith.

Faith is an action, and not by your reasons alone.

Faith is by a command, and not by any other thought.

Listen.

Ye see then how that by works a man is justified, and not by faith only. (James 2:24)

If you have not been taught the Word of God and baptized into the body of Christ's church, your faith is vain and has not done what is required of God.

For all of you who were baptized into Christ have clothed yourselves with Christ. (Galatians 3:27)

Clothing means covering up in baptism by the hands of God or buried in water. A full covering washes away your sin; thus, you come in contact with the blood of Jesus.

> Buried with him in baptism, wherein also ye are risen with him through the faith of the operation of God, who hath raised him from the dead. (Colossians 2:12)

> But if we walk in the light, as he is in the light, we have fellowship with one another, and the blood of Jesus, his Son, purifies us from all sin. (1 John 1:7)

If you began your walk (action) in Christ, he will cleanse you from your sins.

But first you need to start walking.

Romans 10:17.

Anything you say or do might be used against you in your church?

That's completely false because many times folks will run into potholes in the road, and God shall deliver those of sincere minds, provided that you let go of your issues.

Without God, you have no idea where you're headed.

Remember, if it seems worse, God can deliver.

> For all have sinned and fall short of the glory of God. (Romans 3:23)

Leaders who take care of their wives are an example to us. A man who takes care of the church is an important model to God. It all counts with God.

God has already heard you and is working it out for you.

> If you want people to like you, forgive them when they wrong you. (Proverbs 17:9)

> To start a quarrel is to release a flood;
> so, abandon the dispute before it breaks out.
> (Proverbs 17:14)

The start of an argument is like the first break in a dam; stop it before it goes any further.

> A man of great anger must pay the penalty;
> if you rescue him, you will have to do so again.
> (Proverbs 19:19)

In other words, don't go and rescue people that God has disciplined, because God is still working on them; and if you do, you will have to start again.

Wait on God, then you shall see the work he has done in that person's life (1 Corinthians 10:13, Romans 10:17). Except they turn away again to sin.

Faithful

The church is an institution of trust where God walks among his people, who watches over or guards (Revelation 2).

Sure, one may say, "Some bad people are in it." However, I believe some may be lagging behind, not steadily applying their faith and practices.

Matthew 13:34–30.

Look!

Demons are looking for opportunities, and their father is the devil, but remember this: the devil cannot be in the church belonging to Christ; it may appear as demons sit in righteousness, but they are only passing through to see who they can devour.

> Be sober, be vigilant; because your adversary the devil, as a roaring lion, walketh about, seeking whom he may devour. (1 Peter 5:8)

> But in a great house there are not only vessels of gold and of silver, but also of wood and of earth; and some to honour, and some to dishonor. If a man therefore purge himself from these, he shall be a vessel unto honour, sanctified, and meet for the master's use, and prepared unto every good work. Flee also youthful lusts: but follow righteousness, faith, charity, peace, with them that call on the Lord out of a pure heart. (2 Timothy 2:20–22)

Now it appears that some haven't fled youthful lust, and that's the things demon workers are looking for in a well-designed church.

Weakness among its members, catching them, never to recover by their own will.

Listen to your Bible again.

> When an impure spirit comes out of a person, it goes through arid places seeking rest and does not find it.
>
> Then it says, 'I will return to the house I left.'
>
> When it arrives, it finds the house unoccupied, swept clean and put in order.
>
> Then it goes and takes with it seven other spirits more wicked than itself, and they go in and live there.
>
> And the final condition of that person is worse than the first. That is how it will be with this wicked generation. (Matthew 12:43–45)

Why? Because God knows the heart of mankind.

> If they have escaped the corruption of the world by knowing our Lord and Savior Jesus Christ and are again entangled in it and are overcome, they are worse off at the end than they were at the beginning. (2 Peter 2:20)

Don't give the devil an opportunity to pull you back into sin after God has saved you from it (Ephesians 4:27).

Here's the thing.

> And do not bring sorrow to God's Holy Spirit by the way you live.

Remember, he has identified you as his own, guaranteeing that you will be saved on the day of redemption. (Ephesians 4:30)

Stay in your salvation (Psalm 34:15–22).

The church, your work, must be a fantastic stronghold, where many shall gather together to worship God as firmly glued together in Spirit and with truth (John 4:24).

It must be a remarkable place, and its atmosphere, it shall be the greatest, whereby many shall come and say, "We go to church where we are taught of God's commands and how we shall live, and the gospel is applied daily and remembered, and its people rejoice by hearing it, being filled up with the word of God."

Now keep your Bible open. It is written from the pen of David; out of his heart, he says, "I will bless the Lord at all times: his praise shall continually be in my mouth. My soul shall make her boast in the Lord: the humble shall hear thereof and be glad. O magnify the Lord with me, and let us exalt his name together" (Psalm 34:1–3).

Open up your Bible, and let us read together these verses from Ephesians 3:16–20.

That God would grant you, according to the riches of his glory, to be strengthened with might by his Spirit in the inner man;

(Let it be your will to listen and obey the word of God by putting into practice your faithfulness to him)

That Christ may dwell in your hearts by faith; that ye, being rooted and grounded in love,

(Let your heart be of Christ and allow self to deeply think about the things God wants you to do)

May be able to comprehend with all saints what is the breadth, and length, and depth, and height;

> (Growth is a must to any child of his father; without growth, there is no safety [2 Peter 3:18]).

> And to know the love of Christ, which passeth knowledge, that ye might be filled with all the fullness of God.

Now abide faith, hope, love; the greater is the summation of the three.

Where there is no love, no faith, and no hope, whom shall you put your trust in?

Listen again to Romans 8:24, Hebrews 11:1, 2 Corinthians 4:18. For God is love (1 John 4:7–21).

> Now unto him that is able, to do exceedingly abundantly above all that we ask or think, according to the power that worketh in us; unto him be glory in the church by Christ Jesus throughout all ages, world without end.
>
> Amen.

How dedicated are you?

The tongue is something else.

Are you building up the body of Christ with your words or tearing it down?

> He who is not with me is against me, and he who does not gather with me scatters. (Matthew 12:30)

We can be just as much enemies of Jesus with our mouths as we can with our actions. Words are very powerful in the building up or tearing down of the body of Christ, his church.

> The tongue has the power of life and death, and those who love it will eat its fruit. (Proverbs 18:21)

> See to it, brothers, that none of you has a wicked heart of unbelief that turns away from the living God.
> But exhort one another daily as long as it is called today, so that none of you may be hardened by sin's deceitfulness.
> We have come to share in Christ if we hold firmly to the end the assurance, we had at first. (Hebrews 3:12–14)

Notice the *if* here; subsequently to your choice—either for God or away from your Creator.

Practice your faithfulness so that it shall become a daily affirmation to your practical life.

For some, they had to get rid old-age habits forming.

Let God be your light.

Give up smoking.

Give up lying.

Give up debauchery.

Give up drinking.

Give up everything that may separate you from your Creator (Romans 8:35–39).

Your answer should be "Nothing."

Family

The devil has separated families all over the places in America. Don't people care any longer?

You can't be in your own world, omitting your own blood kin.

A little reminder of purpose: Did God tempt Abraham in Genesis 22:1–2? (James 1:13.)

Abraham trusted God, and he believed in the resurrection of Isaac, if anything would happen to his only son; therefore, he believes God (Genesis 22:7–8).

Did not Jesus believe God the Father and believed in his resurrection? Yes.

There is no comparison or an allegory relation between Isaac and Jesus.

Isaac didn't die by the hands of evil men, and it did not please God to bruise him (Isaiah 53:4, 10, and 12). Rather, it was a test of Abraham's faith, and since it was, credit for his actions doing exactly what God wanted Abraham to do, and Isaac subsequently submitted to his father, Abraham.

Isaac yielding to this shows what God intended to do for all today, under great faith (Genesis 22:9ff); he wasn't afraid but concerned. Jesus yielded to his crucifixion, wasn't afraid.

However, God did no harm to Isaac. No.

How many sons did Abraham have at this time?

Two, but God was talking about the son of promise and not the bond woman, but the free woman.

First Love

Staying in the church is important (Hebrews 10:25, Galatians 6:1ff).

Don't let people push you into alcohol or drugs or anything that separates you from the love of God (Romans 8:35–39).

Touch the garment of Jesus. Get healed by faith.

Walk away from the devil and his broken promises.

Heavy hitters, listen. Jesus was vocal about sin but waited until he had demonstrated his love and compassion first before speaking out about it.

That's the proper sequence Jesus modeled for us.

He knew society wouldn't listen to what he had to say about morality unless they understood that he cared about them.

Compassion teaches with strength of the word given by mouths of those who love the Word of God.

Unless you have compassion for people, you have no business teaching otherwise.

How then can they call on the one they have not believed in?

And how can they believe in the one of whom they have not heard?

And how can they hear without someone preaching to them? Or a preacher, normally called to preach the whole counsel of God (1 Peter 4:11)?

And how can they preach unless they are sent? As it is written, "How beautiful are the feet of those who bring good news!" (Romans 10:14–15).

Question comes to you. Do you have good news, or are you nothing but a Goliath wanting to destroy the man coming to God or perhaps lost his way home? (Galatians 6:1ff).

Many have traveled the road of destruction.

Liberal? Yes, but only in terms of economics—generously serving and caring for those in need of help and hope (Matthew 20:28).

Clearly, Jesus was more about heart than rules. Jesus was first and foremost a servant. He led with compassion, healing and feeding everywhere he went.

Jesus expected his followers to do the same, and the church did for the better part of 1,900 years.

Jesus warned us of the potential abuses when political leaders wield too much power, assuming responsibilities that his church was intended to have.

The government cannot provide hope, only help; at the same time, Jesus did not deny the authority of government in society. Researchers have found that, in fact, Jesus went so far as to subject himself to the legal system and pay taxes, because he is the one who put those rulers in place (John 19:11, Romans 13:1).

Parties can divide us, so it is with the world; but we who are of God are not of it.

By faith we are the children of God, not from a particular party.

> For ye are all the children of God by faith in
> Christ Jesus. (Galatians 3:26)

Read 2 Corinthians 4:1–3 and 1 Corinthians 4:1–3.

The terror of the Lord: This is, of the Lord Jesus, who will be seated on the throne of judgment and who will decide the destiny of all people (2 Corinthians 5:10).

Let God help you. Just let him. It's wonderful to know God. Do it.

Let your trust in Jesus be seen of men.

Some folks have simply lost their first love because they judge and cannot accept forgiveness or won't forgive others but pronounce judgment upon others (Revelation 2).

Here's what they do.

Suppose any man or woman marries a fool.

The Bible says,

> The fool says in his heart, "There is no God."
> They are corrupt, their deeds are vile; there is no one who does good. (Psalm 14:1)

What about most non-Christians?

> Do not be yoked together with unbelievers.
> For what do righteousness and wickedness have in common?
> Or what fellowship can light have with darkness? (2 Corinthians 6:14)

Listen, anyone who wants to marry must marry only in the Lord—as with widows. Get yourself someone who is a Christian, a child of God.

Listen.

It may be hard to convert a worldly person who has no need to serve God.

It might take time.

If you are dating someone who is not a citizen in the kingdom of God, you could be facing struggles; and if you marry such a one, it could be devastating and will hurt your life unless you get out of it.

My friends, there are different kinds of faiths apart from the one faith mentioned in the Bible.

The Lord of one faith has been once delivered, and it has been accepted and given to holy apostles of God (2 Peter 1:3).

And that it was given to us and for us to live by and practice (Ephesians 4:5–6).

But other faiths (not mentioned in your Bible) will divide your family as those written in your Bible (Jude 1:3).

> As Solomon grew old, his wives turned his heart after other gods, and his heart was not fully

devoted to the LORD his God, as the heart of David his father had been. (1 Kings 11:4)

But though we, or an angel from heaven, preach any other gospel unto you than that which we have preached unto you, let him be accursed.

As we said before, so say I now again, if any man preach any other gospel unto you than that ye have received, let him be accursed. (Galatians 1:8–9)

The Bible reminds us to be faithful to the Word, but if we are caught up in a trespass (Galatians 6:1), even God shall deliver when others are not available.

No temptation has overtaken you except what is common to mankind (2 Corinthians 10:13).

And God is faithful; he will not let you be tempted beyond what you can bear.

But when you are tempted, he will also provide a way out so that you can endure it.

But some clever student will point you toward 1 Corinthians 7:13–15, where Paul says, "To the rest I say this (I, not the Lord): If a brother has an unbelieving wife and she is willing to live with him, he must not divorce her. And if a woman has an unbelieving husband and he is willing to live with her, she must not divorce him. For the unbelieving husband is sanctified through his believing wife, and the unbelieving wife is sanctified through her believing husband. Otherwise your children would be unclean, but now they are holy."

Are you listening here?

Some say, you see, this is the fool we've been talking about; you are obligated to stay with them. No, they are not called fools.

Read the rest of it.

We are talking about someone who has been a Christian at one time and departed from the faith; or such, as it may be here, left the church.

You cannot possibly turn them around (Galatians 6:1ff).

Listen.

But if the unbeliever leaves, let it be so.

The brother or the sister is not bound in such circumstances; God has called us to live in peace.

Most people are not mind readers or body readers.

Because you didn't know that person was going to let go of God's hand, you should not be strangled by the life that person chose to dwell in.

If they continue to subject their lives to debauchery, night living, drugs, and alcohol as well.

That is the kind of person you should let go of, and especially a fool (Psalm 14:1).

One cannot sanctify a fool (Psalm 14:1).

I sincerely believe that it is talking about someone who was a believer, now apostatized.

Remember where it says,

> If they have escaped the corruption of the world by knowing our Lord and Savior Jesus Christ and are again entangled in it and are overcome, they are worse off at the end than they were at the beginning. (2 Peter 2:20)

Usually a careful devout Christian will not make mistakes going down the path of destruction by choosing their mate outside of Christ.

But remember, any child of God can be fooled as Eve was deceived (1 Timothy 2:14).

And Adam was not the one deceived; it was the woman who was deceived and became a sinner.

I'm saying here even though Adam decided to stay with Eve because there was no one else. Today, most people will not.

You must start paying attention to your spiritual beliefs and not fail in making good decisions.

Just be cautious about everything and take your time.

> And Jacob served seven years for Rachel;
> and they seemed unto him but a few days, for the
> love he had to her. When the seven years were
> fulfilled at last, Jacob spent his wedding night
> only to discover at dawn that it wasn't Rachel,
> but her elder sister Leah whom Laban had deliv-
> ered to Jacob's tent. (Genesis 29:18–30)

Listen, others will then judge you because they simply don't have the full story; they judge you based upon what they see. Bible history is not in question.

People don't mind what we read from scriptures but only to justify what they may see today in our life (none of their business).

Every man stands before God with his own life (Hebrews 9:27).

> For we must all appear before the judgment
> seat of Christ, so that each of us may receive what
> is due us for the things done while in the body,
> whether good or bad. (2 Corinthians 5:10)

God sees and knows all (Hebrews 4:13).

Leave God to judge, not your business (Matthew 7).

Perhaps you might have some little bad secrets that you have hidden from many, but yet you judge your brother.

Don't do it.

Remember, for we walk by faith, not by sight (2 Corinthians 5:7).

To stay with a fool is foolishness, knowing it's is wrong to be living that way.

Rather ask God to begin again.

Other people will mislead your life as if they seem to have a direct revelation from God or something else to judge your life.

Not so, my friends.

Watch them who say, "Oh no, you are stuck with the fool because you cannot marry again, because it would be unscriptural to do so."

Keep your business away from weak people.

The language in 1 Corinthians 7 is that of describing a Christian who has gone back into the world versus an atheist who does not believe in God anymore or a skeptic.

Others will reach to Matthew 19, not knowing the truth about Jewish philosophy and history.

Those who judge you to stay have no mercy or grace and say, "Everything God will forgive except for this one." Not so.

What ignorance.

God forgives any sins that you have repented of as a Christian who may have fallen.

Listen, sin is sin (Romans 6:23).

> I will set out and go back to my father and say to him: Father, I have sinned against heaven and against you. (Luke 15:18)

Ask yourself, did the prodigal son live in debauchery? Yes.

> Not long after he received his inheritance, the younger son got together all he had, set off for a distant country and there squandered his wealth in wild living. (Luke 15:13)

Excessive indulgence in sensual pleasures.

Yes, he repented from his ways, although not married, and came to his senses.

That's what is required.

Hebrews 5:14 does not suggest that we kick people out of church just because they didn't commit sins in their present state (Romans 3:23).

Listen.

> But strong meat belongeth to them that are
> of full age, even those who by reason of use have
> their senses exercised to discern both good and
> evil.

Sometimes it might take a little more teaching.

Just a little bit care and concern for those who don't pay attention or fooled by a fool.

Pray to God and ask to begin again.

> The Lord is not slack concerning his prom-
> ise, as some men count slackness; but is longsuf-
> fering to us-ward, not willing that any should
> perish, but that all should come to repentance.
> (2 Peter 3:9)

Teach people the truth, but if they don't desire the truth, don't find yourself tapped into worldly travelers, by defining your life with a non-Christian.

Stay with Christians no matter how good that person may look.

Remember the devil will offer you something else.

Keep safe in the church.

Holy people.

I have met people who take their friends to family and say, "Look what I got, isn't she beautiful? Or she got what, is it a fool?"

My friends, stay with the church.

Truth seekers, God shall know—not necessarily you can affirm on your own.

Allow God to be first place in your life.

Focus on God

Do you hear God? I mean, what now is your interest?

What sights get before our human eyes, and what words get into our human ears—influence us image-bearers of God and bring deep and lasting impact in the world?

Including how we spend our money.

In a previous generation, the largest companies sold oil and gasoline.

Today, the largest companies sell human attention. Facebook and Instagram want your attention, to sell it to advertisers.

Google and YouTube want your attention for the same reason; and Apple, the largest company of all, created the device that turned all of life into endless possibilities for capturing human attention— the pixelated billboards we now carry around with us all the time.

If you, my friend, want God, ask yourself, what percentage? Are you paying attention to your shame?

Listen, evangelism is the better choice for all Christians to desire. Get your ministry in action today.

> Come now, you who say, "Today or tomorrow we will go to such and such a city, spend a year there, buy and sell, and make a profit" whereas you do not know what will happen tomorrow. For what is your life? It is even a vapor that appears for a little time and then vanishes away. (James 4:13–14)

Follow Jesus

Recompense is a much-needed effort today.
Jesus said,

> O Jerusalem, Jerusalem, you that kill the
> prophets, and stone them which are sent to you,
> how often would I have gathered your people
> together, even as a hen gathers her chickens under
> her wings, and you would not! (Matthew 23:37)

Why?

> Then Jesus told his disciples, "If anyone
> would come after me, let him deny himself and
> take up his cross and follow me."
> For whoever would save his life will lose it,
> but whoever loses his life for my sake will find it.
> For what will it profit a man if he gains the
> whole world and forfeits his soul?
> Or what shall a man give in return for his
> soul? (Matthew 16:16ff)

What does it mean?

It is suggested to say that a condition for discipleship is keeping
our focus on God and not away from it.

The Bible says, "If anyone desires to come after Me, let him
deny himself, and take up his cross daily, and follow Me" (Luke 9:23).

To "take up your cross" is something that has to take place in
your thoughts.

When thoughts that aren't pleasing to God come to your mind during the day, you "put them to death"; in other words, you put them out of your mind.

Example: A judging thought toward your friend comes up, or perhaps a grumbling thought of dissatisfaction for what you have to do today, perhaps work or visiting.

As these thoughts come up in your mind, you choose to analyze and then deny them.

You stand guard at the door of your own heart, and you decide what comes through. When a sinful thought pops up in your mind the first time, it is only a temptation—a suggestion from Satan (1 Corinthians 10:13).

Now, you may choose to deny that thought and not to give it a second thought.

You disagree with it.

You don't dwell on it.

Just let it go.

A firm *no* in your mind.

The psychology of it is you simply don't permit any more to think about it.

My friends, denying these sinful thoughts is how you take up your cross daily.

Did Jesus see the thoughts of Satan through the eyes/mind of Peter?

Yes, Jesus did.

Watch.

> From that time forth began Jesus to shew unto his disciples, how that he must go unto Jerusalem, and suffer many things of the elders and chief priests and scribes, and be killed, and be raised again the third day. Then Peter took him, and began to rebuke him, saying, be it far from thee, Lord: this shall not be unto thee. But he turned, and said unto Peter, get thee behind me, Satan: thou art an offence unto me: for thou

savor not the things that be of God, but those that be of men. Then said Jesus unto his disciples, if any man will come after me, let him deny himself, and take up his cross, and follow me. (Matthew 16:22–24)

What else?

Speak to Jesus. Set your mind goals high upon Christ (Colossians 3:1–3).

Food

Life is too short not to fight for what is good.

First Thessalonians 5:21 says, "Prove all things; hold fast that which is good."

Fight for the good of every soul. And teach the truth, the gospel of Christ, to everyone.

Believers often hinder their growth in grace by not giving themselves up to the spiritual affections raised in their hearts by the Holy Spirit.

Teach, preach, and exhort.

Get your food from the right table (John 6:35).

> But Jesus replied, "I have a kind of food you know nothing about" (John 4:32).

> Your sins are telling your mouth what to say. Your words are based on clever deception. (Job 15:5)

> Examine yourselves to see whether you are in the faith; test yourselves. Do you not realize that Christ Jesus is in you—unless, of course, you fail the test? (2 Corinthians 13:5)

> Don't you realize that your body is the temple of the Holy Spirit, who lives in you and was given to you by God? You do not belong to yourself. (1 Corinthians 6:9)

You, my friends, are God's property.

> So then, do not grieve the Holy Spirit of God, with whom you were sealed for the day of redemption. (Ephesians 4:30)

Foreknowledge

Did you know?

> For whom He did foreknow, He also did predestinate to be conformed to the image of His Son, that He might be the firstborn among many brethren. (Romans 8:29)

God's wisdom is supreme. Now, we human beings, His creation, can only know after the fact, but since Jesus, before the fact, but God knows even before the fact.

The word *foreknow* is from the Greek word *proginosko*, from which we get the word *prognosis*.

When your doctor gives you a prognosis, he's giving you his best opinion, based upon medical science and his years of training and experience.

But when God sees the future, it's not based upon his best educated guess. It's a certainty, because God sees the future more clearly than we can see the present.

God's foreknowledge can best be illustrated like the viewing of a parade.

We live in history, and we see events as they come by one at a time, but God dwells in eternity; He sees the beginning, the end, and everything in between.

And God knows everything; as you face the challenges ahead today, remember you have a Father who loves you and who knows what lies ahead. Trust him for your present and your future (Hebrews 4:13).

Ask yourself this question: When did you learn after the fact?

> Now, we have not received the spirit of the world but the Spirit who comes from God, so that we can understand the things that were freely given to us by God. (1 Corinthians 2:12)

Forgiveness

Be kind and compassionate to one another, forgiving each other, just as in Christ God forgave you. (Ephesians 4:32)

But if you do not forgive others their sins, your Father will not forgive your sins. (Matthew 6:15)

People who are quick to be defensive can overlook someone else's ability to be so.

They get so caught up in the heat of moments that they become oblivious to what might happen; and if the other person pushed aside their ability to be understanding and opted to be defensive, the instigator often wants a tense situation to escalate. Why? Because they believe it justifies their defensiveness.

But if you can remain calm and sensitive in the face of confrontation, then you can do much to help someone else do the same.

Brothers and sisters, if someone is caught in a sin, you who live by the Spirit should restore that person gently. But watch yourselves, or you also may be tempted. (Galatians 6:1)

Impeachment and repentance are two different things.

One is a worldly view and the act of God having an absolute advantage over the world.

Christians cannot be impeached, however rebuked and corrected (2 Timothy 3:16, Hebrews 4:12).

God forgives, the world does not; God convicts your sins but pardons you and forgives.

The god of this world hates forgiving the people of God, but our God has the last word; he is our defense minister in our case.

> If you forgive others their trespasses, your heavenly Father will also forgive you, but if you do not forgive others their trespasses, neither will your Father forgive your trespasses. (Matthew 6:14–15)

Folks within the body of Christ shall be punished if they are not forgiven just as the world.

A design not to compromise.

Watch.

> If your brother or sister sins, go and point out their fault, just between the two of you. (Matthew 18:15ff)

Notice "just the two of you alone."

Now, if they listen to you, you have won them over. "But if they will not listen, take one or two others along, so that every matter may be established by the testimony of two or three witnesses" (v. 16).

Do not take your family or take others you know too well; it could introduce a form of nepotism.

> If they still refuse to listen, tell it to the church; and if they refuse to listen even to the church, treat them as you would a pagan or a tax collector. (v. 17)

Today this could be viewed as partiality, in that you cannot see others in the church today as tax collectors or any other race other than Christians.

Full Armor of God

Listen carefully.

Have you felt like evil has come your way or in your path, but you can't do anything about it?

Just a test of your faith, stand.

> Therefore, put on the full armor of God, so that when the day of evil comes, you may be able to stand your ground, and after you have done everything, to stand. (Ephesians 6:13)

Never take it off.

Never stumble into the hands of your enemies, just see the salvation of the Lord. God is at work.

Stand still.

Don't fall backward, lean forward on Jesus.

> But I say unto you, love your enemies, bless them that curse you, do good to them that hate you, and pray for them which despitefully use you, and persecute you. Just do good. (Matthew 5:44)

> In doing this, you will heap burning coals on his head, and the LORD will reward you. (Proverbs 25:22)

If a man is not devout, teach him how to love God and be a devout Christian. Without controversy, show him how to partake of the Word without offence.

> A servant of the Lord must not quarrel but
> must be kind to everyone, be able to teach, and
> be patient with difficult people. (2 Timothy 2:24)

To be devout is to be deeply devoted to one's religion or to another belief, cause, or way of life.

Absent of gossiping, absent of lying, absent of cheating, absent of hating your neighbors, absent of self-righteousness. No drinking, no drugs, no more partying of any kind.

Listen to your Bible. *Debauchery* meaning "crazy partying and wild nights, usually accompanied by a lot of alcohol."

Debauchery is all about indulging in some of life's pleasures—overindulging, in fact (1 Peter 4:3).

Get Right

Are you ready to totally respect and give yourself over to God? Remember Romans 8:1.

Now, "Do not offer any part of yourself to sin as an instrument of wickedness, but rather offer yourselves to God as those who have been brought from death to life; and offer every part of yourself to him as an instrument of righteousness" (Romans 6:13).

As the old song hymn that was sung years ago,

> Get right with God and do it now
> For He will show you how,
> Right down at the cross
> Where he has shed his blood
> Get right God,
> Get right
> Get right with God

Gifts/Stewardship

T ax season.

Friends, while many may be in attendance of church services, whether regular or fellowship services or special events, many may feel ebullient, and some might even feel the same ways when receiving tax refunds; especially in appropriate times, goals are set forth.

Indeed, many are thankful and blessed to have received, but keeping the Lord in mind is very necessary! Of course, "I will…" is not enough; there has to be an action.

Minimizing any goals for the work of the Lord reduces many efforts to grow. Amen! "For whom much is given, from him much will be required" (Acts, Luke).

The work must go on. Any gifts the Lord has given us, stewardship of those gifts is a righteous act; anything less is unfaithfulness. Amen!

Let all of us remember the Lord first! God bless (Ecclesiastes 5:4).

Gifts

U se your gift, not as the world does but what God has given to each of us (spiritual gifts).

As each one has received a special gift, employ it in serving one another as good stewards of the manifold grace of God.

My friends, teach the Word of God every day that many may be encouraged by it.

> As every man hath received the gift, even so
> minister the same one to another, as good stew-
> ards of the manifold grace of God. (1 Peter 4:10)

The Bible speaks of the manifold grace of God.

What does that mean? It means we can experience God's grace in many ways.

For instance, there is singing grace. When Paul and Silas were in prison, God gave them grace to sing (Acts 16:25).

There is speaking grace. Colossians 4:6 says, "Let your speech be always with grace, seasoned with salt, that ye may know how ye ought to answer every man."

God will give you the ability to speak, even about your troubles, with his grace.

God also gives us strengthening grace. Timothy was often sick with many infirmities. Paul told him to "be strong in the grace that is in Christ Jesus" (2 Timothy 2:1).

Abraham never wavered in believing God's promise. In fact, his faith grew stronger, and in this, he brought glory to God (Romans 4:20); in other words, Abraham didn't walk this way and another way.

Say this prayer: "Lord Jesus, I love you, please come into my heart, forgive me of my sins, I repent. Let me learn of your word, help my heart to establish your principles and that my love abide by it forevermore. Amen."

My friends, this is the first step to get to Jesus: by obedience to faith in baptism for the remission of your sins (Romans 10:17).

Listen, folks, preachers and all.

People will try hard to get people into the body of Christ, and we want them to serve and to evangelize, but there are some who will not let those who has a zeal for God work—some of which will keep others from serving in the church. Why?

Listen, you might have a program set up, but God has accounted all things for his service that are listed in his commands (John 12:48).

There is a percentage of folks who may be protective, sure enough, but it is because you don't want things changed because of their liking.

Each has his own gift, and yours differ from others, step out of the way, allow God's servant to work.

Don't stand in the way of work.

Listen, there is a message here.

> For I say, through the grace given unto me, to every man that is among you, not to think of himself more highly than he ought to think; but to think soberly, according as God hath dealt to every man the measure of faith.
>
> For as we have many members in one body, and all members have not the same office.
>
> So, we, being many, are one body in Christ, and everyone members one of another.
>
> Having then gifts differing according to the grace that is given to us, whether prophecy, let us prophesy according to the proportion of faith;
>
> Or ministry, let us wait on our ministering: or he that teacheth, on teaching;

Or he that exhorteth, on exhortation: he that giveth, let him do it with simplicity; he that ruleth, with diligence; he that sheweth mercy, with cheerfulness.

Let love be without dissimulation. Abhor that which is evil; cleave to that which is good.

Be kindly affectioned one to another with brotherly love; in honour preferring one another;

Not slothful in business; fervent in spirit; serving the Lord. (Romans 12:1–11)

Are you with me?

Every member must work together for the perfecting of the saints.

Completeness is being perfect for the coming of Christ.

Our dangers are when mankind takes matters into their own hands by providing a service for themselves rather than for God.

Don't do that, divisions are not of a command, but perfectly joined together is a command.

Amen.

Giving

Rich young ruler.

He was rich (past/present tense), but Jesus was trying to tell him something, or did he already know?

First things first.

He is rich, no problem. Jesus was not addressing his money or how much. Jesus is not addressing how much he should spend or what to spend his money on or who with.

Jesus is addressing his willingness to give.

Now wait, prior to his answer, wealthy man said, "I have kept these commandments from my youth up. What do I lack?"

Already he has reached the age of maturity and should know how to be honest, plus either his parents or teachers (under the law) must have taught him how to give according to the law of Moses (Deuteronomy 15:7, 8, 10, 11).

Note what he said: "I have kept."

If that was the case, he sincerely must have forgotten or might have been caught up in buying and selling. Notice James 5:1ff.

This whole thing started in such a promising way, but he was not a good listener; however, he loved Jesus (did he?).

This young man was so excited that he literally ran up to Jesus and fell on his knees before him, asking Jesus what he had to do to inherit eternal life.

But he refused to give up his wealth for the sake of following Jesus, and the verse above tells you the end of the story in the Bible.

But of course, it was not the end of the story for this young man. Have you ever wondered what happened to the rich young ruler?

Wait. We know that the apostles carried the word into the world by no means with lots of money.

They risked their lives.

Wait, there is more about the wealthy man.

The rich young ruler, on the other hand, kept his money for himself but lost every cent of it when the Romans destroyed Jerusalem (between AD 68 and 70).

While he was very rich, he wasn't able to buy even a moldy crust of bread to alleviate his starvation during the prolonged siege.

Every Jew who wasn't slaughtered at that time was sold as a slave.

God

Remember, just as Moses did, he came down off the mountain with a radiant glow (Exodus 34:29).

Have you spoken to God? Has the word of God changed you? Beautiful attributes will show the light of God within you (Matthew 5:14–16).

Or could it be that the god of this world influences you his way (2 Corinthians 4:4)?

There comes a point in your life when you have to decide which direction you want to travel on.

Either the narrow way that leads to life or the broad path leading to destruction (Matthew 7:14).

Choose you this day, means to pick a path.

What's your goal?

Who among you fears God and his judgment?

> But only a fearful expectation of judgment and of raging fire that will consume the enemies of God. (Hebrews 10:27)

> For our God is a consuming fire. (Hebrews 12:29, Numbers 16:35)

> Now all has been heard; here is the conclusion of the matter:
> Fear God and keep his commandments, for this is the duty of all mankind. (Ecclesiastes 12:13)

But only fools say in their hearts, "There is
no God."
They are corrupt, and their actions are evil;
not one of them does good! (Psalm 14:1)

God is incapable of misunderstanding, mismanagement, or mistakes.

Deuteronomy 32:4 says "his works are perfect, and all his ways are just."

That means God doesn't get it wrong. Ever.

You and I, on the other hand, are fully capable of making an even greater mess of things.

God Is in Control

That is, the Jews as a people have not obtained what they sought. They sought the favor of God by their own merit; and as it was impossible to obtain it in that manner, they have, as a people, failed of obtaining his favor at all, and will be rejected (Romans 11:7).

Notice that today, the Word of God must be slowly moving in hearts because of the richness and obedience to faith. Not too fast but steady as it goes.

If one or many are led by blind eyes, such are distance in failing to understand God's divine purpose.

Mankind cannot make up stuff by how they want faith to work apart from the written word; it will be rejected every time (John 12:48).

Some men and women are in charge in this world who are Christians and attend church, but then you have those who are not appointed by God to public office but introduced by men. Certainly, they are not of God, but it doesn't mean that God is incompetent of doing his purposes.

This means that God still remains in control of all things (2 Peter 1:3).

Here's my opinion why. Members should not be politicized by the world because of the work God may have appointed them to do and have not his church to become a battleground from evildoers. Christian are not to be blamed for the works of evildoers.

Since God is in control of all things, why can't he use whomever God wishes to fulfill his mission in this world?

> Therefore, God has mercy on whom he
> wants to have mercy, and he hardens whom he
> wants to harden. (Romans 9:18)

The LORD instructed Moses, "When you go back to Egypt, see that you perform before Pharaoh all the wonders that I have put within your power. But I will harden his heart so that he will not let the people go." (Exodus 4:21)

But Sihon king of Heshbon would not let us pass through, for the LORD your God had made his spirit stubborn and his heart obstinate, that He might give him into your hands, as is the case this day. (Deuteronomy 2:30)

For it was of the LORD to harden their hearts to engage Israel in battle, so that they would be set apart for destruction and would receive no mercy, being annihilated as the LORD had commanded Moses. (Joshua 11:20)

He has blinded their eyes and hardened their hearts, so that they cannot see with their eyes, and understand with their hearts, and turn, and I would heal them. (John 12:40)

What then? What Israel was seeking, it failed to obtain, but the elect did. (Romans 11:7)

The others were hardened.
God controls everything.
Everything.
Christians and non-Christians in public places in this world.
If God has put men into places, why does a nonentity have to become a member of the church?
Isn't God in control of all things?

For rulers are not a terror to good works, but to the evil.

Wilt thou then not be afraid of the power? Do that which is good, and thou shalt have praise of the same.

For he is the minister of God to thee for good.

But if thou do that which is evil, be afraid; for he beareth not the sword in vain: for he is the minister of God, a revenger to execute wrath upon him that doeth evil.

Wherefore ye must needs be subject, not only for wrath, but also for conscience sake. (Romans 13:4–5)

He makes nations great, and destroys them; He enlarges nations, and sends them away. (Job 12:23)

You set all the boundaries of the earth; You made the summer and winter. (Psalm 74:17)

By My great power and outstretched arm, I made the earth and the men and beasts on the face of it, and I give it to whom I please. (Jeremiah 27:5)

Why hold on to your bad experiences when you have been born again (2 Corinthians 5:17)?

Let go and let God keep you in faithfulness.

If a man has a hundred sheep and one of them wanders away, what will he do? Won't he leave the ninety-nine others on the hills and go out to search for the one that is lost? (Matthew 18:12)

Question: do you know anyone who has left the ninety-nine?

If any man accomplishes anything, he has to put in effort.

So why are there so few of man who do not put in effort?

Knowing that a few is part of the whole.

Christ needs the totality of the body to make all parts work together.

When it doesn't, the link is not as strong as the whole.

Somebody knows of someone who has not been showing up. My friends, that is a voice that needs to be heard.

We are family, and family should miss others who have not been around lately.

Won't a concerned citizen call the authorities to find that lost person in society? I think yes.

Shouldn't our elders be concerned about a missing member? I believe they would.

It has been said that if one or more elders were missed from the body, shouldn't its members care?

I think yes.

Then we have work to do where lack has taken over.

Thinking on Jesus, then act on your faith (Romans 10:17, Galatians 6:1ff).

Godly Life

Listen, you cannot make or change the doctrine of God from the things already written.

The Holy Spirit wrote down those things approved by God and have been given to us by the apostles and prophets, so how could you rewrite the things of God?

Here's the point. Apostle Paul said, (First you cannot,) "unlike so many, we do not peddle the word of God for profit. On the contrary, in Christ we speak before God with sincerity, as those sent from God" (2 Corinthians 2:17).

It's not for sale. When Simon saw that the Spirit was given at the laying on of the apostles' hands, he offered them money (Acts 8:18).

Lastly, certification of my first point.

> We also have the prophetic message as something completely reliable, and you will do well to pay attention to it, as to a light shining in a dark place, until the day dawns and the morning star rises in your hearts.
>
> Above all, you must understand that no prophecy of Scripture came about by the prophet's own interpretation of things.
>
> For prophecy never had its origin in the human will, but prophets, though human, spoke from God as they were carried along by the Holy Spirit. (2 Peter 1:19–21)

And finally, verse 3: "His divine power has given us everything we need for a godly life through our knowledge of him who called us by his own glory and goodness."

Here's the message: don't change anything that God has given his apostles and prophets to write down as instructions for us.

These men were appointed by God (1 Corinthians 4:1–2, John 12:48).

Some men and some women are making money off the Word by selling it to you at their cost to bear.

The Bible says explicitly to you that faith comes by hearing—and hearing the Word of God (Romans 10:17).

No admission fee to hear it. It's all free.

Now watch this.

> Get the truth and never sell it; also get wisdom, discipline, and good judgment. (Proverbs 23:23)

Some translations use "by the truth, and sell it not," which in figurative language depicts "whatever you have to give up"; don't give up the truth after you have received it from the mouth of God.

This is where many denominations and others have mistranslated the Word by taking things against you to give money, more of yours, and by saying, "Give your alms or 10 percent to God."

Read 2 Corinthians 8:12 or 2 Corinthians 9:7; his plan as he shall consider, by 10 percent as under the law of Moses.

Listen to your Bible…

> Is anyone thirsty? Come and drink—even if you have no money! Come, take your choice of wine or milk—it's all free! (Isaiah 55:1)

Watch out for those who don't believe the Bible, who try to buy themselves into heaven, who take you alone with them.

For their life is to enjoy the present time they are living, but they don't give a whole lot about how you are living.

Godly Minded

And he gave some, apostles; and some, prophets; and some, evangelists; and some, pastors and teachers; For the perfecting of the saints, for the work of the ministry, for the edifying of the body of Christ: Till we all come in the unity of the faith, and of the knowledge of the Son of God, unto a perfect man, unto the measure of the stature of the fulness of Christ: That we henceforth be no more children, tossed to and fro, and carried about with every wind of doctrine, by the sleight of men, and cunning craftiness, whereby they lie in wait to deceive; But speaking the truth in love, may grow up into him in all things, which is the head, even Christ: From whom the whole body fitly joined together and compacted by that which every joint supplieth, according to the effectual working in the measure of every part, maketh increase of the body unto the edifying of itself in love. (Ephesians 4:11–16, KJV)

When you serve God, give it your all, or stay out of it.

Nothing is worse than a subtle pretense, meaning the practices of claiming to have moral standards or beliefs to which one's own behavior does not conform (Matthew 15:14, 2 Peter 2:20).

To be religious means to be godly minded, and apart from godliness are worldly attributes that result in friendship with the world.

Listen.

> You adulterous (non-religious) people! Do
> you not know that friendship with the world is
> enmity with God? Therefore, whoever wishes to
> be a friend of the world makes himself an enemy
> of God. (James 4:4)

City leaders should have knowledge of its surroundings. Don't give your city any name but rather a good name, and make it a good place where all can be prosperous and enjoy.

There are some ghost towns because there was lack of trust and service in its entirety to the people.

Make your city a good community of godly attributes and not of a normality of one kind.

The same people who go to church are not the same behavior practices they are doing outside of the body of Christ.

There be some who are but subtle minds who pretend to be in religious circles but are far from having the attributes of godliness among men.

Your goods are worth nothing if you don't have a good relationship with your city, both inside and outside your city, especially the church.

> A good name is more desirable than great
> riches; favor is better than silver and gold.
> (Proverbs 22:1)

In keeping with the words of Jesus, his servant is not a small thing. Say what you want against my walk with God, but if you speak against the Holy Spirit that dwells inside of me (Luke 3:22) you blaspheme; you shall be forgotten and not be forgiven (1 Corinthians 3:16, Romans 8:14, John 1:12).

> Anyone who speaks a word against the Son
> of Man will be forgiven, but anyone who speaks

against the Holy Spirit will not be forgiven, either in this age or in the age to come. (Matthew 12:32)

Do not speak against God's servants.

It is speaking against God, and God's anger will be kindled against you.

Listen, Romans 15:4 is our reminder.

Why then were you not afraid to speak against my servant Moses? And the anger of the LORD was kindled against them (Numbers 12:8–9).

And the cloud departed from off the tabernacle; and, behold, Miriam became leprous, white as snow: and Aaron looked upon Miriam, and, behold, she was leprous. (Numbers 12:10)

Every day is a blessing of God that you can see, hear, taste, and touch.

Offer your prayers to God continually, day after day; the whole creation praises God.

Do not be anxious about anything, but in every situation, by prayer and petition, with thanksgiving, present your requests to God. (Philippians 4:6)

All the earth worships you and sings praises to you; they sing praises to your name. (Psalm 66:4, Romans 12:1, Romans 8:1)

If you are proud of yourself being a Christian servant of God, tell it wherever you go (Matthew 10:33).

God's Commandments

God says, "If you love Me, keep My commandments" (John 14:15).

God's will is in his word, his commandments.

For example, God commands me to put away "all bitterness, wrath, anger, clamor and evil speaking."

Fix what you have accused.

> For the eyes of the Lord are on the righteous and his ears are attentive to their prayer, but the face of the Lord is against those who do evil. (1 Peter 3:12)

The Lord Rebukes Job's Friends

> After the Lord had spoken these words to Job, the Lord said to Eliphaz the Temanite.
>
> "My anger burns against you and against your two friends, for you have not spoken of me what is right, as my servant Job has."
>
> Now therefore take seven bulls and seven rams and go to my servant Job and offer up a burnt offering for yourselves.
>
> And my servant Job shall pray for you, for I will accept his prayer not to deal with you according to your folly.
>
> For you have not spoken of me what is right, as my servant Job has."

> So Eliphaz the Temanite and Bitdad the
> Shuhite and Zophar the Naamathite went and
> did what the Lord had told them, and the Lord
> accepted Job's prayer. (Job 42:7–9)

Don't lose your wisdom while tampering around with something else or wrongdoings.

Take a hold of your own mind—not to deceive yourself.

If hell is where you are going, don't bother others who are striving for heaven.

That narrow gate, into which you strive to enter, is the gate of life, the gate of heaven (Luke 13:24).

And consequently, if you strive effectually, you will gain admission into the mansions of everlasting joy John 14:1–2

Notice now Luke 13:25.

> Once the owner of the house gets up and
> closes the door, you will stand outside knocking
> and pleading, "Sir, open the door for us." But
> he will answer, "I don't know you or where you
> come from."

God the Father will decide the end of the earth.

> But about that day or hour no one knows,
> not even the angels in heaven, nor the Son, but
> only the Father. (Matthew 24:36)

> Because straight is the gate, and narrow is
> the way, which leadeth unto life, and few there
> be that find it. (Matthew 7:14)

Be in the few that find the gateway to heaven.

But there will be heretics on their way to hell because they refuse to follow the word of God (2 Timothy 4:3–4).

Let Jesus embrace you into his love everlasting.

Listen, don't let others tell you there is something wrong with Trump, while you have no faults of your own (Matthew 7:1ff).

He deserves to be saved as you once were—without hope and without Christ (1 John 1:7, 8).

> The time will come when they will not endure sound doctrine; but after their own lusts shall they heap to themselves teachers, having itching ears; and they shall turn away their ears from the truth and shall be turned unto fables.

In other words, let things alone that you cannot change, because God has already removed the candlestick. God is in control over all the affairs of mankind.

Matthew 12:48.

As iron sharpens iron, so one man sharpens another (Proverbs 27:17).

Jesus is your friend.

> Forever, O Lord, thy word is settled in heaven.
>
> Thy faithfulness is unto all generations: thou hast established the earth, and it abideth.
>
> They continue this day according to thine ordinances: for all are thy servants. (Psalm 119:89–91)

Godly Character

N ow listen, godly character of the older woman in the faith is this: Romans 12:1ff.

> Bodies presented as living sacrifices, holy, acceptable to God, not conformed to this world, but with transformed and renewed minds, in bodies that are temples of the Holy Spirit glorifying God in your body and spirit, which are God's; (no longer living for yourself), but Christ living in you.

They must present themselves to the Lord daily, and they have begun to live life the way God asked them to live—as a walking temple of God (2 Corinthians 5:17).

Nowhere are women in the Bible or in Titus sent out to hold meetings.

Character change is a command and not a position.

But the way she should live and walk (1 Peter 2:21).

When you invent new innovations, denominational groups are appreciating you more.

Why? Because that's what they do from the pulpit daily.

God's People

We think of the church as a people, and some may think of it as a building or a place.

Church comes from an English term; it refers to a place. Not so in the Greek.

Christ's building is his people, and a holy building is designed by the Word of God.

Church is a figure of speech, as some would refer to a people or a body of people. Today, we are God's people, built up in victory, the Word of God.

Abraham was confidently looking forward to a city with eternal foundations, a city designed and built by God (Hebrews 11:10).

Listen to Jesus.

> Nor will they say, "See here!" or "See there!"
> For indeed, the kingdom of God is within you.
> Or in your midst. (Luke 17:21)

To my understanding, Jesus is coming back to get his people who are "called out," sanctified, to be presented to the Father (1 Corinthians 15:24).

It's means no matter where you might be in the world, whether you are in worship or busy at work, the body or the called out will respond to the end. Wherever your life may be (Matthew 24:39–41).

One body, one mind, of one spirit (John 12:48).

> Instead, they were longing for a better
> country, a heavenly one. Therefore, God is not

ashamed to be called their God, for He has prepared a city for them. (Hebrews 11:16)

Church is *ekklesia* in Greek.

Absolutely, the called out by the Word of God.

Church is not any Greek term. Congregation is meaning a group of people as to the commands of God. Gathering.

Oh, how I love Jesus.

He's been so good to me.

I walk and talk in the new Jerusalem way.

Knee at the cross.

Jesus is all the world to me.

Have you been to Jesus for the cleansing power?

Let Jesus be the center of your life.

God is the head of the church and should be the head in your life.

You have rights to live, act, and do as righteousness in an ethical way; thus, perhaps you may work for Jesus.

Who are these people? Don't they know our president must be respected (Romans 13)?

Swallow your pride and say, "God will help."

I have the right to defend the Word of God (Romans 1:16, John 12:48).

I write what the Bible says.

God is always concerned with the unbelievers.

God exists.

Nothing offends God more than others who don't believe in him (John 1:1ff).

I have the right to defend the Word of God (Romans 1:16).

The Bible is right.

The fool says in his heart, "There is no God." They are corrupt, they do abominable deeds; there is none who does good. (Psalm 14:1)

God's Promise

The promise God gave to Moses and the Israelites when they crossed over the Red Sea is found in Exodus 19:3–13.

> Then Moses went up to God, and the LORD called to him from the mountain and said, "This is what you are to say to the house of Jacob and what you are to tell the people of Israel. 'You yourselves have seen what I did to Egypt, and how I carried you on eagles' wings and brought you to myself. Now if you obey me fully and keep my covenant, then out of all nations you will be my treasured possession. Although the whole earth is mine, you will be for me a kingdom of priests and a holy nation. These are the words you are to speak to the Israelites." (vv. 3–6)

> So, Moses went back and summoned the elders of the people and set before them all the words the LORD had commanded him to speak.
> The people all responded together, "We will do everything the LORD has said." So, Moses brought their answer back to the LORD. (vv. 7–8)

> The LORD said to Moses, "I am going to come to you in a dense cloud, so that the people will hear me speaking with you and will always put their trust in you." Then Moses told the LORD what the people had said. (v. 9)

And the LORD said to Moses, "Go to the people and consecrate them today and tomorrow. Have them wash their clothes and be ready by the third day, because on that day the LORD will come down on Mount Sinai in the sight of all the people.

Put limits for the people around the mountain and tell them, Be careful that you do not go up the mountain or touch the foot of it.

Whoever touches the mountain shall surely be put to death. He shall surely be stoned or shot with arrows; not a hand is to be laid on him. Whether man or animal, he shall not be permitted to live.' Only when the ram's horn sounds a long blast may they go up to the mountain." (vv. 10–13)

But we preach Christ crucified, unto the Jews a stumbling block, and unto the Greeks foolishness.

But unto them which are called, both Jews and Greeks, Christ the power of God and the wisdom of God. (1 Corinthians 1:23–24)

Go to the Word for answers; don't distance yourself from God.

It is good to see that religious leaders are fighting to put back God in the schools and over the building.

In God we trust.

We sincerely appreciate bishops who feed the church of God.

We thank them daily in prayer for keeping us safe, comfortable, and sound.

By it we grow and keep growing up into a mature culture in Christ.

Following the lead is important to any successful Bible student.

Good Name

A good name is better than precious ointment, and the day of death than the day of birth. (Ecclesiastes 7:1)

Good News

My friends, don't wait too late wherein you may not be able to talk about Jesus.

Speak while you can.

Life can change for you at any time.

God knows who you are (i.e., those who are weak) or how whole you are (those who are strong).

Listen.

> Righteousness exalts a nation, but sin is a
> reproach to any people. (Proverbs 14:34)

As good stewards of the manifold grace of God, each of you should use whatever gift you have received to serve one another (1 Peter 4:10).

Moreover, it is required in stewards that one be found worthy (1 Corinthians 4:2).

When any man has served in the church for over fifty years faithfully and has been accounted as a good steward in the work of the Lord, notice, my friends, leave him alone in serving the Lord; he is using the gift God has appointed him to have.

Such a one is not to be treated as a novice.

Perhaps you may learn something from him, if you so desire.

> But encourage one another daily, as long as
> it is called "Today," so that none of you may be
> hardened by sin's deceitfulness. (Hebrews 3:13)

Don't give up your fight for salvation, stay with God.

You shall inherit eternal life with God (John 3:36); otherwise, condemnation.

The Gospel

God invites as many as are willing to come eat at his table and to "taste and see that the Lord is good" (Psalm 34:8).

Tragically, however, not everyone who is welcomed and called to enter into God's kingdom will do so. Although the invitation is an open one, not all people will take it to heart.

Why? Let's discover more.

Some people, however, will not respond to God's call, but others will take full hold of the salvation.

The gospel is calling for all sinners to obedience in Christ.

God knew, before the foundation of the world began, those who will be chosen (Ephesians 1:4).

> But you are a chosen people, a royal priesthood, a holy nation, God's special possession, that you may declare the praises of him who called you out of darkness into his wonderful light. (1 Peter 2:9)

Will you show up (Matthew 22:14)?
Those who are called, and few who are chosen.
Let's look.
We understand 2 Corinthians 5:18–20,

> And all things are of God, who hath reconciled us to himself by Jesus Christ, and hath given to us the ministry of reconciliation;
> To wit, that God was in Christ, reconciling the world unto himself, not imputing their tres-

passes unto them; and hath committed unto us the word of reconciliation, (to wit means mental sharpness and inventiveness; keen intelligence.)

Now then we are ambassadors for Christ, as though God did beseech you by us: we pray you in Christ's stead, be ye reconciled to God.

(ambassador means from God's point of view; it indicates a person who acts as a representative for God).

Such as those who are called (1 Thessalonians 2:4).

When you come or if you come to the invitation of Christ called by the gospel, whether or not, a few who hear will be chosen, although a great many are called but will not show up (Matthew 22:14).

Gossip

Frank T. McAndrew, Ph.D., and Cornelia H. Dudley Professor of Psychology at Knox College in Galesburg, Illinois: "Everyone gossips."

He says, is it that particular knowledge, helped people to get ahead socially; and people who were not interested in it were at a disadvantage, McAndrew says.

'They were not good at attracting and keeping mates or maintaining alliances.

The ones who weren't interested in the goings on of other people sort of got weeded out."

We tend to think of gossip as a negative behavior—when, for instance, we tattle on someone or share information behind someone else's back that may show them in a bad light.

But it's really not.

Damageable heresy is not fitting to be spoken of in cases to enlighten to respect and peace and inform. Hurting people is bad gossip.

Good talks are basically tossing and gossiping about things shared; and meant to share, rather than to destroy reputations.

Sort of like the stock market or seeking employment, or as scientists sharing information about a particular thing.

Some will not call it gossip, but it is definitely definitive.

By definition (at least the definition social scientists who study gossip use), gossip is any talk about someone who isn't present, it's usually about something we can make a moral judgment about (meaning you tend to approve of the information or disapprove), and it's entertaining, meaning it doesn't feel like work to do it; you tend to want to share or hear the information.

Psychologists say gossiping is a social skill. It's how to know.

Gossip is actually one of the societal forces that brings us together and helps maintain social order.

Could it be? In a general thought, let's see.

However, the Bible talks about a bad gossip.

A good gossiper is someone who people trust with information and someone who uses that information in a responsible way.

When you find out the person your friend has a crush on has a bad reputation for cheating, you let your friend know, not to hurt your friend, but as a warning.

You find out someone in your company is not a team player and you let other coworkers know so that they can try to avoid working with that colleague.

Key is that you're sharing information in an appropriate way that's helping others.

Teams has found that gossip is actually one of the forces that promotes cooperation among groups, too.

Experiments inside of teams (from educators) have suggested that any threat of being gossiped "about" in a bad sense, often deters untrustworthy behaviors; once people have been gossiped about for behaving in an untrustworthy way, they tend to reform their behavior.

Education is shared by informers who are putting forthright information on the basis of learning.

And gossip helps people know who to avoid and not trust.

Bad practices tell others who not to listen to.

Normally called bad gossip.

Government

> There is neither Jew nor Gentile, neither slave nor free, nor is there male and female, for you are all one in Christ Jesus. (Galatians 3:28)

A tax collector's job in the past like unto today is to collect taxes due to the government.

Listen.

> Jesus said, "Render to Caesar the things that are Caesar's; and to God the things that are God's." (Matthew 22:21)

> And He said to them, "Whose image and inscription is this?" They said to Him, "Caesar's." (vv. 20–21)

Then give to its government.

> Let every person be in subjection to the governing authorities. (Romans 13:1)

The Great Commission

> For if people do these things when the tree
> is green, what will happen when it is dry? (Luke
> 23:31)

People believe in the Great Commission of Christ, but evildoers oftentimes talk about why it's not necessary. Don't discourage anyone from filling it. Rather, do what God says. Save a soul from spiritual death.

Greek Words

Grace—Xa'pn
Mercy—Eleos
Sister—Athelfi
Brother—Athelfo's
Food—Trofi
Water—Nero'
Humble—Tapino's
Strife—Diama'he
Fool—Ano'etos
Trust—Embistosini
Believe (verb)—Pist'evo
Belief—Pisti
Salvation—Soter'ia

A Greek Armenian woman spoke and wrote this language.

The best type of preaching is expository and textual concepts combined.

It shall expand upon systematic theological significance of the scriptures.

The word of God is a system of beliefs by which all of Scripture is given by the inspiration of God and is profitable.

Jesus himself shows the expository method in Luke 4 and Luke 24.

Most people are schooled in the church from preachers or teachers who had or have higher learning.

I think at times we should teach folks a little Greek and logic by which one can learn the deeper meaning of words and actions of words from doing a daily word study.

One cannot become a follower of other men all their lives.

Christ needs workers and leaders out front, not ghost leaders hidden from others that cannot be seen.

Take your place.

Leaders must be tested and approved by its congregation and not in secret (Mark 16:15–16).

In other words, get yourself off the shelf and go serve.

Because of elderly men and elect ladies, many have taught us how important Christ's mission is really supposed to be.

Your soul salvation is that important.

Remember Acts 10:2. Cornelius was a devout man.

He had to do something with himself.

Others may be the same, and you should be responsible to teach them the words of God, by which they should be saved.

Students will learn that God does not show favoritism, and he has always planned for all people to receive the good news about Jesus.

You want to preach or teach, get schooled, then you will be tested and approved (2 Timothy 4:1ff).

They need a deeper understanding of Christian theology. Many are limited, and some are just theology ignorant.

Unclear and *unlearned* spells *uncertain.*

Logic is "reasoning conducted or assessed according to strict principles of validity."

A valid inference is one where there is a specific relation of logical support between the assumptions of the inference and its conclusion.

Fallacy: "In philosophy, a formal fallacy, deductive fallacy, logical fallacy or non sequitur (Latin for "it does not follow") is a pattern of reasoning rendered invalid by a flaw in its logical structure that can neatly be expressed in a standard logic system, for example propositional logic."

Law: "Laws of thought, traditionally, the three fundamental laws of logic: (1) the law of contradiction, (2) the law of excluded middle (or third), and (3) the principle of identity. That is, (1) for all propositions p, it is impossible for both p and not p to be true, or symbolically p."

When something is, it cannot be what it is not.

I'm not an expert in logic, but without it, most will make excuses or find fifty different preachers to explain their beliefs.

Grow in Knowledge

Let me share with you an experience I've never forgotten.

Unless you've been there, in spirit and truth, you never understand its meaning.

In Navy boot camp, you are instructed to learn twelve general orders.

Practice is a must; read and reread until you learn them.

When inspection comes, the commanding officer will stand in front of you, eye to eye, and ask you any number that comes to his mind, and without stumbling, you must say that general order with conviction and enthusiasm, and by his wish, he might ask you to give him more than one if not all of them.

And if you don't learn those general orders as required, you are put out, showing no growth.

What a wasted moment in life.

What could you say to the God in heaven if you decided not to grow in grace, knowledge, and truth (2 Peter 3:18)?

Everyone will stand before truth.

> For we must all appear before the judgment
> seat of Christ, so that each of us may receive what
> is due us for the things done while in the body,
> whether good or bad. (2 Corinthians 5:10)

What do you expect will come at your judgment?

Many will say, "But have they done or practiced what they learned?"

It is so important that we hear and do. There are many Bible examples of people who hear and do.

Examples are important.

Putting your faith into practice is important.

Romans 10:17.

Ephesians 4:1ff; read also chapter 2.

Where are you at in life, and where are you headed?

As for me and my house, we will serve the Lord without hypocrisy.

Did you know that trespasses can destroy your life outside this earth?

To live with Jesus, overcome transgressions by repentance of sins.

Jesus is the only God of heaven who offers you a door to salvation.

Take it.

> And she shall bring forth a son, and thou shalt call his name JESUS: for he shall save his people from their sins. (Matthew 1:21)

Growth

Matthew 5:17–20.

Some people usually express their philosophical posture in simple ordinary language; whereas, those willing to learn (Matthew 5:6) are those who learn languages. Why?

The philosophical expression of the sum may feel less obligated to study and are sometimes called capricious or fragmentary to an extent, than those who seek higher learning, because of deep studies to organize their position to a systematic life of thinking for all mankind (Ephesians 4:29–32; 2 Timothy 2:14–17).

Growth is necessary for the church. Any expression of languages must be understood by all mankind to hear, learn, and understand, to be saved. Apart from that is just question after question after question. But if the sum is left behind, it is simply because of choice.

Can you manage your mind? Or is someone else doing it for you? Which?

Study the Greek language to define the original meaning of words from the new covenant of God.

Not all, but those used to help you in your work (preaching or studies).

Can any belong to a Tare Society and not know it (Matthew 13:26ff)?

What are tares (Matthew 13:26)?

This symbolic diagnosis tares, as it relates our own conventional practices thereof, causes a great deal of nervous energy when it comes to other related issues, such as gossip, believing a lie, filthy talking, all sorts of ungodly business, such as some in speaking with our neighbor(s) (Colossians 3:8–11).

Let's be clear, could God be happy with our performances?

God will not be happy with those who cannot identify what anger is, and how it comes in terms to truth. Anger is not a term agenda. In most situations, folks would rather exchange the truth to unrighteous behaviors.

Such practices influence newly elected members in the body.

Remember that God will consider those whom you offend; such practice will not go unpunished. God will bag up those who sin for eternal punishment.

"Bag up" means to bundle together and burn up (Matthew 13:30). This not to say, "Well, we just leave them (tares) alone."

No! We are to teach the Word of God together; we understand its power and his will to obey. Amen.

Repentance is necessary for salvation; therefore, repent.

People will miss the mark at times by trying to fix things without the Word.

These hand-me-down ignominies are not of God.

Mankind will enable himself to foolish behaviors if not careful, proven to not fit for the kingdom or not fit for heaven.

It is time to know the differences between truth and error. Why would anyone believe something any angry person says in relation about another without proven facts (Matthew 18:15ff)? Investigate.

This isn't about just knowing (Galatians 6:1ff) what I am discussing here and is not revile or dissipation but actually the difference between a reprehend in terms of someone who doesn't know facts but only by what others are saying in gossip; now their relationship to God is dissipated because of matters unproven in a society before us today (2 Thessalonians 2:11ff).

The strength of sin is in the company of its own society, whether some family, some friends, some church folks, or even outside influences from the community of God's people; many ought to recognize its power and come to terms that this is not of God.

This retrovirus can only kill the Word in people who strive to perfect the company of believers.

Many should be unwilling to destroy the flow of the communion with God (fellowship).

Instead, some will run to gossip. If we know a thing, we recognize it and turn to prayer and trust in the Word of God (Matthew 18:15ff, Galatians 6:1ff, 2 Thessalonians 13–17).

If any man commits a sin not leading to death, pray forgiveness, then it should be left to God and forget and not left by mankind (Matthew 7:1ff).

Tares. God will bundle up to burn, sure enough, but our responsibility is to persuade men (2 Corinthians 5:11), to believe in God, trust in his Word, walk by faith. Amen!

Prayers are your needed efforts daily to God.

Hear

Leap into the Word of God and trust others to lead you.

Romans 10:14 says, "How then can they call on the One in whom they have not believed? And how can they believe in the One of whom they have not heard? And how can they hear without someone to preach?"

Verse 17: walking with Jesus every step of the way.

> Rescue others by snatching them from the flames of judgment. Show mercy to still others, but do so with great caution, hating the sins that contaminate their lives. (Jude 1:23)

Remember Galatians 6:1ff.

Heaven

Don't worry about having an important role in the church, just be a Christian.

Perhaps that's what God wants you to be…

Anything else he would open up doors for you, naturally.

What will we look like in heaven? You will look like the best self you could have ever imagined.

We will be changed, so quickly, so beautiful, we will look like what God wants us to look like.

Heaven is unlike our earthly tabernacle; this tent will be resolved in a moment (1 Corinthians 15:47–52).

What a day of rejoicing that will be.

Get yourselves ready.

One day, God is coming, and you will not know it.

Always be ready to receive your supernatural body.

Serve the Lord with gladness.

> That He might present her to Himself a glorious church, not having spot or wrinkle or any such thing, but that she should be holy and without blemish. (Ephesians 5:27)

Question: Are you made for heaven?

I mean, have you been listening to Jesus and walking in Word and in truth?

> Jesus said "I am the way and the truth and the life. No one comes to the Father except through me." (John 14:6)

Can you be used by God in the end of your life?

Going to God, will he say to you, "Well done, good and faithful servant"? Or will he say, "Your work is worthless. You are incapable of paying attention to details from my word"?

Matthew 7:22.

Jesus said, "I'm the word" (John 1:1).

> Then shall he say to the faithful, "Come on in because you were faithful with a few things. I will put you in charge of many things. Enter into the joy of your master." (Matthew 25:23)

If not, then prepare yourself to go to heaven.

Holy Spirit

But God hath revealed them unto us by his Spirit: for the Spirit searcheth all things, yea, the deep things of God.

For what man knoweth the things of a man, save the spirit of man which is in him? Even so the things of God knoweth no man, but the Spirit of God.

Now we have received, not the spirit of the world, but the spirit which is of God; that we might know the things that are freely given to us of God.

Which things also we speak, not in the words which man's wisdom teacheth, but which the Holy Ghost teacheth; comparing spiritual things with spiritual. (1 Corinthians 2:10–13)

The Home

Proverbs 25:24, 21:9.

Problems within a home.

The usual conversation but escalated into an unreasonable manner, and putting blame could be in the wrong place.

Ecclesiastes 7:29.

But he isn't listening. Perhaps not, because he is yelling back.

Listen carefully, she is not a slave to her husband but a coequal in marriage.

Now many attempts to correct her, you may be met with failures, for her pride cannot be submissive in cases of shouting matches.

It is a common problem today, especially in this rebellious age, when women or men no longer know their God-ordained place. It is a dangerous trap and cannot set examples for others.

Baits and other similar issues set a standard for others to copy intellectual foolishness, however unfit for to live by. Some may think these similarities, but how do you reconcile with your mate if there is no communication? No reasoning, no comparison, no understanding.

In view of what Solomon was trying to say in his day and age, does it make a comparison to our own given situation today?

Why, because he has lots of wives, so what can he compare?

Some say it is better to stay in the workshop or visiting friends than to try to have any peace or pleasure with your mate, knowing that no working relationship is in the house.

That's not a way to define a relationship between each other today.

However, if either spouse causes damages to their marriage, perhaps it is not fitting the two belong together (not like Adam and Eve, being one parent, or two people on earth).

Read 2 Timothy 2:23ff.

Leaving is an option depending upon how critical your situation may be.

Drugs, alcohol, lying, cursing, stealing, unfit living conditions, nasty, filthy, fornication, adultery—either of these few things can cause a marriage breakup by law today.

Read 1 Corinthians 10:13.

It is not uncommon for people to act in defense of their lives.

Now, families who pray together stay together; otherwise, put the blame where it belongs. God has called us to peace (1 Corinthians 7:15).

Stop being a slave in your own house.

When you share quarters with your mate (i.e., spiritual spouse), you are not each other's slave.

Further your responsibility by keeping peace at home.

Correct your life daily with God (Romans 6:23).

Honor

Remember two immutable things: You must honor your mother and your father (Ephesians 6:1ff).

No matter whatsoever you think. Those two things are written for God's purposes, and not for any to decide otherwise.

Read Ecclesiastes 12:1.

Whatever the cost, get it done for the sake of saving your house, your property, where you both can enjoy.

So, what about your commitment toward each other? Your body is a temple of the Lord.

> Don't you realize that your body is the temple of the Holy Spirit, who lives in you and was given to you by God? You do not belong to yourself. (1 Corinthians 6:19)

When things go wrong in your marriage, will you not make things right, or will you have a temper tantrum, putting your investment in jeopardy?

Marriage is incredibly powerful and must be protected at all cost, just like your property.

There are laws in living and building a house, just like relationships.

If your investment comes to problems?

Will you not fix it?

That's the way it's supposed to be done.

Don't labor in vain your house.

Stay away from things that cause dangers to your house.

Fix it, right!

No matter what the cost, make it right before it falls down and gets destroyed.

God will help you in your building, only if you allow him to come inside.

Without God, we are nothing. Great houses have been erected by ambitious men; but like the baseless fabric of a vision, they have passed away, and scarce a stone remains to tell where once they stood.

How will you stand?

House of God

For a day in thy courts is better than a thousand. I had rather be a doorkeeper in the house of my God, than to dwell in the tents of wickedness. (Psalm 84:10)

Husbands and Wives

When you quit listening to your mate, you, my friend, are going to fail.

Partnership is a plus to any people who desire to work together for a long future.

Understand this: The first sign of mental illness in a relationship is dominated with failures. Quit overlooking these flags. Pay attention to your life.

The thing to do is keeping it alive and wait on each other. Keeping your word is important for all objectives.

Listen to your Bible.

> Trust in the Lord with all your heart and lean not on your own understanding; in all your ways submit to him, and he will make your paths straight. (Proverbs 3:5–6)

> For husbands, this means love your wives, just as Christ loved the church. He gave up his life for her. (Ephesians 5:25)

> Therefore a man shall leave his father and his mother and hold fast to his wife, and they shall become one flesh. (Genesis 2:24)

> He who loves his wife loves himself. (Ephesians 5:28)

> For the husband is the head of the wife as
> Christ is the head of the church, his body, of
> which he is the Savior. (Ephesians 5:23)

Now, one cannot be the head of the wife if the wife follows her own dreams, to exclude her husband; that's not of God, but of man.

That's what the world does, not Christians.

Christians keep the commandments of God. At all cost.

Jesus says, "If you love me, keep my commandments" (John 14:15).

When one leaves God, such creates a different administration and admonition to the world.

Read 2 Peter 2:20. Thus leaving your sanctification to your Creator and his word.

Pococurante means "someone who is careless and or indifferent."

Stay with God. Deeds are not overlooked (Jeremiah 23:24).

Hypocrisy

Let Jesus embrace you into his love everlasting.

> Remember that at that time you were separate from Christ, excluded from citizenship in Israel and foreigners to the covenants of the promise, without hope and without God in the world. (Ephesians 2:12)

Christians are attacked all day long; they even are called hypocrites, but hypocrites go to church where transformation begins into the image of Christ, but hypocrites in the world don't get transformed.

They remain in hypocrisy and criticize God's people.

Under the breath of false accuser, they remain lost (Psalm 1:1ff, Romans 15:4).

Reread and understand: things that may affect you today affected those in times past.

> Alexander the coppersmith did great harm to me. The Lord will repay him according to his deeds. (2 Timothy 4:14)

> My enemies say with malice: "When will he die and be forgotten?" (Psalm 41:5)

> He will reward my enemies with evil. In Your faithfulness, destroy them. (Psalm 54:5)

Idols

J osiah was eight years old when he began to reign, and he reigned in Jerusalem one and thirty years.

And he did that which was right in the sight of the Lord, and walked in the ways of David his father, and declined neither to the right hand, nor to the left.

For in the eighth year of his reign, while he was yet young, he began to seek after the God of David his father: and in the twelfth year he began to purge Judah and Jerusalem from the high places, and the groves, and the carved images, and the molten images.

And they broke down the altars of Balaam in his presence; and the images, that were on high above them, he cut down; and the groves, and the carved images, and the molten images, he brake in pieces, and made dust of them, and strewed it upon the graves of them that had sacrificed unto them.

And he burnt the bones of the priests upon their altars, and cleansed Judah and Jerusalem.

And so, did he in the cities of Manasseh, and Ephraim, and Simeon, even unto Naphtali, with their mattocks round about.

And when he had broken down the altars and the groves, and had beaten the graven images into powder, and cut down all the idols throughout all the land of Israel, he returned to Jerusalem. (2 Chronicles 34:2–7)

Impatience

> If you have run with the footmen, and they
> have wearied you, then how can you contend
> with horses? And if in the land of peace, wherein
> you trusted, they wearied you, then how will you
> do in the swelling of Jordan? (Jeremiah 12:5)

Yahweh rebukes Jeremiah's impatience, showing him by two pro-
verbial sayings that there were still greater trials of faith in store for
him. (You got to watch your step.)

Refer to Jeremiah 12:1–4.

Stop complaining so much about nothing.

The prophet is compelled to make an answer to himself, and
the voice of Jehovah is heard in his inmost soul rebuking his impatience. What are the petty troubles that fall on him compared with
what others suffer, with what might come on himself?

Good question.

Prosperous wickedness is after all a mere ordinary trial, a mere
"running with the footmen"; he will have to exert far greater powers
of endurance.

And if in the land. Rather, "and in a land of peace you are secure;
but how will you act when the pride of Jordan swells?"

If thou can feel safe only where things are tranquil, what will
you do in the hour of danger?

The "pride of Jordan" is taken to mean the luxuriant thick-
ets along its banks, famous as the haunt of lions (Jeremiah 49:19,
Jeremiah 50:44, Zechariah 11:3).

What will the prophet do when he has to tread the tangled maze
of a jungle with the lions roaring round him?

We allow small things to stop us from our blessings with God because we complain about the smaller matters.

You can't run with horses if you can't walk in the mist of footman. Listen to Hebrews 12:3–5.

> Consider Him who endured such hostility from sinners, so that you will not grow weary and lose heart.
>
> In your struggle against sin, you have not yet resisted to the point of shedding your blood.
>
> And you have forgotten the exhortation that addresses you as sons: "My son, do not take lightly the discipline of the Lord, and do not lose heart when He rebukes you."

Oftentimes adversities will come upon us. God sees and knows why. Because others (his may have caused them, that may affect even the smallest mountain of people) make bad judgments.

Jesus

I can verify that Jesus is the Son, and I love the son of God.

The Bible is your textbook and autobiography to set guide against Paradox defects that cause problems in our generation.

Without proper understanding, mankind tends to fail in seeking spiritual guidance.

Howbeit that God today is the same yesterday and forever (Hebrews 13:8)?

Right now, God speaks to us by the work. Take a look then, review your life again.

God is still offering salvation for all mankind today.

I look to the world for spiritual guidance.

Look above. Colossians 3:1–3.

> The god of this age has blinded the minds of unbelievers, so that they cannot see the light of the gospel that displays the glory of Christ, who is the image of God. (2 Corinthians 4:4)

Are you really a friend of Jesus?

> You are My friends if you do what I command you. (John 15:14)

> Jesus Christ The Only Begotten Son of God. Who, being in the form of God, thought it not robbery to be equal with God.

But made himself of no reputation, and took upon him the form of a servant, and was made in the likeness of men.

And being found in fashion as a man, he humbled himself, and became obedient unto death, even the death of the cross.

Wherefore God also hath highly exalted him, and given him a name which is above every name;

That at the name of Jesus every knee should bow, of things in heaven, and things in earth, and things under the earth;

And that every tongue should confess that Jesus Christ is Lord, to the glory of God the Father. (Philippians 2:6–11)

For in him all things were created: things in heaven and on earth, visible and invisible, whether thrones or powers or rulers or authorities; all things have been created through him and for him. (Colossians 1:16)

Memorize this.

Have a deep trust for Jesus. The existence of God came to us for a little while on earth. His created earth.

Until I come, devote yourself to the public reading of Scripture, to preaching and to teaching. (1 Timothy 4:13)

John 14:19. Keep that deep trust. Romans 8:9.

Judgment

Proverbs 11:30 is what love means to God. Doing his work, daily.

John 3:16 means that God always loves his created man. What about you?

Jesus said, "I must work the works of him that sent me, while it is day: the night cometh, when no man can work" (John 9:4).

Matthew 28:18–20.

When you pass from this life, you shall be judged by the life you lived, from your Creator, God.

Read Hebrews 9:27. After that, the judgment. Ecclesiastes 12:14.

Notice your Bible.

> This will come to pass on that day when God will judge men's secrets through Christ Jesus, as proclaimed by my gospel. (Romans 2:16)

> Therefore, judge nothing before the appointed time; wait until the Lord comes.
>
> He will bring to light what is hidden in darkness and will expose the motives of men's hearts.
>
> At that time each will receive his praise from God. (1 Corinthians 4:5)

Even if mankind makes his own way but seems to manage his life apart from the Creator's Word.

Listen to the Word and live your life according to God's standards. He loves you and wants his created man to be saved; but apart from that, there is no salvation.

Amen.

Now, John 12:48 tells us that many will choose their own course of life (Hebrews 9:27, Matthew 7:14), or one can submit to the word that brings life back to his soul.

Hebrews 9:14.

Stay with the Lord.

Psalm 148:1–6.

King David

The paw of the lion, bear, and the Philistines (1 Samuel 17:37).

David, anointed king of Judah (2 Samuel 2:1–9) by the House of Judah. Now Saul was dead, while he liveth; if he thought someone was strong, he took him (1 Samuel 14:52); but in the day of Saul when God himself appointed David king, he saw a young lad to be leader among his people, who is humble, concerned for the work that has been appointed for him to do.

Saul in talking approved David going to battle; and as he went out, he took off the armor, took it off, and used a staff and five smooth stones, but when he approached the Philistines, they laughed. "Am I a dog that you come to me with sticks?" (1 Samuel 17:26–51).

But the Lord was with David, who was carrying stones; when he took a stone out of his bag and slung it around and struck the Philistine in the forehead, and he fell on his face to the earth, with a single shot, so David prevailed over the Philistines with a sling and a stone, putting that Philistine to the grave.

No sword in the hand of David. But he ran over to the Philistine, took his sword, and finished the job, while the others fled; all the people rejoiced (1 Samuel 17:48–52). Amen!

Knowledge

Guessing yourself right is not defined as a cognitive function to increase information.

In matters of religion and knowledge.

Growing in the grace and knowledge requires to read and study 2 Timothy 2:15.

Cognitive functioning refers to multiple mental abilities, including learning, thinking, reasoning, remembering, problem-solving, decision-making, and attention.

> But grow in the grace and knowledge of our
> Lord and Savior Jesus Christ.
> To him be glory both now and forever!
> Amen. (2 Peter 3:18)

> But speaking the truth in love, we should
> grow up in all things into Him who is the head,
> Christ. (Ephesians 4:15)

No man nor woman can whip any people into church.

Don't beat yourself and others up by teaching them words belonging to God. John 12:48 is active today.

Be gentle, soften your vowels, engage your tone to serve others with the inspired word of God in a gentle manner.

> A servant of the Lord must not quarrel but
> must be kind to everyone, be able to teach, and
> be patient with difficult people. Unless you too
> be tempted to be difficult. (2 Timothy 2:24)

But watch yourself, or you also may be tempted.

Carry one another's burdens, and in this way, you will fulfill the law of Christ.

If anyone thinks he is something when he is nothing, he deceives himself.

Each one should test his own work.

Then he will have reason to boast in himself alone, and not in someone else.

For each one should carry his own load.

But the one who receives instruction in the word must share in all good things with his instructor. (Galatians 6:3ff)

Have you ever spoken with someone and it felt like every time you talk to that person, it sounds like someone was stabbing you with their words?

That's harsh. And can sound damaging to the ears.

Words are needed to take a more proactive approach in a professional manner.

Hearers are in exchange to its receivers. Counter actively in response.

To get ahead requires a gentler approach. Not actions of intimidation to win.

Perhaps you might be subject to lose an argument if unprepared.

All of us are being subjected to his own resurrection, as plan to our departure.

We were blessed to have great parents, but that is still not the end. There is a someday soon.

Then shall the dust return to the earth as it was: and the spirit shall return unto God who gave it. Vanity of vanities, saith the preacher; all is vanity. And moreover, because the preacher was wise, he still taught the people knowledge; yea, he gave good heed, and sought out, and set in order many proverbs. (Ecclesiastes 12:7–9)

Dictionary meaning relating to or being a work (such as a book or recording) whose production cost is paid by the author or artist.

Who shall receive from his works?

What does vanity mean in the Bible?

According to Strong's Concordance, the word *vain* or *vanity* has the idea of vapor or breath.

Much more to consider: whereas the more you preach, less likely are your listeners to consider the Word of God in its entirety.

So then Solomon is right; vanity, vanity, today—is it all the same as before?

New Testament calls it vainglory.

Let us not be desirous of vain glory, provoking one another, envying one another. (Galatians 5:26)

Let nothing be done through strife or vainglory; but in lowliness of mind let each esteem other better than themselves. (Philippians 2:3)

Vainglory means "inordinate pride in oneself or one's achievements; excessive vanity."

Read 2 Corinthians 2:10.

These are the things God has revealed to us by his Spirit.

The Spirit searches all things, even the deep things of God.

In the simplest terms.

Read 2 Samuel 12:3.

But now that he has died, why should I go on fasting?

Can I bring him back again?

I will go to him, but he cannot not return to me.

My dad was a good writer and a good speaker.

Converted a great number of people over the course of his life.

Even from his workplace, he taught and converted mankind to the gospel of Christ.

Think about it, one cannot convert every man, but some will listen to the Word of God.

> But small is the gate and narrow the road
> that leads to life, and only a few find it. (Matthew
> 7:14)

The question of your concern is not to anybody else, but where are you headed, and where are you misleading another to go?

Crazy people will never be a civilized society because they refuse to become rightfully minded.

Here's what they think.

> Those who say that evil is good and good
> is evil, that dark is light, and light is dark, that
> bitter is sweet and sweet is bitter. What sorrow.
> (Isaiah 5:20)

It is all in their actions

Self-evidences prove that ignorance will not seek the righteousness of God, until divine retribution, supernatural punishment is inflicted upon a person or groups of people by being rebellious against God, who seek their own philosophies in life.

Many cultures have a story about how a deity exacted punishment upon previous inhabitants of their land, causing their dooms. We learn from previous things written (Romans 15:4).

Some take matters into their own hands away from God.

They fail and never recover from stumbling.

What sorrow it is to see such failures among the Babylonians.

> For I have not held back from announcing
> to you the whole purpose of God. (Acts 20:27)

> Whoever speaks, as one who speaks oracles of God; whoever serves, as one who serves by the strength that God supplies—in order that in everything God may be glorified through Jesus Christ. To him belong glory and dominion forever and ever. Amen. (1 Peter 4:11)

The church has become a changed people, "some of which" (might have), who once were denominational people, were not a people, but a behaving people who didn't want to let go of false teachings and false worship from past experiences; they have changed completely to serve God in a rightful way.

It takes time if you were not raised up in the body of Christ.

Read Galatians 6:1ff.

All this is to say God is at work today, using our minds and our physical abilities in doing his work.

From heaven, Christ uses us in his work.

Listen.

> The Lord is not slow in keeping his promise, as some understand slowness.
>
> He is patient with you, not wanting anyone to perish, but everyone to come to repentance. (2 Peter 3:9)

Bear in mind that our Lord's patience means salvation, just as our dear brother Paul also wrote you with the wisdom that God gave him.

Changed people are God listeners (2 Timothy 3:16).

A few constituents have changed from past doctrines.

And we should be aware of other circumstances that surround us, although there are a few who hold on to their taught doctrine and practices; maybe among you today, but within our groups, they're learning the truth and right way—by changing and to know the truth (John 17:17).

Read John 10:1ff, including 1 Timothy 4:1ff and 2 John 1:10.

Ministry is a work.

> Jesus said I must work the works of my
> father that sent me, while it is day: the night
> cometh, when no man can work. (John 9:4)

The question is, are you in Christ?
The church believes in the exact doctrine of God, his way, no other reason.

> All this is from God, who reconciled us to
> himself through Christ and gave us the ministry
> of reconciliation. (2 Corinthians 5:17–18)

My friends, yes, there are some who hold on to old habits learned, from those who practice denominational problems; but now they are free through the truth.
John 4:24.
Remember what Jesus said.
Listen

> I have other sheep that are not of this sheep
> pen.
> I must bring them also.
> They too will listen to my voice, and there
> shall be one flock and one shepherd. (John 10:16)

Those who have let go are completely washed and sanctified, made themselves a good vessel for the master's use.
Because they have learned the kind differences between truth and errors.

> As it is written: "How beautiful are the feet
> of those who bring good news!" (Romans 10:15b)

Will you, my friends, today see the differences?

Others are halfway there, and you could be a voice in deciding the differences in their life.

My friends, if you did not help a brother or sister from their errors, you have violated the Word of God.

And if you have problems talking with others who have errors, don't approach them alone because you have become a stumbling stone to yourself.

It takes a skilled person to convince others to turn away from errors.

And since others might have knowledge of your harsh language and unchanging practices, you are not the person prepared to go for Jesus.

Don't let the power of the Word of God leave you because you see others changing the doctrine of Christ to a better way in service to them who do error.

Leaders

Some folks are Scripture settlers; they know nothing more than history, lacking application to the Word.

> But blessed is the one who trusts in the Lord, whose confidence is in him.
> They will be like a tree planted by the water that sends out its roots by the stream.
> It does not fear when heat comes; its leaves are always green.
> It has no worries in a year of drought and never fails to bear fruit. (Jeremiah 17:7–8)

When you discover application, you will come in the presence of God's eternal purpose in life.

When you know God's needed efforts, you will come to emotional means to do.

That's real.

> Nothing in all creation is hidden from God's sight. Everything is uncovered and laid bare before the eyes of him to whom we must give account. (Hebrews 4:13)

Life

Life is a series of moments; what footprints have you left behind for many to remember?

What changes have you made to better serve others?

Don't forget how important your life is with God.

> Why, you do not even know what will happen tomorrow. What is your life? You are a mist that appears for a little while and then vanishes. (James 4:14)

Remember at birth, you were given the breath of life from God. And you, my friend, became a living soul.

Thank God for your life today.

Read Revelation 4:11.

> For You formed my inward parts;
> You covered me in my mother's womb.
> I will praise You, for I am fearfully and wonderfully made;
> Marvelous are Your works,
> And that my soul knows very well. (Psalm 139:13–14)

Light and Darkness

Keep your chin up, God is still in control.

There are some folks who are afraid to step/walk into the light with God because such are afraid of being exposed.

First John 1:7 says, "But if we walk in the light, as he is in the light, we have fellowship with one another, and the blood of Jesus, his Son, purifies us from all sin."

Hebrews 4:13 tells everyone who is exposed to light, and has been drawn thereof, knows that God does not like or approve habitual sinners.

> If any man sees his brother sin a sin which is not unto death, he shall ask, and he shall give him life for them that sin not unto death. (1 John 5:16)

There is a sin unto death; I do not say that he shall pray for it.

Then you have those who step into the light but don't give a good answer why they have, because such wanted to only see what happens if they do. For one, such will find Christians; they look upon to see who might be weak and might want to deceive.

> Do not be deceived: God cannot be mocked.
> A man reaps what he sows. (Galatians 6:7)

Christians know the enemy of God.

The devil's triangle is this: himself, demons, and evil man.

Don't be fooled, some of which actions are of atheist minds who don't believe in the Word of God (Psalm 14:1).

Why? The devil makes parades against righteous people and does harm to innocent mankind; he maketh lies and colors deceit with words of encouragement, which are lies and bring bloodshed (John 8:44).

> Woe unto them that call evil good, and good evil; that put darkness for light, and light for darkness; that put bitter for sweet, and sweet for bitter! (Isaiah 5:20)

There are background evils that surround us; we have much more work to do in saving sinners from the fire.

Then they will come to their senses and escape from the devil's trap (2 Timothy 2:26).

For they have been held captive by him to do whatever he wants.

God made colors for his particular purpose.

It is not for anyone to redesign God's eternal purpose.

Careful of your walk in this world.

You could design your own destiny (Hebrews 2:1).

All of God's designs belong to his secrecy (Deuteronomy 29:29).

You cannot figure out God; that's not going to happen (Revelation 4:11).

In fact, God has made us smart to understand his plan, not his mind. Just do what we are told (John 12:48).

Don't worry your minds.

Trust God.

Man, shut up!

> God forbid yea, let God be true, but every man a liar; as it is written, that thou mightest be justified in thy sayings, and mightest overcome when thou art judged. (Romans 3:4)

Guns are okay for the right case of defense.

A right to defend yourself and family.

Be your brother's keeper.

Don't be a wobbly wheel in this country, design yourself to walk in the Word of God (1 Peter 2:21); otherwise, you will not be accepted into eternal life with our Creator.

> The eyes of the LORD watch over those who do right; his ears are open to their cries for help. (Psalm 34:15)

> Remember anything against God is of the devil. (John 8:44)

> Jesus said—Do you think I cannot call on my Father, and he will at once put at my disposal more than twelve legions of angels? (Matthew 26:53)

The Light Is On or Off, Which?

Do you remember being told in school to pay attention?

Perhaps you were daydreaming; if so, don't be reluctant to admit it. I happen to be one of those who believe daydreaming is a good thing.

Nevertheless, the teacher wanted you to focus on what she or he was teaching because the teacher knew you would need to know the material—either in life or at test time or both. We should never miss anything that will prepare us for the workplace, marketplace, or the homeplace.

Well, how about God? I mean, why do we miss so much information or put into practice those things given from God that keep our soul salvation secure?

Proverbs 1:33 in the Living Bible says, "But all who listen to me shall live in peace and safety, unafraid."

Relax, God's got you.

Stay focused.

Paying attention to his wisdom unleashes his blessing flow.

Have you ever asked your children if they were paying attention to what you were saying?

You can tell the light's on, but there's nobody in the house. How do you think God feels?

Jeremiah 17:23 says, "But they didn't listen or obey. They stubbornly refused to pay attention and be taught." or

"But they obeyed not, neither inclined their ear, but made their neck stiff, that they might not hear, nor receive instruction."

Wisdom comes from paying attention to your father.

Proverbs 4:1 in the Amplified Bible says, "Hear, my sons, the instruction of a father, and pay attention in order to gain and to know intelligent discernment, comprehension, and interpretation of spiritual matters." In other words, listen carefully.

God wants us to pay attention to the Word, evangelism, instead of the world economy.

First John 4:5–6 in the Amplified Bible says,

> They proceed from the world and are of the world; therefore, it is out of the world its whole economy morally considered that they speak, and the world listens pays attention to them.
>
> But remember, we are children of God, and we listen to God. Whoever is learning to know God, is proactive and perceive, and recognize, understand God, by observation from the word, by experience, and to get an ever-clearer knowledge of Him. Please listen, and he who is not of God does not listen or pay attention to us or Him (God).
>
> By this we know (recognize) the Spirit of Truth and the spirit of error.

If we look to the world system for answers to all our problems, to help us through every adversity, we are removing God from the equation.

Listen, folks, it's time to pay attention.

Light of the World

Who can be better by exhorting the brethren than Jesus?

Matthew 5:14 says, "You are the light of the world—like a city on a hilltop that cannot be hidden."

You, my friend, are built upon the promises of God, never hidden from the world.

You are set before a front line of witnesses that cannot be hidden, crucified or not, and that your love and appreciation for God and his word continues.

Refer to 1 Corinthians 15:58 and Ephesians 2:1, 6, 8.

Pay attention to verse 6.

> And hath raised us up together, and made us sit together in heavenly places in Christ Jesus:
>
> That in the ages to come he might shew the exceeding riches of his grace in his kindness toward us through Christ Jesus.
>
> For by grace are ye saved through faith; and that not of yourselves: it is the gift of God. (vv. 6–8)

Aren't you glad to receive your gift?

Read again Romans 8:1; you can know that you are saved if you continue in his Word (1 Corinthians 15:58).

Listen

Question: How long should the Word of God take effect in your life after you hear it?

Listening to God can take effect immediately (Romans 10:17, Hebrews 4:12).

When asked a question that you don't know, a reasonable response would be, "It's just beyond my purview."

Some would say, "It's beyond my pay grade."

There is no "almost being saved."

You must go all the way.

How can you just think about it?

Listen to God, be conformed to the likeness of Christ.

It's all in the Word.

I met a visitor in the mall, and in talking to him, I mentioned, "With that power in your voice, you should be preaching." He said someone else told him likewise.

He said he wanted to repent, get right with God, and be saved according to the Word of God, and he will look further into the ministry of God.

I told him, "Jesus needs you and will help you to become a great teacher."

Just a little encouraging goes a long way.

Read Hebrews 13:2 and 1 Corinthians 3:6–8.

Listen to Teachers

Listen carefully to your teachers. You can't override their minds by teaching their class.

Teachers have a way to ask probing questions to stimulate your mind.

Furthermore, just listen. Answer or comment when necessary; otherwise, don't say anything.

Plato quote: "Wise men speak because they have something to say; fools because they have to say something."

> A wise man will hear, and will increase learning; and a man of understanding shall attain unto wise counsels. (Proverbs 1:5)

> All spoke well of Him and marveled at the gracious words that came from His lips.
> "Isn't this the son of Joseph?" they asked! (Luke 4:22)

Let men say this of you.
Wise to feed.
Trust will serve.
We have great friends, hope yours are great as well.
Glory to God.

> A man that hath friends must shew himself friendly: and there is a friend that sticketh closer than a brother. (Proverbs 18:24)

How about you?

People that come into our lives or people we choose to be part of our lives are chiefly of four kinds: confidants, constituents, comrades, or commanders.

Confidants are people who are around you because they are into you.

Confidants buy into you as a person and therefore are willing to be by your side whether you are up or down, in victory or defeat, right or wrong. They are however wise enough to tell you when you are wrong.

Constituents, on the other hand, are those who are around you because they are for what you are for.

They are people pursuing the same destination that you are pursuing, are going the same place you are going, and are therefore travelling the same path you are travelling. They are only with you because you both have the same destination in mind.

Commanders, on their part, are in your life because you have a resource that can take them to where they are going. They are not in your life because you are going where they are going but because you have a resource or skill that they consider important in helping them arrive at their destination.

Comrades, finally, are those who are around you because they are against what you are against. They are those who are around you because you share the same enemy. They are only with you to see the greater enemy fall.

Now ask yourselves the big question: What kind of people are you listening to?

First, share your thoughts with God, then share your thoughts with any man.

Careful how you answer everyone.

Amen.

Listening

Romans 12:10–13.
The Bible says,

> Be kindly affectionate to one another with
> brotherly love, in honor giving preference to
> one another; not lagging in diligence, fervent in
> spirit, serving the Lord; rejoicing in hope, patient
> in tribulation, continuing steadfastly in prayer;
> distributing to the needs of the saints, given to
> hospitality.

Now each one should practice what they say in love.
Remember Galatians 6:1–10.
God knows that we can remember more from reading than
words spoken in a moment in time.
Over and over again we can reread what was already spoken for
our better relationship with God.
Reading God's words should put us into action by his spoken
words before.
Refer to John 1:1ff and 2 Peter 1:20–21.

> Behold, the Lord's hand is not shortened,
> that it cannot save; neither his ear heavy, that it
> cannot hear:
> But your iniquities have separated between
> you and your God, and your sins have hidden
> his face from you, that he will not hear. (Isaiah
> 59:1–2)

Listen, God sees and hears everything (Hebrews 4:13).

But God will not pay attention to your cry for help if you are not listening to his word.

Who else would?

Living for Christ

Friends who are Christians, the best to speak about (1 Thessalonians 5:11).

> Speaking to one another in psalms and hymns and spiritual songs, singing with grace in your heart to THE LORD IN HEAVEN.

Praying together with our hearts and hands high above our heads to God in heaven.

Teaching ourselves to be more like him.

Living our lives, the best we know how, learning from the Word of God.

Therefore, encourage one another and build each other up, just as in fact you are doing.

I manage to get this far in life, and no one will change this mind. I'm Christian Marcel, made from God.

I have trusted God with my whole heart, and in him will I keep my trust.

How about your story?

Living Sacrifice

T hugs are not of us.
We respect all authority regardless of what others may feel.
Listen to your Bible: Romans 13, Matthew 22:37.
Listen.

> I urge you, brothers and sisters, in view of
> God's mercy, to offer your bodies as a living sac-
> rifice, holy and pleasing to God-this is your true
> and proper worship. (Romans 12:1)

A living sacrifice is not a dead man. It is a new creation in God
(2 Corinthians 5:17).

> Wherefore he (God says) saith, Awake, thou
> that sleepest, and arise from the dead, and Christ
> shall give thee light. (Ephesians 5:14)

> If you belong to the world, you are not of
> God. You might have been physically created by
> God; but you chose to be of the devil. (John 8:44)

> Jesus said "Come to me, all you who are
> weary and burdened, and I will give you rest.
> Take my yoke upon you and learn from me, for I
> am gentle and humble in heart, and you will find
> rest for your souls. For my yoke is easy and my
> burden is light." (Matthew 11:28–30)

> He that hath knowledge spareth his words:
> and a man of understanding is of an excellent
> spirit. Even a fool, when he holdeth his peace,
> is counted wise: and he that shutteth his lips is
> esteemed a man of understanding. (Proverbs
> 17:27–28)

Question: Will anyone buy a dirty animal at an auction?

Or would you buy a dirty dress or a dirty towel for your family?

Or could you say to some waiter in a restaurant who wears dirty clothing, "Come serve me"?

I say no, it must be presented to sell and look good enough to serve.

Mankind must represent Jesus in the most unique way.

Living sacrifice.

Here's my point.

Why present yourselves any ole way to God?

Jesus is going to present those who present themselves as a living sacrifice to his Father.

Without spot or blemish and without blame to his Father.

Listen these words.

Revelation says, "So that he might present the church to himself in splendor, without spot or wrinkle or any such thing, that she might be holy and without blemish" (Ephesians 5:27).

Now, any leader or leaders must first be tested; and then if there is nothing against them, let them serve as deacons (1 Timothy 3:10).

So shall their wives as well.

Both are considered one body in Christ.

Notice Romans 12:1–2.

> Therefore, I urge you, brothers and sisters,
> in view of God's mercy, to offer your bodies as a
> living sacrifice, holy and pleasing to God—this is
> your true and proper worship.

Do not conform to the pattern of this world but be transformed by the renewing of your mind.

Then you will be able to test and approve what God's will is—his good, pleasing and perfect will.

If a leader must present, then you must do the same.

As Stephen (a man of God) once said, "There's a difference between being in Christ and being with Christ."

Read Galatians 3:27 and Romans 6:3.

Listen: *In Christ* means "salvation"; *with Christ* means "to bring you to obedience for your salvation."

If one is not in Christ, you are lost (Romans 8:1).

In Christ, you are saved by obedience to his word.

Living Water

John 7:37–39.

Yet a simile or a metaphorical saying emphasizing the use of words by Jesus. Indicating a heavenly meaning yet an earthy saying—however, not a parable and yet a literal receiving.

Read Acts 1.

Notice.

> Now on the last day, the great day of the feast, Jesus stood and cried out, saying, "If anyone is thirsty, let him come to Me and drink. He who believes in Me," as the Scripture said, "From his innermost being will flow rivers of living water."
>
> But this He spoke of the Spirit, whom those who believed in Him were to receive; for the Spirit was not yet given, because Jesus was not yet glorified.

It takes place when Jesus was in Jerusalem for the Feast of Tabernacles, not the Feast of Weeks (Pentecost).

Some say that Jesus awaited glorification when he ascended to the Father.

I think.

This takes us to the rolling away of the stone, at his resurrection.

Our God can do anything he sees fit to finish his work, even today.

The Word and by the Holy Spirit actively participating in lives today,

> The veiled character of the glory of the Risen Jesus during this time is intimated in his mysterious words to Mary Magdalene: "I have not yet ascended to the Father; but go to my brethren and say to them, I am ascending to my Father and your Father, to my God and your God."
>
> No one has ascended into heaven but he who descended from heaven, the Son of man.

Look closely, when you have been rising with Christ, your citizenship is being raised to glorify the Father in heaven.

But you are still in ministry of God on earth until such time of your departure (Hebrews 9:27).

So, work out your soul salvation.

Matthew 28:18–19.

There Christ permanently exercises his priesthood, for he "always lives to make intercession" for "those who draw near to God through him."

As "high priest of the good things to come," he is the center and the principal actor of the liturgy that honors the Father in heaven.

> Therefore, he is able, to save completely those who come to God through him, because he always lives to intercede for them. (Hebrews 7:25)

Reading treasures from the Bible.
Prayers that teach us how to dwell in the house of the Lord.
Words of encouragement printed.

> Create in me a clean heart, O God, and renew a steadfast spirit within me.

Do not cast me away from Your presence, and do not take Your Holy Spirit from me.

Restore to me the joy of Your salvation and sustain me with a willing spirit. (Psalm 51:10–12)

Logical Conclusions

J esus says, "If you do not remain in me, you are like a branch that is thrown away and withers; such branches are picked up, thrown into the fire and burned" (John 15:6).

Colossians 1:9–12.

Spiritual growth means growing to know how God wants us to live so that we seek to please him in all things.

> The meek shall eat and be satisfied: they
> shall praise the Lord that seek Him: your heart
> shall live forever. (Psalm 22:26)

Question: Have you ever wondered why people stumble?

Here's why: Psalm 1:1ff.

Perhaps some might struggle in that area.

Don't get hooked on sin.

Why?

It is you not feeding on Jesus, the Word of God.

Men will seek satisfaction in the evil pleasures of this world rather than the eternal promises of eternity.

Suppose you just finished a wonderful meal, and somebody knocks on your front door.

You answer it, and they give you a plate of stale crumbs, saying, "Take this. Eat."

You would say, "No, thank you, I don't need that. I'm already satisfied."

When you feast on the goodness of Jesus, you won't go down a dark alley eating from cans with the devil's billy goats.

What does it mean to "feast on the goodness of Jesus"? It means to find your contentment in Jesus.

How will you find that? You're going to find Jesus in the Word.

Jesus said, "Search the Scriptures, these are they which testify of Me."

You're not going to be pure until you put your eyes upon Jesus, the one who's altogether lovely, and gaze into his face in the Word of God.

> And Jesus said unto them, I am the Bread
> of life: he that cometh to Me shall never hunger;
> and he that believeth on Me shall never thirst.
> (John 6:35)

Lord's Supper

Does Luke's research of Paul suggest that the Lord's communion be taken on the first day of every week (Acts 20:7)?

Or as often as the church comes together.

What does *often* mean? How many times?

What did the other apostles do after the resurrection of Jesus?

Necessary inference suggests *oftentimes* when taking the Lord's Supper (1 Corinthians 11:23ff).

Question: When Jesus instituted the communion with the Twelve, how often did he take it after his crucifixion?

After the resurrection, how often did Jesus participate in the reason given (Matthew 26:26)?

The Lord's Supper was instituted by Jesus Christ during his last week before his crucifixion (Matthew 26:17–30).

This week fell during the time of the Jewish holidays, the Passover feast and the week of Unleavened Bread (Matthew 26:17).

> And as they were eating, Jesus took bread, blessed and broke it, and gave it to the disciples and said, "Take, eat; this is My body."
>
> Then He took the cup, and gave thanks, and gave it to them, saying, "Drink from it, all of you. For this is My blood of the new covenant, which is shed for many for the remission of sins. But I say to you, I will not drink of this fruit of the vine from now on until that day when I drink it new with you in My Father's kingdom." (Matthew 26:26–29)

Love

Love never changes; it works together. It lives in truth, lives for God, sits in righteousness.

Hate is a different thing; it dies in hypocrisy and lives with lies, conquer, deception, and evangelizes to destroy mankind.

> Love is patient, love is kind. It does not envy, it does not boast, it is not proud. It does not dishonor others, it is not self-seeking, it is not easily angered, it keeps no record of wrongs. Love does not delight in evil but rejoices with the truth. It always protects, always trusts, always hopes, always perseveres. (1 Corinthians 13:4–7)

Have you ever been carried away by foolishness after a while when things go south?

Some have and some have not, but we all been taught how to love God; and if we do, we shall not turn a blind eye against the truth.

In teaching ourselves, we say to others, "Hold up, wait a second, did I just hear you say such and such? Well, I thought you were a just man, what happened to your just?"

Did it go south, just as the devil teaches to listen?

Don't, listen, pay attention to where it's going.

When people love you, learn to love back, not with ill feeling or caustic remarks, corrosive explosive behavior, but with godliness (Ephesians 4:24ff).

In John 13:34, Jesus taught, "A new command I give you: Love one another. As I have loved you, so you must love one another."

Then he added, "By this everyone will know that you are my disciples, if you love one another" (verse 35). How do we do this? What does it mean to love one another?

To believe in Jesus and do what he says. Practice makes perfect. Sad to say that hate will keep a person out of heaven, whereas doing what love does causes you to love God evermore (John 12:48).

> Let brotherly love continue.
>
> Be not forgetful to entertain strangers: for thereby some have entertained angels unawares.
>
> Remember them that are in bonds, as bound with them; and them which suffer adversity, as being yourselves also in the body. (Hebrews 13:1–3)

There are some people who are bound because such cannot have a mind to get out of it.

So, they are stuck.

Do you walk and talk in the new Jerusalem way?

And do you press along the way? Well, a few will find it.

Thank you, Lord, thank you, Lord, I just want to thank you, Lord.

You've been soooooo good.

Folks may say, "Love your neighbor."

Jesus told us to love our neighbor (Mark 12:31).

Who is thy neighbor?

Jesus gave a great example in Luke 10:29ff.

Question: Can you find a neighbor in church today?

Perhaps, and perhaps not.

People get to busy in their everyday lives to pay attention to the most important message Jesus gave us today.

Here it is, written in the Word of God: James 2:14–26.

Neighbors are your friends who are so belonging to Christ (1 John 2:2).

You know who your friends are today, this minute?

And certainly, you know who your neighbors are, so why don't you do the will of God and forget about how weird the world behaves toward neighbors today?

Remember that the world is not sanctified. But you are, totally.

My friends, be the light, the salt, and engine God wants you to become for his purpose.

God's plan is needed.

Even I must pray every day for God's plan to work in me.

Listen: Get serious with God outside of the walls to which you worship.

When you leave church, it means go to work (Mark 16:15–16).

Worship is giving your sincere appreciation and love for your Creator.

Question: Will you let him down?

As for me, I can't.

I can only do as much as God allows.

Be sanctified and a peculiar people, set apart for good works.

Amen.

Love is the principal thing.

> Jesus replied: "Love the Lord your God with all your heart and with all your soul and with all your mind." (Matthew 22:37)

Never let your heart turn away from God. In every case, acknowledge him—morning, noon, or night.

> But to you who are listening I say: Love your enemies, do good to those who hate you, bless those who curse you, pray for those who mistreat you. If someone slaps you on one cheek, turn to them the other also.
>
> If someone takes your coat, do not withhold your shirt from them. Give to everyone who asks you, and if anyone takes what belongs to you, do not demand it back. (Luke 6:27–30)

At times, it's better to give, because someone might need something.

Here's the point: It's not in our day and age a literal slap, as if you stand up and let someone haul off and slap you, but you turn the other side of your face and let them pop you again.

No! That's not it.

The meaning is hyperbole in that it suggests that you don't participate in deciding to defend yourself, but in decency of mind, be sober and reasonable in your decision.

Walk away, and if someone steals your coat by force, don't risk your life on materialist things.

Let them have it, go buy something else.

Not worth it, no matter the value, don't give up your life.

Listen.

> Do not take revenge, my dear friends, but leave room for God's wrath, for it is written: "It is mine to avenge; I will repay," says the Lord. (Romans 12:19)

Now, this verse 31, what does it suggest?

> Do to others as you would have them do to you.

Some might say, "How do you do that? I am fearfully getting my stuff back no matter my pride. I'm not letting anybody take my stuff or slap me, no way. I'm not stupid, I have a right to defend myself against evildoers."

Yes, you do have that right indeed. But the more you think about it, it eventually dies, and you are best healed by staying away from foolish people or keeping them away from you. Mankind has changed.

Back in the days, families would handle their business, no playing around, but we've all gotten a little better than most.

Christians protect their children and families.

Thank the Lord, imagine giving up your freedom. It was easy back then to protect our family; nobody messed with family, but then some friends and family act like the wind has carried them into the world and not toward God.

Treating the family as if it has little value.

What's up with that?

Listen, one must set the standards of righteous behavior for God in this life. It is he that has given you tools to follow. His commandments have strength, use them (not all men can accept these sayings, but to those who are chosen, but many are called.)

> For this is the love of God, that we keep his commandments: and his commandments are not grievous. (1 John 5:3)

> Therefore, brothers, be all the more eager to make your calling and election sure. For if you practice these things you will never stumble. (2 Peter 1:10)

Loyalty

D ual loyalty does not fly.

> Those who bow down on the roofs to worship the starry host, those who bow down and swear by the LORD and who also swear by Molek. (Zephaniah 1:5)

> So these nations worshiped the LORD but also served their idols, and to this day their children and grandchildren continue to do as their fathers did. (2 Kings 17:41)

> Their hearts are devious; now they must bear their guilt. The LORD will break down their altars and demolish their sacred pillars. (Hosea 10:2)

> You, adulterous people, don't you know that friendship with the world means enmity against God? Therefore, anyone who chooses to be a friend of the world becomes an enemy of God. (James 4:4)

You can't have it both ways.
Worldliness versus godliness.
Dual loyalty.

Dealing with a Case of Incest

It is actually reported that there is sexual immorality among you, and of a kind that even pagans do not tolerate:

A man is sleeping with his father's wife.

And you are proud! Shouldn't you rather have gone into mourning and have put out of your fellowship the man who has been doing this? (1 Corinthians 5:1–3)

For ye have need of patience, that, after ye have done the will of God, ye might receive the promise. For yet a little while, and he that shall come will come, and will not tarry. Now the just shall live by faith: but if any man draw back, my soul shall have no pleasure in him. But we are not of them who draw back unto perdition; but of them that believe to the saving of the soul. (Hebrews 10:36–39)

Marriage

Take notice, my brethren, if a woman who is going to be married but does not submit to her father in the Lord, how could she submit to her husband, in the Lord?

She will not.

Angry women tend to withhold her duty to exercise submission in the Lord.

A father should be able to submit and present his precious gifts to the man who she wants to marry.

She is sanctified.

She belongs to the body of Christ.

She is graced with the blessing of God; however, if she turns her heart away from God, how can this woman believe in the Word of God? A woman cannot presume to present an unsanctified body to another man believing in God (2 Corinthians 6:14).

One's actions should be of trustworthiness.

The values of sanity are in the Word of God and not by self-determination.

Secondly, a mother cannot give away her daughter in marriage; that is not her responsibility.

A woman by the command of God can never occupy the office of headship in a family, because she is a wife.

If she was to remarry or not, she cannot swap out a command of God to make herself head.

Perhaps a manager of his (family) affairs, or if her husband either dies or becomes ill wherein he cannot perform. She is still either a wife or widow.

Furthermore, if she doesn't follow the commands of God, neither will her daughter.

Historically, in Jewish marriages, this is unheard-of in the first century where a wife is called head of her family.

Modern-day evangelical propaganda is not biblical—contrary to the Word of God.

People will get contaminated by following a deception; anything that is not a command, that places itself alongside command, is but a sin.

A controversial thing that is popular today.

We must find and follow the commands of God.

Don't let the world be your CEO for your marriage.

Let God tell you the marriage he wills on earth to compare with in heaven.

A godly man shepherd his household in the Lord (Ephesians 5:25).

The responsibility is in the home.

Results are defined in the home (Ephesians 6:1).

We have a duty to protect and take care of our parents.

> Honor your father and mother, so that your days may be long in the land the LORD your God is giving you. (Exodus 20:12)

Rejoice in the Lord, let all the saints of God shout out his name. Amen.

It has been said that if a man or woman who has an ex who tried to write your life off and lied to your child/children or anyone else after she asks you to leave because she wanted to move on, then told everyone that you left her (saying you ran off and left as though she hasn't done it herself), that is nothing but unfruitful acts of darkness.

That's what is called a damnable lie that destroys a whole city.

Things can reverse itself where folks can discover what the truth really is.

In working both ways in a dysfunctional marriage, a man can be physically present, but she could be spiritual absent; thus, she has already left the stage into serving the world. Same as a man.

But what does the Bible say?

> Wives, submit yourselves to your own husbands as you do to the Lord. For the husband is the head of the wife as Christ is the head of the church, his body, of which he is the Savior. Now as the church submits to Christ, so also wives should submit to their husbands in everything. (Ephesians 5:22–24)

When she does not believe God, she does not belong to God; and when he does not define his purpose, he fails over time.

But still it is commanded that she suffers the marriage to perfection.

Listen to your Bibles.

Paul telling the church at Corinth:

> Be ye followers of me, even as I also am of Christ.
>
> Now I praise you, brethren, that ye remember me in all things, and keep the ordinances, as I delivered them to you.
>
> But I would have you know that the head of every man is Christ; and the head of the woman is the man; and the head of Christ is God. (1 Corinthians 11:1–3)

This usually will happen with a couple who has been married for the first time, where careers are at stages of separation.

A person who at the stage of grace will weigh by providing for themselves or children without their partner's participation; this often pushes their mate aside.

Researchers deem this as the art of dysfunctional behavior.

For all my prayer warriors, keep on doing the commands of God.

Are you married to Christ? If not, who are you married too?

Ancient Jewish couples were betrothed to each other for one or more years before they had a wedding ceremony and consummated their marriage. Yet this betrothal period was not anything like modern "engagements" that can be easily called off. The betrothal period was a time when the bride and groom were supposed to prepare themselves for the life they were going to soon share together.

The husband often went away and prepared a home for the future family while the woman would engage in practices that prepared her for her future life as a wife and mother.

This betrothal period is presupposed in many of Jesus's teachings, such as his parable about the virgins who hadn't prepared themselves for the returning bridegroom.

Jesus was also alluding to this betrothal period when he told his disciples that he was "going away to prepare a place for them" so that they could always be where he was (John 14).

Once he'd made his declaration of love and pledge of life by dying on the cross, he would have to go away and prepare a place for him and his bride to live together.

This betrothal period is also presupposed in the New Testament's teaching about the need for the bride to "make herself ready" (Revelation 19).

In ancient Jewish culture, a man initiated the process of getting married by pledging his life to his prospective bride on the condition that she will accept his offer and reciprocate his love and pledge.

This is what God does toward us in Christ. Jesus's incarnation, ministry, and death on our behalf is God's declaration of love toward us.

Yet God doesn't pledge his life toward us on the condition that we reciprocate.

Rather, "while we were yet sinners Christ died for us" (Romans 5:8).

God makes the ultimate sacrifice up front, in hopes that this will win the heart of his potential bride and she will reciprocate.

Christ's sacrifice is thus God's invitation to join him at "the marriage supper of the lamb."

While this may be understood, have you by the invitation of the Lord taken his word as truth?

And will God help you understand the differences between worldly marriage and heavenly marriage?

Can a man in a brothel be anybody's business?

Listen to the Word of God.

> Marriage should be honored by all, and the marriage bed kept pure, for God will judge the adulterer and all the sexually immoral. (Hebrews 13:4)

The Bible uses no language as cheaters.

But calls it sin.

We speak where the Bible says all sin is transgressions against God.

If she is a Christian, why divorce?

Both you and your spouse knew the difference.

However, if one spouse is not fully converted, you may with consent be reconciled at a certain time.

But if an unbeliever, that marriage cannot be made in heaven; marriages are made in heaven with two Christians.

The devil knows how to destroy marriages after a spiritual struggle.

Pray about it, ask God in private for guidance.

If a man is to be fruitful and multiply, how can he reproduce if he makes himself a eunuch?

Then how can they marry?

It is a choice of mankind to have children.

Will a surrogate mother be exempt from having children?

Yet from another's body because of sexual relations with her husband?

The law permits, but it depends upon circumstances in which our medicine perhaps has allowed.

I took Matthew 19 from commentaries as you, until I carefully researched its Greek meaning and Jewish behaviors in marriages.

Perhaps you should likewise.

Commentaries tend to copy each other's work and so write it.

Research. Jesus is speaking about Jewish behaviors in how they treat their women.

Remember, he is being tested, but Jesus goes right to the heart of the matter.

I've said enough. I pray you research in your findings.

Since you are in a public discussion, my question has always been "Can God forgive sins?"

Second, will God allow you to begin again?

Or no matter what happens in a union unfit, will God allow to be set within a body of evil faith?

Or will God allow you to escape (1 Corinthians 10:13)?

No man can go back and get his divorced wife after she belongs to another.

When you divorced her or him, you completely separated yourself from the marriage.

When you ignorantly fell into trespasses and sins, you may be forgiven from God and begin again, when you repent.

This sin can be repented of.

It is not an unpardonable sin.

Jewish men have more than one idea of marriage and more than one wife.

They used marriages as a thing to swap out or get from.

Jesus knew their acts of disobedience; wherefore, the logical things to do was to remain unmarried, but you cannot go back and get your wife if she has willfully married another man today.

To begin again means you ask God for a covenant relationship with him, thus repent of your sins.

Most, but not all, might have had an interpersonal relationship with their date before they became their spouse.

Or outside of marriage had a child.

Did God forgive those who did before entering into a union?

Yes, if repented.

Temptations can come to you when the devil knows your condition.

Pay attention to your life (Ephesians 4:27).

If you are going through some extreme sins (whatever those may be), you surely know how difficult it is being lost.

Your conscience will convict you.

Listen.

> For the wages of sin is death; but the gift of
> God is eternal life through Jesus Christ our Lord.
> (Romans 6:23)

Don't misunderstand the passage; in another place, it says, "We all sin." That means everyone sins at one time or another (Romans 3:23).

It does not mean that you have to stay in it as if living the life.

Get out of it, know what sin faith can do to you.

Sin will literally rob you of your eternal destiny, and everything has one.

God can help you; in fact, God will help his children through it if you let him.

If you find the window of opportunity to leave your sin, go, and you forfeit your opportunity, then temptations will overwhelm your conditions (1 Corinthians 10:13).

The Bible is clear.

> If when you have escaped the corruption
> of the world through the knowledge of our Lord
> and Savior Jesus Christ, only to be entangled
> and overcome by it again, their final condition is
> worse than it was at first. (2 Peter 2:20)

Now, this is when people reproach mankind and say within their hearts and in the presence God "that I have no sins."

Listen your Bible.

> If we say we have fellowship with Him yet
> walk in the darkness, we lie and do not practice

the truth. But if we walk in the light as He is in the light, we have fellowship with one another, and the blood of Jesus His Son cleanses us from all sin. If we say we have no sin, we deceive ourselves, and the truth is not in us. (1 John 1:6–8)

Decision is ours to make.

Don't give opportunity to the devil (Ephesians 4:27).

The world may be your problem, but it's not always your fault. Stay faithful to God.

"Can two walk together except they be agreed?" (Amos 3:3). The answer is yes.

But what happens if it becomes a problem? You can't agree.

Results without reservation—it means you simply have two different opinions and cannot agree upon your findings. With anything, be careful that your disagreements don't get your separation, and you become desperate to unite again.

The question is, what have you resolved?

Find your happiness to define your purpose.

If you are not happy in your relationship with your spouse, how in the world did you marry?

Now, if she or he decides to be unhinged in a relationship, what caused the problem?

Christian or non-Christian?

Perhaps to better understand, what caused the car to flip over?

Reckless driving in a marriage is not the thing to do.

You must be a defensive coordinator rather than an offensive driver.

Figure of speech is offered here to simply illustrate your need, to take a look at your potentials.

Furthermore, unhinged means playing wild games with each other; that includes also cursing, lying, and stealing.

Not the thing to do. There must be a presidential action in a marriage. Without controversy, some of which goes into a marriage blindly, ignorantly, and selfishly (money, looks, property, citizenship, etc.).

Man needs to recreate his thoughts before entering into a union; otherwise, he's not ready to see the potholes or unexpected things that show up unknowingly.

After carefully reviewing marriage, it tends to be all the same when two are together in love but requires much more; it's definitely definitive to work out our own soul salvation with fear and trembling.

My friends, before you build a car, read the blueprint.

A woman cannot be made without man, and there would not be an us without woman (Genesis 2:18).

It was all in the mind of God before creation.

His eternal purpose and will.

Jesus came by an agent, a woman whom God saw fit to reproduce his Son; she was a divinely ordained, called woman. That's how important woman is to God.

Woman should use her body to bring forth an offshoot from her husband.

Husband and wife.

A branch is an offshoot (i.e., we call an offspring from man). A stem that originated from a beginning.

Now listen carefully.

> The LORD God said, "It is not good for the man to be alone. I will make a helper suitable for him."

A helper suitable is in all aspects of her divinely designed body. She is looked upon by God as carefully made to reproduce us. No woman, no us.
Out of man comes woman, out of woman comes us.
Designed only from the Godhead.

> Husbands love your wives, just as Christ loved the church and gave himself up for her. (Ephesians 5:25)

"Gave himself up" is an operative phrase, as so defined.

It means to sacrifice yourself or give yourself up for her.

Just as Christ gave himself up for us.

To sanctify means cleansing to make a fitted vessel for the use in God's kingdom (John 17:17).

Husbands are called to love their wives differently than wives love their husbands.

For instance, the Bible calls husbands to submit in marriage.

When it says a husband must live with his wife "in an understanding way," what things should he understand?

A word for husbands from 1 Peter.

> Likewise, husbands, live with your wives in an understanding way, showing honor to the woman as the weaker vessel, since they are joint heirs with you of the grace of life, so that your prayers may not be hindered. (1 Peter 3:7)

One reason to say that the command here "to honor" has already been given to all Christians (1 Peter 2:17).

These husbands are being addressed as exiles and sojourners who live and are married in a foreign world.

The experience example is given to today, no matter where you are at or what country you are in.

> As obedient children, do not be conformed to the passions of your former ignorance, but as he who called you is holy; you also be holy in all your conduct. (1 Peter 1:14–15)

All honor and pride belong to the message of God's eternal purpose.

This plan is fully funded in eternal life.

To inquire eternal life, one must not misunderstand God, however, rather submit to the Word.

Final.

Husbands are now called, likewise as others, to submit in marriage in a way that's particular to their role (1 Peter 3:7); that is, male and female are created by God in the womb of a woman.

Now verse 22, plain and simple.

> Wives submit yourselves to your own husbands as you do to the Lord.
>
> For the husband is the head of the wife as Christ is the head of the church, his body, of which he is the Savior.
>
> Now as the church submits to Christ, so also wives should submit to their husbands in everything.

What does this all mean?

Woman, stay with your godly husband.

Husbands who are of God follow the commands of God.

Otherwise, they apostatize and has decided to live under a different administration (the world's view).

This is what happens when marriages are not in the upgrades.

It should be that each one teaches another in marriages.

But when folks have difficulty talking, passion is not a factor.

Partnership must be deeply involved in passion and not just having a living mate.

Conversation is a must, rather than being scared to speak to your marriage partner about improving your marriage.

Some people live in a marriage but don't speak when something is on their mind. So, they box themselves in, unwilling to make it right with their partner.

Nor use reasoning when things get out of hand.

Quiet thoughts are most devastating when reasoning has been set aside.

Nothing gets resolved.

Some people run to the Bible for answers, but even Jesus used parables.

Some church people will always use Bible history or autobiographies from the Bible to temporarily fix their problems.

Know how to get professional help.

Compliment your spouse daily.

Buy them their favorite drink, Starbucks, or tea.

Or simply make some coffee and eat apple pie.

Reach for their hand when watching TV.

Talk about the little things.

Don't keep secrets.

Initiate sex.

Apologize when you're wrong. Take a walk hand in hand. Go to bed together.

Start committing to the "sixty-second blessing."

Send flirty texts and emails throughout the day.

Read a marriage book together.

Appreciate all that your spouse does.

Give more and expect less.

Simplify your life so you have more time for connection.

Schedule date nights regularly.

Ask for what you want and need; your spouse isn't mind reader.

Stay healthy and try to look your best.

Best college education I ever had.

Learn to start over and trust again.

Take your concerns to your mate instead elsewhere.

Work out your own soul salvation together with God.

Otherwise, you make everyone part of your life, which usually ends up in a hot mess, and it's your choice in making.

Careful your work.

The Word of God must be honored, no matter what is seen on television or heard on radio or parades from the streets, of even laws given by the government. God's Word shall not return to him as having no meaning (Hebrews 4:12–13).

> So shall my word be that goeth forth out
> of my mouth: it shall not return unto me void,
> but it shall accomplish that which I please, and

it shall prosper in the thing whereto I sent it.
(Isaiah 55:11)

Listen.

There is no such thing as two husbands or two wives in a homosexual relationship.

Can two devils be married? Yes.

A gay man married to another man calls his mate husband, then who is he?

And a gay woman married to another woman calls her mate a wife, then who is she?

You see how a worldly order differs from God's order.

> And said, for this cause, shall a man leave
> father and mother, and shall cleave to his wife:
> and they twain shall be one flesh? (Matthew 19:5)

> Wherefore they are no more twain, but one
> flesh. What therefore God hath joined together,
> let not man put asunder. (v. 6)

There cannot be two of the same sex in a marriage according to God's standards.

One man and one woman, his wife and her one husband.

That's it.

> For your Maker is your husband, the Lord
> of hosts is his name; and the Holy One of Israel
> is your Redeemer, the God of the whole earth he
> is called. (Isaiah 54:5)

If any man forfeits his claim on the Word of God to live in sin, that person has chosen God not to be his father.

See how great a forest a little fire kindles, and the tongue is a fire, a world of iniquity (James 3:5).

Have you ever heard as a child that someone called or said that you are stupid, ugly, ignorant, or crazy? Or perhaps even as an adult?

Suppose you have a friend, and a friend of a friend speaks ill of you. News has its way of getting around. Well, if you grow out of it, a good thing.

Death and life are in the power of the tongue.

Proverbs 18:21 puts it this way: "The tongue has the power of life and death."

The stakes are high. Your words can either speak life or your words can speak death.

Our tongues can build others up, or they can tear them down.

I am talking about bad gossip—things people don't like about you or jealous of somehow.

Truth is truth, but not to damage one's reputation. Perhaps the person you might be talking about damaged their own reputation, and you are adding more to it. Law- and policy-making has a different opinion if it affects our outcome.

It was a boy that had a bag of feathers, and he took them out of the bag and dumped them on the street.

When his mother found out about it, she said, "Go gather up those feathers and put them back in the bag." (You know better.) The boy tried, but he couldn't; and so is our gossiping of people. You can't gather all those feathers or take all that stuff back that was dumped on the streets. Because they blow all over the place.

Words have a way of making false claims.

Every family has strong leaders, and families grow much stronger in most cases.

Not a lot of empty talk with strong families.

Why, loose lips sink ships.

Strong men build a house. "The Wise and Foolish Builders" (Matthew 7:24–27).

God created one man and one woman. How did the Bible approve or allow polygamy (Genesis 4:19) before it came to terms of one wife only?

Because man had several wives at one time, will they be punished for polygamy?

Against Original Purpose

Though practiced, polygamy has always been against the original purpose of marriage that God ordained in the Garden of Eden. God specifically told the kings of Israel that they were not to multiply wives:

Neither shall he multiply wives for himself, lest his heart turn away Deuteronomy 17:17.

How could Adam and Eve go from God's presence if God is everywhere (Genesis 3:8)?

Proverbs 15:3 declares that "the eyes of the LORD are everywhere, keeping watch on the wicked and the good."

"The eyes of the Lord," could it mean his angels or himself?

It's a symbolic gesture the garden represents heaven, God's ultimate presence. When they disobeyed God, he put them out of the garden the way he put Lucifer out of heaven. To sin against God puts one out of his presence (Isaiah 59:2). Yes, God is everywhere, yet his presence is not among sinners.

It sounds good, but its purpose, like validity, does not support its conclusion.

What was the earth for?

Because of sin. Consider Jesus on the cross when he took upon himself the sins of the world. What did he cry out to God? (Mathew 27:46.) God can have nothing to do with sin. When we sin, we cut ourselves off from God.

He won't even listen to our prayers until we repent (John 9:31, Isaiah 59:2).

How can two people who see the same things come up with different results? And then one will lie over it.

But even the archangel Michael, when he was disputing with the devil about the body of Moses, did not himself dare to condemn him for slander but said, "The Lord rebuke you!" (Jude 1:9)

Believe and let God work in your life.
Give yourself over to God today.

> For he remembered that they were but flesh;
> a wind that passeth away, and cometh not again.
> (Psalm 78:39)

Then give ear to his word, submit to his commands—although you have a choice, but if I were you, I call attention to his word (John 12:48).

> Nevertheless, they did flatter him with their mouth, and they lied unto him with their tongues. (Question: but how often have you lied to God and to yourself?)
> For their heart was not right with him, neither were they steadfast in his covenant. (Psalm 78:36–39)

How many times have you made promises to God and did not follow through?

> But he, being full of compassion, forgave their iniquity, and destroyed them not: yea, many a time turned he his anger away, and did not stir up all his wrath. (Psalm 78:38)

> For Christ also suffered once for sins, the righteous for the unrighteous, to bring you to God. He was put to death in the body but made alive in the Spirit. (1 Peter 3:18)

Military/Soldiers

U pon entering military duties, when you first enlist, the recruiter is welcoming you in. All smiles and handshakes, you get sworn in.

Now.

In Navy boot camp, they yell at you and make you perfectly fit and then give you school, but in regular service after boot camp, no yelling; you are trained as a professional worker in your field of expertise.

In the church, you get trained in the Word of God—no yelling, screaming, just inviting you to think and develop your self—fitted for service of God (Romans 12:1–2).

But in the world, things are entirely different; at times you are yelling and screaming and acting foolish—all because one is not trained in the Word of God.

Never stops (i.e., gossiping, backbiting, outbursts of anger) in every profession.

Today we should not have such acts of disobedience in the house of God (1 Peter 4:17).

If one hears the Word (Ephesians 4:31–32), he is a fitted vessel (2 Timothy 2:20–21).

We know and read that.

> For everything in the world—the lust of the flesh, the lust of the eyes, and the pride of life—comes not from the Father but from the world. (1 John 2:16)

> We understand that all Scripture is God-breathed and is useful for instruction, for convic-

tion, for correction, and for training in righteousness, so that the man of God may be complete, fully equipped for every good work. (2 Timothy 3:16–17)

The Bible says, "Everyone who serves is a soldier."

A student in the Church of Christ keeps himself from becoming entangled in the world's business so that he may satisfy the officer (Jesus, the captain of our salvation) who enlisted him (2 Timothy 2:4).

For it became him, for whom are all things, and by whom are all things, in bringing many sons unto glory, to make the captain of their salvation perfect through sufferings. (Hebrews 2:10)

Equip you with everything good to do his will, working in us what is pleasing in his sight, through Jesus Christ, to whom be glory forever and ever. Amen. (Hebrews 13:21)

When you have the skills and confidence to take action against the biggest problems that stop your church group from becoming dead works, it makes outsiders apart from your group eager to be a part of your plan.

Now you got their attention.

The Bible is your teacher.

Question: You want to teach? (Luke 6:40).

Here's the idea.

Lectures should go from being like the family singing around the piano to high-quality concerts.

Get in tune with the whole thing (Ephesians 4:16).

Who will follow Jesus, who will stand for him?

As we look ahead into the next century, leaders will be those who empower others.

Don't break a leg trying to impress others, do for Jesus.

Let your light shine before all men.

In the next life, your enemy will find out who's in change.

Your enemies will take a seat in high places in this world, having no idea that God will not be pleased with such performances.

If a man is an enemy to other pride performers, then pray for them; love your enemies as God says to (Matthew 5:44, Proverbs 25:22).

For your enemies are not mine, but yours.

I will pray for them as well and do good as God has said.

> Therefore, as we have opportunity, let us do
> good to all people, especially to those who belong
> to the family of believers. (Galatians 6:10)

And because your enemies are not to be trusted, never underestimate your own will to protect and defend your own rights.

The idea here is to not be like them, but better, as God intended you to become—humble but stronger than your adversary, your enemy. (As someone has said, "In other words, don't let my shoe size fool you.")

Minister

In Christianity, a minister is a person authorized by a church to perform, and ordained by God to preach unto his word and too organization, to perform administration functions, to wit, teaching; setting things in order, and leading services that may include weddings, baptisms, funerals; or otherwise providing spiritual guidance to its community.

Sometimes other religions bodies don't get involved with wedding or funeral services in the building because they have personal reasons only and treat their building or property as if sacred.

The term *minister* is taken from the Bible, meaning "servant."

Latin also introduces it as "servant," "attendant."

Read 1 Corinthians 4:1–3 and 2 Corinthians 4:1–2.

A preacher must have more than Bible college; and when it comes to gender, they (he or she) must specialize in certain acts within the body of Christ. For example, experts within their field, except for preaching, whereas the Bible does not allow women to perform.

Anything else may be permitted, in a quiet manner.

Where there are but little or no higher education experiences, one is taught within the counsel of that body, by preachers/ teachers, including elders and deacons to do things in a biblical way.

Members can play a much larger role in this administration of God.

Remember a woman is not reduced to be a Christian only or pew sitter, she can be involved in the administration of its work.

One is preparation.

Two, secretarial duties.

Three, classes where children are taught.

Four, by showing a good example to younger women.

Although some will see these things as small efforts, they are not larger than we think.

Making the body work as it was intended.

> From whom the whole body fitly joined together and compacted by that which every joint supplieth, according to the effectual working in the measure of every part, maketh increase of the body unto the edifying of itself in love. (Ephesians 4:16)

God loves women, but because women in biblical times were not allowed to do things, it does not necessarily mean they were exempt from God or divorced from God; they had a part, but not to preach nor in the services authorized from God, because of 1 Corinthians 14:34, where it says (plural) *women* and (singular) where it says *a woman.*

Tough saying, but from the authority of God (2 Timothy 3:16).

No man has any rule over the authority of God nor can place himself above what is written (1 Corinthians 4:6).

Notice.

There are some failures; that is, people who do exasperate by themselves and whole, not the Word of God as written.

So, they allow where God has not allowed.

Most call themselves apart from God, denominational groups who form opinions away from the authority of God.

Folks who do that think what they are doing is right.

They will say, "Lord, we tried to do what was right."

> On judgment day many will say to me, "Lord! Lord! We prophesied in your name and

cast out demons in your name and performed many miracles in your name." (Matthew 7:22)

Important here is verse 23: "But I will reply, 'I don't know you. Get away from me, you who break God's laws.'"

Remember our Creator can reject or rejoice in your performance of his will (John 12:48).

Where do you stand?

Ministry

M inistry is our work (2 Corinthians 6:1–10).

God has always wanted us to be like him (Genesis 1:26); since Genesis, mankind still can, by conforming to his Son.

Read Philippians 2:5–11 and Romans 8:30. In that, mankind fails. God (John 1:1ff) still found a way to make it possible for his people to be called by his word (Romans 10:17) and name.

"That in the dispensation of the fullness of the times" (Ephesians 1:10) gives reference to God's rules in his house, meaning his economy, that administration (Matthew 16:18ff), his arrangements for all to fulfill his plan of salvation.

So where is it we go to meet God's need?

His Word.

The church (Romans 10:14)! What is going on in the church? God's Word is being studied. It is a place where all come to an understanding (2 Timothy 2:15). The Bible says, "A wise man will hear and increase learning, and a man of understanding will attain wise counsel" (Proverbs 1:5).

Let's all get back to building our own families, in that we spent countless hours all over the place. This is not to be thought of as selfish intent, but at times, we neglect our own because of busy schedules.

We then will find that our loved ones are dearly missed or have passed on.

What matters here is vacancy, drifting apart. At times, it leads to separation; however, an agenda is needed that will strengthen or align ourselves with what really matters again, and that in times past, it might have been viewed as an unbalanced wheel, which might even concerns others.

Many times, persons will distance themselves from others, for some unknown reasons, but family must be connected; wherefore, it may be true, leaving things undone can cause damages to our future by not keeping in touch.

Then again if your family doesn't connect with you because of religious matters, do not worry about it.

Pray about their recovery.

It may be that some could assume, that one or two members should or consider carrying the load.

This is unthought-of; discussions must be considered when all else fails.

And just leaving this alone will omit parts that really matter to all family.

Here's what is needed: calling, visiting, connecting, and planning events, just to know who's who and what others may be doing and why these days, having fun times again.

Praying and singing in the Lord help members to grow in the Word.

This is a concern to every family, my sincere request!

We all want to talk about new additions; that is, cousins 1, 2, 3 keep in touch and that no one can be left out. It will take all parts to help.

Just a thought!

Have you met a few family members who can't accept you from your adulthood till now?

Here's why: change is not in their agenda.

Pray for them, perhaps let them be. Only God can reduce their minds to serve him. Not you. Just be kind, tenderhearted.

But change is necessary for growth in the Word.

Everyone in a church has the right to speech in asking questions without interruption from others, who may feel some questions are less important; and at times, someone in a class could always grasp the center of attention and pontificate on politics rather than the discussion at hand.

Now, discouragement or arguments would be the first thing some may employ, but to handle this with responsibility should come by the order of its teacher, or it comes to order by appointed leaders and not from an opportunistic party.

The class should at no time appoint a time to excommunicate that person by two important reasons:

1. Those persons are members or visitors.
2. They give, they sing, they serve.

Learning together is the most important gain to any spiritual growth.

It helps when many practice their interdependent skills as well as independency in sharing information studied; thereby others grow (Ephesians 3:1–21). Amen!

Questions not part of the original discussion can be answered or discussed in private (Acts 18:26). Always putting a little ointment on it, fixing to perfect.

Faith is the issue here.

Remember, faith without works is dead.

It takes hard work at times to convince understanding.

If you get frustrated, how can you persuade mankind of the work of God?

The vineyard of the Lord.

Sometimes some are willing to discuss within the realm of their own groups, dialogues, and things to which are narrated concerning the Bible, leaving the idea of evangelism out, and unwilling to prepare to work in neighborhoods, so then some may be willing to stay within their circle of influences. This is not the way the teaching of Jesus is set up (Mark 16:15–16).

We have experiences—it's the best teacher, and not by our same old, same old routines.

What has happened to leading by example? Even the NAACP says, "Each one teaches one." What are some expected to accomplish by following routines of the same? The Bible says, "What profits a man who says, I have Faith but have not Works, can Faith save him" (James 2:14ff).

Some may say, "Well, I have a full schedule," and usually that is required of many; whereas, others may have none, it's not too late to add one more to the schedule.

A soldier in battle for truth fights the good fight of faith (1 Timothy 6:12), or even athletes compete to win in a race (2 Timothy 2:3ff). We are all in this race to win, so then let no one discourage you or stand in your way. You have a robe, mansion, and crown!

Now.

Changing it up is a plus—empty seats or not filled from daily norms in your life. What can you do tomorrow that hasn't been done today? MUCH! As the ole song sung in some Churches of Christ, "There is much to do, there's work on every hand." Here am I, send me.

Thanking Jesus for all the work done on our behalf and for those in the vineyard today (1 Peter 2:21).

Amen!

Take the ethical approach to life.

Listen to Jesus.

When a preacher leaves a pulpit and another is hired, they don't attack each other.

Serve a time in your ministry.

Leadership is an ongoing challenge.

It works best for some, until the mind has no additional growth (i.e., when you can't implement or delegate knowledge); well, no need to challenge, just?

There are but a few men and their mates who can best serve in growth.

But the called out must trust and be given a chance to prove that growth will succeed.

Church growth is never compromise.

It is seen in its original attributes or its original form.

Respectable people when running for office don't attack people that are in office.

Keep it civil, best to work.

Just present your best efforts to lead.

And pick yourself a best team in leading.

What can wash away my sins? Nothing but the blood of Jesus.

What can make me whole again? Nothing but the blood of Jesus.

What precious blood.

Every saved person has a position in the church of God as he so appoints (Ephesians 4:11–16).

For the perfecting of the saints, for the work of the ministry, for the edifying of the body of Christ (v. 12).

In the book of Numbers, men were given certain things to do in the tabernacle of the congregation or tent of meeting.

The Levites were instructed to the duties in the tabernacle of God.

Now we are not to compete with God over who does what in the church.

In Numbers 2, it teaches us many things we can learn from God.

Solomon is fulfilling the dream of his father, David, in building the house.

Now everyone is not chosen from God to build a house.

You cannot mock others by building a house of God based upon what you see.

One might be a watcher but not a unique builder.

Here's a unique builder.

Bezalel, the artisan and architect who oversaw the building of the tabernacle.

> See, I have called by name Bezalel the son of Uri, the son of Hur, of the tribe of Judah.
>
> Our portion describes Bezalel as filled with divine spirit (ruach elohim), and endowed with wisdom (chochmah), discernment or technical know-how (tevunah) and with knowledge of every kind of work (uVda'at u'vchol melachah).
>
> The products that Bezalel makes further highlights his special characteristics. (Exodus 31:2ff)

In Exodus 31:1–6 and chapters 36 to 39, Bezalel, Bezaleel, or Betzalel (Hebrew: _____), was the chief artisan of the Tabernacle and was in charge of building the Ark of the Covenant, assisted by Aholiab.

In the Hebrew Bible, Oholiab (Hebrew: _____, "father's tent"), son of Ahisamakh, of the tribe of Dan, worked under Bezalel as the deputy architect of the Tabernacle and the implements which it housed, including the Ark of the Covenant.

We understand that Jeremiah was called while in the womb (chapter 1).

Before I formed you in the womb, I knew you, before you were born, I set you apart; I appointed you as a prophet to the nations.

See, today I appoint you over nations and kingdoms to uproot and tear down, to destroy and overthrow, to build and to plant.

Jeremiah was chosen and not appointed by men.

God has to choose one to become a leader for him.

You have to believe that you cannot place men where God has not approved.

Natural talents come from being anointed into that position, for the purpose of God's will.

God was telling Israel how to set up their camp (Numbers 2).

The Levites will encamp all around the tabernacle to do the service in the tabernacle.

Not any other tribes.

The eleven would tithe to the one tribe.

God gave the order.

Listen.

When we sing songs today, every person has a unique personality in singing their note as they're supposed to sing it, by making the whole song sound beautiful.

But when folks are singing up and down, going all over the place, songs don't sound as beautiful as it should because others don't sing their notes as they should.

God gave certain voices for his services.

Stay in your lane.

Getting out of your lane makes the whole song sound like a myth.

Notice.

> If the whole body were an eye, where would
> the sense of hearing be?
> If the whole body were an ear, where would
> the sense of smell be? (1 Corinthians 12:17)

Man cannot be everything that God did not give a talent to.

It doesn't matter how large or small the church is, God has appointed someone to have their place (Romans 11:4).

Jobs are easy commandments for you.

Do it and live.

My friends, our elders are the best people I've ever met in this area.

Perhaps you have great bishops yourselves.

Leaving from military experience to regular life with regular people, transition takes time.

So, all ye, help and understand for all things that matter to reestablish a military person's mind.

Go slow.

For some, it could be very difficult to explain why a military man's mind is not going the way you should think.

Just go slow and lead to transitional change.

Church is the best place for any transitional change.

Be active in the Lord's church.

When an order is given from God, get it done.

Oftentimes mankind will back up rather than go forward with the Lord's work.

Think about it.

Jesus came, fulfilled his mission, went back to heaven, and watched who had listened in order to save his own soul from spiritual death.

I get it and hope you will continue to see how important your life on earth is by doing the will of him who made you (Revelation 4:11).

You can have the best job, you can have the best talent, and you can even be a good person; but if you don't do the Lord's work, you will not accomplish his purpose by which you were made to do.

That is to serve God.

Now that's not too much to ask for, because God allows you to live your lives and have the right kind of fun doing it.

Remember that obedience to God will get you to heaven (2 Peter 2:20).

Mission Work

Fewer churches are in mission today.

The Churches of Christ must salute each other by reason of being connected to growing population.

When you have a church in long-standing progress of mission work, whether oversees or local, why not be connected to that source of responsibility ongoing?

Giving and receiving benefits from sources puts you in fellowship with the mainstream of things.

We all need to be connected to mission responsibility. Give to those who are in present active mission today.

One of the most ridiculous songs I ever heard, yet popular:

> You ain't nothing but a hound dog
> Been snoopin' round my door
> You can wag your tail
> But I ain't gonna feed you no more.

Do you know what this means?
It is saying, "You are no good for me to give my attention to."
Ungodly.

Mothers

Love your mama, you only have one.

She is God's special revelation to you.

Oh, how that women who love their families should be appreciated.

Start shopping now, fellows.

Name

Shipe is a name that was formed by the Anglo-Saxon society of old Britain.

The name was thought to have been used for someone who once worked as a person who worked as a shepherd, the guardian of the sheep.

Shipes
A family name

Known in the southeast USA as a very influential family with strong ties to the community.

Influential; some of which shall be political; very giving to the community.

What Does Name "Shipe" Mean

We are spiritually intense and can sting or charm.

Our name brings love and new starts into life and attracts money, in business, we are the creator and promoter of original ideas and usually enjoy considerable financial success.

We are intuitive and might be interested in the arts, drama or science.

Creative and outgoing, we are always looking for an opportunity to show your abilities, especially before audience.

We are very flexible and likes to feel appreciated.

Make it godly right.

Look now, for all ye women who have multi-last names, to whom are you married to?

If you are married to Christ, to whom do ye belong to?

Listen.

The New Testament calls Christ the bridegroom and the church his bride. To understand what this means can change your life.

For we don't take upon worldly attributes while having the mind of Christ.

> For your Maker is your husband. (Isaiah 54:5)

And if your husband is the head of his house, why are you using your father's last name and his too?

That's two heads. So, then who are you married to?

> For I feel a divine jealousy for you, since I betrothed you to one husband, to present you as a pure virgin to Christ. (2 Corinthians 11:2)

Some say, "Well, I want to keep my father's name so folks can find me on FB or by other means."

Don't kid yourself; when you marry, you change houses, which includes your last name.

Anything else you come up with is nonsense. When you marry, no children are attached to multiple last names.

Who will know who you are, except identified as a nutcase?

You leave and cleave to your husband.

Husbands are glued together with their wife. Likewise, for all who are in Christ.

One Lord, one faith, Christian.

Some folks still are using their father's and mother's last names and are married and have moved away to establish a home with their spouse; the woman is using two last names from back home.

Do you know your station in life?

Did anyone tell you your new name?

If so, why are you married to your father's last name?

Did your mother school you in marriage?

And if you think otherwise, a liberal or covenant breaker.

One name equals one song.

One Lord, one faith equals NT practices.

> You shall be a crown of beauty in the hand of the Lord, and a royal diadem in the hand of your God.
>
> You shall no more be termed Forsaken, and your land shall no more be termed Desolate, but you shall be called My Delight Is in Her, and your land Married; for the Lord delights in you, and your land shall be married.
>
> For as a young man marries a young woman, so shall your sons marry you, and as the bridegroom rejoices over the bride, so shall your God rejoice over you. (Isaiah 62:3–5 ESV)

New Creation

The Lord said, "Come to me, all you who are weary and burdened, and I will give you rest" (Matthew 11:28).

> Therefore, if anyone is in Christ, he is a new
> creation. The old has passed away. Behold, the
> new has come! (2 Corinthians 5:17)

This new creation comes by obedience to the gospel (Romans 10:17).

Hearing then leads you to act (Mark 16:15–16).

Your actions are rejoiced from heaven.

> Just so, I tell you, there is joy before the
> angels of God over one sinner who repents.
> (Luke 15:10)

This means, "For all of you who were baptized into Christ have clothed yourselves with Christ" (Galatians 3:27).

Don't put off any longer, arise and be baptized, wash away your sins (Acts 22:16).

Oaths

Y ou shall not misuse the name of the Lord your God, for the Lord will not hold anyone guiltless who misuses his name. (Exodus 20:7)

You must not swear falsely by My name and so profane the name of your God. I am the LORD. (Leviticus 19:12)

You shall not take the name of the LORD your God in vain, for the LORD will not leave anyone unpunished who takes His name in vain. (Deuteronomy 5:11)

Fear the LORD your God, serve Him, and take your oaths using only His name. (Deuteronomy 6:13)

You are to fear the LORD your God and serve Him. Hold fast to Him and take your oaths in His name. (Deuteronomy 10:20)

Obedience

Jeroboam made for himself priests and prophets (1 Kings 13:11–25). Who were not of God?

When you tell a lie, that means you have to tell another one to cover up the first one that you just told. Never stops, does it?

Change is necessary for obedience.

The Bible is right; judgment is pronounced upon all unrighteous (Hebrews 9:27).

> And all liars, shall have their part in the lake
> which burneth with fire and brimstone: which is
> the second death. (Revelation 21:8b)

Never extend your hands to an unethical person in conversation. Anyone who acts foolishly is not a Christian.

> I will greatly rejoice in the Lord; my soul
> shall exult in my God, for he has clothed me with
> the garments of salvation; he has covered me with
> the robe of righteousness, as a bridegroom decks
> himself like a priest with a beautiful headdress,
> and as a bride adorns herself with her jewels.
> (Isaiah 61:10)

> I put on righteousness, and it clothed me;
> my justice was like a robe and a turban. (Job
> 29:14)

> If one blesses his neighbor with a loud voice early in the morning, it will be counted to him as a curse. (Proverbs 27:14)

> Do not drag me away with the wicked, with those who do evil, who speak cordially with their neighbors but harbor malice in their hearts. (Psalm 28:3)

All that God has given us today is in written form (2 Peter 1:3).
In these words, read what was written (2 Timothy 3:16).
Become a doer of his Word.
James 1:22 says, "But don't just listen to God's word. You must do what it says. Otherwise, you are only fooling yourselves."
Why was Adam and Eve banished from the garden?
Here's why!

> And the LORD God said, "The man has now become like one of us, knowing good and evil.
> He must not be allowed to reach out his hand and take also from the tree of life and eat and live forever."
> So, the LORD God banished him from the Garden of Eden to work the ground from which he had been taken.
> After he drove the man out, he placed on the east side of the Garden of Eden cherubim and a flaming sword flashing back and forth to guard the way to the tree of life. (Genesis 3:21–24)

So, we have two trees: the tree of life and the tree of knowledge. Adam and Eve ate from the tree of knowledge and not the tree of life.
They disobeyed God, who created them, and he removed them from their choice again to eat from Eden.
God expects obedience today.

You cannot go on disobeying God and he does not know about it.

Don't drive yourself away from your new life in Jesus (2 Corinthians 5:17).

Be obedient to God right now, today.

In another place, God has said,

> "At just the right time, I heard you.
> On the day of salvation,
> I helped you."
> Indeed, the "right time" is now.
> Today is the day of salvation. (2 Corinthians 6:2)

Obey God

Do exactly what God says to do (Romans 15:4).

Do you remember Uzzah?

Well, Uzzah didn't do what God told him to do.

Let's look.

First of all, the ark of the covenant was supposed to be carried by Levites and not on a new cart.

"A new cart" (2 Samuel 6:3).

As the ark was being transported, the oxen pulling the cart stumbled, and a man named Uzzah took hold of the ark. God's anger burned against Uzzah, and he struck him down, and he died (Numbers 4:15).

> Then Moses wrote this law and gave it to the priests, the sons of Levi, who carried the ark of the covenant of the LORD, and to all the elders of Israel. (Deuteronomy 31:9)

> And the Levites carried the ark of God with the poles on their shoulders, as Moses had commanded in accordance with the word of the LORD. (1 Chronicles 15:15)

> Insert the poles into the rings on the sides of the ark, in order to carry it. (Exodus 25:14)

But they didn't.

> And the anger of the LORD burned against
> Uzzah, and He struck him down because he had
> put his hand on the ark. So, he died there before
> God. (1 Chronicles 13:10)

God said "carry"; he did not say "build a cart."
You have to do exactly what God says, and Uzzah did not.

> When they came to the threshing floor
> of Nakon, Uzzah reached out and took hold
> of the ark of God, because the oxen stumbled.
> The Lord's anger burned against Uzzah because
> of his irreverent act; therefore, God struck him
> down, and he died there beside the ark of God.
> (2 Samuel 6:6–7)

Then David was angry because the Lord's wrath had broken out against Uzzah, and to this day, that place is called Perez Uzzah.
Consider your loved ones today.
If they don't do as God tells them in the Word, how can you get mad at God for punishing them who violate his commands?
You can't.
God is the Creator, and we are the created.

> If they have escaped the corruption of the
> world by knowing our Lord and Savior Jesus
> Christ and are again entangled in it and are over-
> come, they are worse off at the end than they
> were at the beginning. (2 Peter 2:20)

> There is a judge for the one who rejects Me
> and does not receive My words: The word that I
> have spoken will judge him on the last day.

> I have not spoken on My own, but the Father who sent Me has commanded Me what to say and how to say it.
>
> And I know that His command leads to eternal life.
>
> So, I speak exactly what the Father has told Me to say. (John 12:48–50)

Pray for your ruler (Psalm 72).
Good morning, saints, beloved of God.
Have a wonderful day.

> This is the day the Lord has made; Let us rejoice and be glad in it. (Psalm 118:24)

We will rejoice and serve Jesus.

Get your evangelism on by writing comments about Jesus on FB.

Use your time wisely.

Paul cautioned the saints, "Be very careful, then, how you live—not as unwise but as wise, making the most of every opportunity, because the days are evil" (Ephesians 5:15–16).

Time management is important because of the brevity of our lives. Our earthly sojourn is significantly shorter than we are inclined to think.

David said, "You have made my days a mere handbreadth; the span of my years is as nothing before you. Each man's life is but a breath" (Psalm 39:4–5).

Even for a little while.

Make the most of your day's importance by saving lives for Jesus, even your own.

Amen.

> Who is among you that feareth the Lord, that obeyeth the voice of His servant, that walketh in darkness, and hath no light? Let him

trust in the name of the Lord and stay upon his God. (Isaiah 50:10)

Book for today: Jude 1–25. A short book.

One Body

For as we have many members in one
body, and all members have not the same office.
(Romans 12:4)

What does it mean?
Stay in your own lane.
It is God's will that men have special gifts. Not for any to decide.

The body is a unit, though it is comprised
of many parts. And although its parts are many,
they all form one body. So, it is with Christ. (1
Corinthians 12:12)

Get it! Amen.
Leave the body to God (Luke 4:16–30).

And he gave some, apostles; and some,
prophets; and some, evangelists; and some, pastors and teachers;
For the perfecting of the saints, for the work
of the ministry, for the edifying of the body of
Christ:
Till we all come in the unity of the faith,
and of the knowledge of the Son of God, unto a
perfect man, unto the measure of the stature of
the fulness of Christ:
That we henceforth be no more children,
tossed to and fro, and carried about with every

wind of doctrine, by the sleight of men, and cunning craftiness, whereby they lie in wait to deceive;

But speaking the truth in love, may grow up into him in all things, which is the head, even Christ:

From whom the whole body fitly joined together and compacted by that which every joint supplied, according to the effectual working in the measure of every part, maketh increase of the body unto the edifying of itself in love. (Ephesians 4:11–16 KJV)

When we serve God, give it your all, or stay out of it.

Nothing is worse than a subtle pretense, meaning the practices of claiming to have moral standards or beliefs to which one's own behavior does not conform (Matthew 15:14, 2 Peter 2:12).

One God

If the Bible says there is one name above all names, and one faith and one baptism, one God, then why are there so many faiths today (Ephesians 4:1ff)?

It certainly wasn't that many in the first century.

Why now?

> Very truly I tell you Pharisees, anyone who does not enter the sheep pen by the gate, but climbs in by some other way, is a thief and a robber. (John 10:1)

Pentecost is not a name of any church, neither is it a name of any person; it is a day.

> When the "day" of Pentecost came, they were all together in one place. (Acts 2:1)

Pentecost means "fiftieth day" or Feast of Weeks. *Shavuot*, a Hebrew word, means a Jewish holiday.

Folks should stop telling others about a Pentecostal church that is not named in your Bible.

The only church that is named in your Bible is the Church of God or Christ, that which Christ is God; it is the only name, none other (John 1:1, Romans 16:16, Acts 4:12).

Shavuot in Hebrew is known as the Feast of Weeks in English and as Pentecost in Ancient Greek; it is a Jewish holiday that occurs on the sixth day of the Hebrew month of Sivan, meaning it may fall May 15–June 14.

> Yahweh, the God of the Israelites, whose name was revealed to Moses as four Hebrew consonants (YHWH) called the tetragrammaton...
>
> Although Christian scholars after the Renaissance and Reformation periods used the term Jehovah for YHWH, in the 19th and 20th centuries biblical scholars again began to use the form Yahweh.

I strongly suggest that God's name be spoken as wonderful to be said loosely.

The name *Yeshua* appears to have been in use in Judea at the time of the birth of Jesus.

How strong are you in the Lord? Have you ever asked yourself this question (2 Corinthians 13:5)?

One People

Did you know that racism will get you hell? That's right, skin that God has given as covering to mankind has been frowned on by some ignorance of mankind.

Ole sinner, why go against the covering of God? Foolishness needs to be dropped.

Listen to your Bible.

> And hath made of one blood all nations of men for to dwell on all the face of the earth, and hath determined the times before appointed, and the bounds of their habitation. (Acts 17:26)

Something else. Just as an atheist who says there is no God. Therefore, actions preclude their beliefs against God.

How can you practice evangelism the right way while living with a cold heart?

> The fool hath said in his heart, there is no God. They are corrupt, they have done abominable works, there is none that doeth good. The Lord looked down from heaven upon the children of men, to see if there were any that did understand, and seek God.
>
> They are all gone aside, they are all together become filthy: there is none that doeth good, no, not one.

> Have all the workers of iniquity no knowl-
> edge? Who eat up my people as they eat bread,
> and call not upon the Lord?
>
> There were they in great fear: for God is in
> the generation of the righteous. (Psalm 14:1–5)

Listen, Jesus welcomes all people, never discriminates against any people.

> Jesus wants all people to be saved and to
> come to a knowledge of the truth. (1 Timothy
> 2:4)

When Apostle Peter wrote these words, just who do you think he was referring to?

You atheist, or you who practice racism? May it never be.

> What shall we say then? Shall we continue
> in sin, that grace may abound?
>
> God forbid. How shall we, that are dead to
> sin, live any longer therein?
>
> Know ye not, that so many of us as were
> baptized into Jesus Christ were baptized into his
> death?
>
> Therefore, we are buried with him by bap-
> tism into death: that like as Christ was raised up
> from the dead by the glory of the Father, even so
> we also should walk in newness of life.
>
> For if we have been planted together in the
> likeness of his death, we shall be also in the like-
> ness of his resurrection:
>
> Knowing this, that our old man is cru-
> cified with him, that the body of sin might be
> destroyed, that henceforth we should not serve
> sin. (Romans 6:1–6)

But you are a chosen people, a royal priesthood, a holy nation, God's special possession, that you may declare the praises of him who called you out of darkness into his wonderful light. (1 Peter 2:9)

Listen, change is necessary for salvation to begin. Reconstruct your life and your face and your actions before God.

Overthrow Sin

> Now Joshua was dressed in filthy garments as he stood before the Angel. (Zechariah 3:3)

Sins removed by a command.

> If it is burned up, he will suffer loss. He himself will be saved, but only as if through the flames. (1 Corinthians 3:15)

> "Some of you I overthrew as I overthrew Sodom and Gomorrah, and you were like a firebrand snatched from a blaze, yet you did not return to Me," declares the LORD. (Amos 4:11)

Be proactive every day in the work of the Lord.

Every day, there is a person that needs to be reborn or delivered. Amen.

Parables

Y ou should worry about it; Jesus said these words in a parable. A parable is an earthly story with a heavenly meaning. Watch.

> The owner's servants came to him and said, Sir, didn't you sow good seed in your field? Where then did the weeds come from? An enemy did this he replied. So, the servants asked him, do you want us to go and pull them up? No, he said, if you pull the weeds now, you might uproot the wheat with them. Let both grow together until the harvest. At that time, I will tell the harvesters: First collect the weeds and tie them in bundles to be burned; then gather the wheat and bring it into my barn. (Matthew 13:27–30)

> He did this to present her to himself as a glorious church without a spot or wrinkle or any other blemish. Instead, she will be holy and without fault. (Ephesians 5:27)

Prepare yourselves for heaven.
Get into Christ (Galatians 2:27).

Parents

Remember two immutable things: You must honor your mother and your father (Ephesians 6:1ff).

No matter whatsoever you think.

Those two things are written for God's purposes and not for any to decide otherwise.

> Remember your Creator in the days of your youth, before the days of trouble come and the years approach when you will say, "I find no pleasure in them." (Ecclesiastes 12:1)

Whether Christian or not, these words shall remain forever.

> Heaven and earth will pass away, but my words will never pass away. (Matthew 24:35)

When one becomes a deciding factor against God's Word, such a person has placed self in the Creator's chair; thus, these are mandated actions against the Word of God.

Consider this: why follow after hate and the inventor of hate?

We who are truthful expose wrongdoings.

Everything will be brought to light.

Things in the dark are exposed.

Patience

For ye have need of patience, that, after ye have done the will of God, ye might receive the promise. For yet a little while, and he that shall come will come, and will not tarry. Now the just shall live by faith: but if any man draw back, my soul shall have no pleasure in him. But we are not of them who draw back unto perdition; but of them that believe to the saving of the soul. (Hebrews 10:36–39)

Seek the Lord, all you humble of the land, you who do what he commands. Seek righteousness, seek humility; perhaps you will be sheltered on the day of the Lord's anger. (Zephaniah 2:3)

Put in some time and stay in your patience.
Wait for the Lord at all times.
Amen.

Pay Attention

Nothing is too complicated with the Bible, so why do men make the Bible so complicated?

Your thoughts for just a moment. What is the difference between a predetermined act and an absolute holy feeling as it relates to your service of worship to God in a public place (church)?

Folks tend to say in unemotional groups, "One cannot show emotions while in worship to God."

Except for the satisfaction of saying *amen.*

One cannot raise hands to the heavens praises to God, nor pat their feet or give a testimony or that women can't say amen.

Tell me, where do men get this stuff from by saying you can show predetermined acts of obedience in public but not be emotional?

Nonsense, folks, get your praise on.

Allow no one to tell you otherwise; it is decent and in order to God.

But it has to be given as it is to receive.

When it hits you, say "thank you, Lord," raise hands, say amen.

But don't play loud music and flip around or whistle really loud, over-shouting, wearing larger hats than your neighbors' or even putting on too much perfume; you then become a distraction to others who are there to learn.

Pay attention to yourselves.

> Pay close attention to yourself and to your teaching; persevere in these things, for as you do this you will ensure salvation both for yourself and for those who hear you. (1 Timothy 4:16)

Remember there are some who go into confusion by overdoing it in church, and there are some who sit and do nothing besides nothing.

Under the law, Jesus could save anybody as he wishes and heal and deliver from demonic actions; could Jesus save a deathbed confession, a final departure, without baptism today?

When Jesus was baptized to fulfill all righteousness (right thing to do), and the thief—no record of one baptism, then how could the criminal be saved?

This day and always, I shall love our God, my family, and especially to those who are of the household of faith, my friends, and our neighbors.

The Lord hates everyone who is arrogant; he will never let them escape punishment.

Be loyal and faithful, and God will forgive your sin. Obey the Lord, and nothing evil will happen to you.

When you please the Lord, you can make your enemies into friends.

It is better to have a little, honestly earned, than to have a large income, dishonestly gained.

Celsus, a Greek philosopher, believes that Christians are ignorant people worthy of their God. Christians show that they want to convert only foolish, dishonorable, stupid people, and only slaves, women, and little children.

There are no escapes to this ghostly kind of images and ignorance of men today.

Some preachers, if you look closely, have a disbelief in the existence of God; therefore, they are preaching only what others want to hear.

To the extent where the sum total of those have no emotional feelings, nor will it move such a many to omit repentance.

There are those who are still living under the conditions of lies invented and invested by those who refuse to change completely for the cause of Christ.

There is a book called *The Religious Instruction of the Negroes in the United States*, written by Charles Concock Jones.

Charles Concock Jones Sr. (1804–1863) was a Presbyterian clergyman, educator, missionary, and planter of Liberty County, Georgia.

While in the North, Jones agonized over the morality of owning slaves, but he returned to Liberty County to become a planter and a missionary to slaves.

He served as pastor of the First Presbyterian Church of Savannah, Georgia 1831–32, Professor of church history and polity at Columbia Theological Seminary, Columbia, South Carolina, 1835–38, returned to missionary work in 1839, and was again Professor at Columbia Seminary 1847–50.

He spent the remainder of his life supervising his three plantations.

Besides many tracts and papers, Jones published The Religious Instruction of the Negroes in the United States (1842) and a History of the Church of God (1867).

His Catechism of Scripture Doctrine and Practice (1837) was translated into Armenian and Chinese.

Mr. Jones, the author of this volume, had for years manifested a deep interest in the religious improvement of his colored fellowmen.

He was a minister of the gospel, resident in Georgia, and connected ecclesiastically with the Presbyterian denomination.

Mr. Jones weighs well all objections to the course proposed and meets them on Scriptural grounds: so that it must be difficult for a minister of the gospel or a private Christian to read and not be reproved.

Under the head of the obligations of the church to the negroes, the author speaks out plainly and forcibly, first to the church in slaveholding states on their duties to the slaves, then to Christians in the free states on their duty to afford the gospel to free negroes within their limits.

To the former he says:

"We cannot cry out against Papists for withholding the Scriptures from the common people, if we withhold the Bible from our servants, and keep them in ignorance of its saving truths, which we certainly do whilst we will not provide ways and means of having it read and explained to them."

The way it was, it is not the way it was with Jesus.

Sad how men will go into judgment with toxic minds uncleaned from waste of within hearts.

Best believe that when a lie sells and swells among mankind, it is thus manufactured into minds of their youth.

Friends, stay safe; remember safety is important to friends and family.

God bless.

All bus drivers are trained to stay alert.

So shall all of you pay attention to everything. Stay alert.

People

Definitely secure your life with God.

Now define what you look like?

Read 1 Corinthians 13:12 and James 1:23.

Loads of values.

They are chiefly of four kinds: confidants, constituents, comrades, and commanders.

Borrowing from Jake, he explains types of people; everything defines its value.

Listen.

Confidants are people who are around you because they are into you.

They buy into you as a person and therefore are willing to be by your side whether you are up or down, in victory or defeat, right or wrong. They are however wise enough to tell you when you are wrong. (Unless you wave them out of your life, you have lost a true friendship.)

Constituents, on the other hand, are those who are around you because they are for what you are for.

They are people pursuing the same destination that you are pursuing, are going the same place you are going, and are therefore travelling the same path you are travelling.

They are only with you because you both have the same destination in mind.

Commanders, on their part, are in your life because you have a resource that can take them to where they are going.

They are not in your life because you are going where they are going but because you have a resource or skill that they consider important in helping them arrive at their destination.

Comrades, finally, are those who are around you because they are against what you are against.

They are those who are around you because you share the same enemy.

They are only with you to see the greater enemy fall.

From my desk: There are certain kinds of people that are asleep in the church.

They cannot define what religion is all about. They are just there to be present; hopefully they might see what God is all about and how he works in their lives without any kind of emotional feelings.

These Nobel laureate individuals are nothing but assumptions to themselves.

They will always speak with you, but their hearts are far from what your purpose with God is, because they really don't understand how God works.

They will never understand the real meaning of Christlikeness.

Just to be aware, they are Christians, but will still grow as long as you carry them with you.

The people that really want to grow are let down by the people who don't appreciate your purpose.

Because they don't understand how God works.

> Wherefore he saith, awake thou that sleep-
> est, and arise from the dead, and Christ shall give
> thee light. (Ephesians 5:14)

Listen, you cannot be everyday world (in the world but not of the world) without definition of your purpose.

People perhaps will bring substance of the world into their attitude and then to the church.

They have a different character apart from what they have been taught from the Holy Word.

Question: But why?

Simply because someone might be afraid to be reborn into the spirit realm of God (John 17:17).

People who are afraid of the effects of God's love are unwilling to make necessary changes in their lives. So, they think by faking it as much as they can until it is acceptable.

People should share on FB things concerning importance.

Get your evangelism in action and refrain from making excuses.

Do you have a purpose? If so, why is it taking you long to get there?

Don't dine or contaminate with the world; things begin with inventive stories against you, from people who you don't know (John 8:44).

> Unfaithful people! Don't you know that to be the world's friend means to be God's enemy? If you want to be the world's friend, you make yourself God's enemy. James 4:4

Misleading friends come with much contamination.
After a while, one can be covered with stench.
Where they cannot smell as well as others who do.

> A man that hath friends must shew himself friendly: and there is a friend that sticketh closer than a brother. (Proverbs 18:24)

> Now all has been heard; here is the conclusion of the matter: Fear God and keep his commandments, for this is the duty of all mankind.

> For God will bring every deed into judgment, including every hidden thing, whether it is good or evil. (Ecclesiastes 12:13–14)

The Plan

A purpose plan (Ephesians 3:14–21)!
Written on August 9, 2016.
Friends.

In the beginning was the Word. (John 1:1–5)

There are things we can learn from Ezra.

Ezra knew as well as many of God's followers how important God's work is, even this date; today's character building is for all mankind.

What about you? Could selective building be an issue or a lack of love and respect toward some people?

It could be a problem, of course.

Indeed!

And for lack of a better term, I believe mankind can learn responsibilities of Ezra (3:10–11).

Ezra and the congregation were serious minded.

Did you read what had happened? The foundation was laid; they all rejoiced. Wow (v. 12b)!

All is important here: No bitterness. Just. All.

Let's be clear: Those who respect leadership today follow through with leadership.

Could some leaders not be leaders but rather job seekers? Could it be that some may try a position for a while then quit (Luke 14:28)?

What about those minds that are not as sharp as some may think? It really doesn't matter what one may think about God's decision, for he is in control (Matthew 16:18).

Ask yourself these questions: are they (leaders) still there? Then let them continue to lead with the wisdom provided by or given by God (James 1:5, 16). But if not, then a social decision has been made only based upon what one may think, rather God.

Any leader should have serious concerns for the work of God's house (John 17:23). Jesus is requesting believers to be mature (Colossians 3:17).

The church is a family of believers. It doesn't belong to bishops, deacons, or preachers, but all may accomplish the purpose of God's work together (Ephesians 3:14–21). Amen!

Build some more.

The Potter's Hand

Get your head in the right direction.
Refuse listening to "tarted-up" favors.
Sneaky suspicions will not get you into heaven.
Genuine love is the key.
Acts 5 tells the fact.

> Then the word of the Lord came to me, saying: "O house of Israel, can I not do with you as this potter?" says the Lord. "Look, as the clay is in the potter's hand, so are you in My hand, O house of Israeli." (Jeremiah 18:5–6)

We are priests in the kingdom of God (Revelation 1:6–7).
Yes, I'm a priest in the kingdom of God.
And so are you.
So be thou what God has given you.
I have been charged by the elders at the Bible institution to which I graduated from 1992.
Read 2 Timothy 4:1–2.
I'm asking you to keep the Word of God near to your heart.

Praise God

I will praise God even when not at church.

> I will bless the LORD at all times, his praise shall continually be in my mouth.
>
> My soul makes its boast in the LORD; let the humble hear and be glad.
>
> Oh, magnify the LORD with me, and let us exalt his name together! (Psalm 34:1–3)

Prayer

Pray for men everywhere, especially the household of faith.

For all my prayer warriors, keep on doing the commands of God.

There is only one God, known by his people, so how does anyone else call upon God if they are not his doers?

Ignorance belongs to a clear class of itself.

Although God's people may sin from time after time (Romans 3:23, 6:23), God allows his people time to repent.

Staying focused upon the Creator, God in heaven.

> If my people, which are called by my name, shall humble themselves, pray and seek my face and turn from their wicked ways, then I will hear from heaven, and will heal their land. (2 Chronicles 7:14)

We know that God moved in response to Nehemiah's prayer, allowing him to use his position of influence with the king to get Artaxerxes to support the rebuilding of Jerusalem.

But Nehemiah didn't start with his position. He started with prayer—providing the link between God, Nehemiah's problem, and his position.

If you see something in our nation or political leaders that is broken, is prayer the first thing you do or the last thing you do?

If it's the last thing you do, more than likely you will have wasted your time on other things. If prayer comes last, then so will the solution to the problem.

God does not like being last.

If we are going to turn our communities and nation around, congregations are going to have to join in a unified, national solemn assembly (Joel 1:14) to repent and to throw themselves before the face of Almighty God.

We could save a lot of time and worry if we spent time praying first.

In Nehemiah's case, the crumbled walls of Jerusalem were a pressing problem, something that cried out for immediate and decisive action.

But Nehemiah fasted and prayed first. So, my question to you is, "What wall is crumbling?"

The answer: America.

Have you come to a dark place in your life, and you can't get out of it?

Talk to Jesus.

Remember his words (Ephesians 5:8, Isaiah 50:10).

Preach

Matthew 10:14.

> For if someone comes to you and preaches a Jesus other than the Jesus we preached, or if you receive a different spirit from the Spirit you received, or a different gospel from the one you accepted, you put up with it easily enough.
>
> I do not think I am in the least inferior to those "super-apostles."
>
> I may indeed be untrained as a speaker, but I do have knowledge. We have made this perfectly clear to you in every way. (2 Corinthians 11:4–6)

Stay focused on the Word of God.

Preachers, keep in mind that your lessons are very good, so when you preach, remember that if there wasn't a mess, you wouldn't have a job.

"Why such a mess in the church?" was our lectureship theme in the year of 2000.

Lectureship director: Christian Marcel.

Every church has a different way of doing things.

Many conduct their services in the best possible way, workable to their own needs, except where changes are necessary to apply.

There is no place like the church.

Where families are grouped together for a better time in serving the Lord.

One particular way to educate yourself is to study the Bible.

Higher learning is handed down by those who inform their students learnings.

Thus, earning a good report on better education values.

Going to church is important; sharing in your groups is most important.

Teaching people how to increase their values apart from their social norm.

To keep learning drives you to share (Acts 26:24).

Keep on sharing no matter what.

> For the Spirit God gave us does not make us timid, but gives us power, love and self-discipline. (2 Timothy 1:7)

Proclamation and Affirmation

Listen, are you with me?

Jesus desires all people to be saved and to come to the knowledge of the truth (1 Timothy 2:4).

Not some, but all come to the knowledge of truth.

We must look a little further, brethren, and pay attention to things coming our way.

Amen.

Here's the point: Oftentimes man will spend more time destroying other religious organizations or leaders rather than to pay attention to leaders in our government who need Jesus and think they have him; rather, some of which are in need of being delivered.

Amen.

Listen, pay attention to who's talking rather than creating an argument that you are the only one fighting.

Listen, in Mark 9:38–40, John said to him, "Teacher, we saw someone else driving out demons in Your name, and we tried to stop him, because he does not accompany us." But Jesus replied, "Do not stop him. No one who performs a miracle in My name can turn around and speak evil of Me."

For whoever is not against us is for us.

Proclamation and affirmation work together in love.

That is, practices without hypocrisy.

If any man like Cornelius who loves God, how be it that you treat him as he doesn't love God?

> One day at about three in the afternoon he
> had a vision. He distinctly saw an angel of God,
> who came to him and said, "Cornelius!"

Cornelius stared at him in fear. "What is it, Lord?" (Acts 10:3–4)

Now, what could you say about an angel who approached Cornelius?

Real or not real?

If you say real, then stop bringing people down when they are seekers of truth.

If you say not real, you are calling the Bible a lie.

Watch yourself.

Love never changes; it is always the same as it has always been before. God is love, and we should work together in truth. Love lives in truth. God sits in righteousness, and so shall we be examples of right living for God.

Hate is a different thing; it lives and dies in hypocrisy and lives with lies, conquer, deception and evangelizes to destroy mankind.

Psalm 1:1ff explains.

Prodigal Son

Mockers hate to be corrected, so they stay away from the wise (Proverbs 15:12).

Let's be clear: you can't beg someone to come to attention if it is not in God's will.

It is not your call to discipline but God.

Prayers, yes, if God permits.

He is in control of things we can't see.

Remember the prodigal son.

> When he came to his senses, he said, "How many of my father's hired servants have food to spare, and here I am starving to death!" (Luke 15:17)

Why, because pride caused him to leave home and waste his money on things he wasn't educated to do. In other words, he played the fool.

> Stern discipline awaits anyone who leaves the path; the one who hates correction will die. (Proverbs 15:10)

A man or woman has to come to themselves alone, but if God has to show you (the one who's worrying) in a different way, it could be asking for a bad future. You get what you ask for. Allow God to do his work, leave things to God.

Then all things work together for the good (Romans 8:28).

To endure the Christian struggle against evil, we must understand what Scripture teaches about God's loving discipline.

> And have you forgotten the encouraging words God spoke to you as his children?
>
> He said, "My child, don't make light of the LORD'S discipline, and don't give up when he corrects you, because the Lord disciplines the one, he loves, and he chastens everyone he accepts as his son." (Hebrews 12:5–6)

Psalm 32:1 says, "Blessed is he whose transgression is forgiven; whose sin is covered."

But if they are uncovered, sins are transparent among God and men.

Hebrews 4:13 reminds us, "And there is no creature hidden from God's sight, but that all things are naked (transparent) and open to the eyes of Him to whom we must give account."

God sees all things; his eyes are everywhere.

Remember again Proverbs 15:3, "The eyes of the LORD are everywhere, keeping watch on the wicked and the good."

Step out of the way of God.

> He that tilleth his land shall have plenty of bread: but he that followeth after vain persons shall have poverty enough. (Proverbs 28:19)

> But those who hope in the Lord will renew their strength. They will soar on wings like eagles; they will run and not grow weary, they will walk and not be faint. (Isaiah 40:31)

Prophecy

And the voice which I heard from heaven spake unto me again, and said,

Go and take the little book which is open in the hand of the angel which standeth upon the sea and upon the earth.

And I went unto the angel, and said unto him, Give me the little book. And he said unto me,

Take it and eat it up; and it shall make thy belly bitter, but it shall be in thy mouth sweet as honey.

And I took the little book out of the angel's hand and ate it up; and it was in my mouth sweet as honey: and as soon as I had eaten it, my belly was bitter.

And he said unto me,

Thou must prophesy again before many peoples, and nations, and tongues, and kings. (Revelation 10:8–11)

What works?

Your works.

Your work to Him.

And all your efforts in demonstrating that you are giving your all to obey his word.

Read Revelation 10:2.

John was making known the world empires and what God tends to do or have done about it.

Let the Bible speak, read it, love it, meditate on it.

> We also have the prophetic message as
> something completely reliable, and you will do
> well to pay attention to it, as to a light shining in
> a dark place, until the day dawns and the morn-
> ing star rises in your hearts
> Knowing this first, that no prophecy of the
> scripture is of any private interpretation.
> For the prophecy came not in old time by the
> will of man: but holy men of God spake as they
> were moved by the Holy Ghost. (2 Peter 1:19–21)

Acts 19, 1 Corinthians 12, now in chapter 14, verse 3, God shows that languages were used for a divine purpose to prove something to show Israel that God is keeping his will.

It was understood, and that if at any time the divine language was spoken, it was to evangelize and give every soul at that particular time to save many.

No one today can copy the work of the divine Holy Spirit, who gave the message in a language so important as it were in those times. So, if your Bibles has unknowns, it is not in the original translation. It was added by a translator.

The Bible teaches us that everyone heard one another in in their own language (or tongue) guided by the Holy Spirit from God.

God has never created a tongue that could not be understood to save a generation of people.

Today, God has given us the Word in written form.

Read Romans 15:3 and 2 Peter 1:3.

It is not like it was in the first century, so gather your thoughts to the reasoning of God.

Now if a man or woman speaks in a foreign tongue, let them do two things:

1. write it down
2. tell the church what you just said

Now take the paper and tell them to do it again.

And if he or she can't do either of these two, get rid of that person, who might affect the whole church in believing such a lie.

Tongues are called languages, not anything that cannot be understood.

There are lots of languages, and every language is understood by its people (Acts 2:6).

Propitiation

When I think about the Lord's church, I think about his supper. Everything that Jesus did on behalf of all mankind gave his family of believers the opportunity to reflect on his life.

> And He is the propitiation for our sins, and not for ours only, but also for the sins of the whole world. (1 John 2:2)

Propitiation is an action meant to regain someone's favor or make up for something you did wrong.

You might offer your mom a plate of chocolate chip cookies in propitiation for killing all her houseplants while she was away.

Propitiation comes from a form of the Latin verb *propitiare*, which means "to appease."

Proverbs

Now there lived in that city a man poor but wise, and he saved the city by his wisdom. But nobody remembered that poor man. (Ecclesiastes 9:15)

Watch out, there are dogs outside.

Watch out for those dogs, those evildoers, those mutilators of the flesh. (Philippians 3:2)

Do not answer a fool according to his folly, or you yourself will be just like him. (Proverbs 26:4)

A man of great anger must pay the penalty; if you rescue him, you will have to do so again. (Proverbs 19:19)

Don't take it on yourself to repay a wrong. Trust the Lord and he will make it right. (Proverbs 20:22)

Discipline your children while they are young enough to learn. If you don't, you are helping them destroy themselves. (Proverbs 19:18)

People who do not get along with others are interested only in themselves; they will disagree with what everyone else knows is right. (Proverbs 18:1)

Foolish children bring grief to their fathers and bitter regrets to their mothers. (Proverbs 17:25)

Only someone with no sense would promise to be responsible for someone else's debts. (Proverbs 17:18)

Anyone stupid enough to promise to be responsible for a stranger's debts ought to have their own property held to guarantee payment. (Proverbs 20:16)

If you want people to like you, forgive them when they wrong you. (Proverbs 17:9)

The start of an argument is like the first break in a dam; stop it before it goes any further. (v. 14)

Psychology

Then disorders are decided upon one's findings between the better road and the lesser responsibility.

>As Christians, we need to know how to diagnose and treat these disorders to restore the person to physical, psychological, and spiritual health.
>
>Persons who are depressed often feel distant from God or even feel judged by God for their depressive symptoms.

Life begins by studying your Bible.

>Psychology is the science of behavior and mind. Psychology includes the study of conscious and unconscious phenomena, as well as feeling and thought.

We all know a little about psychology; it is part of standard practices in our lives.

Sort of like philosophy, because we practice things by which our minds grasp through knowledge and understanding.

A great deal of individuals have wisdom, unused wisdom, because they have closed mouths and reserved hearts in sharing the gift within them.

Note, philosophy is not a way of life.

Every person does not have his or her own philosophy.

Philosophy is not simply a theory about something, nor is philosophy a belief or a wish.

Philosophy is an activity: a quest after wisdom. Philosophy is an activity of thought.

The more you learn, the better understanding you'll have of life.

Don't you just want to ignore folks who have nothing to share with you but trashy thoughts and opinions that have nothing but little value and truth.

One can see right through the thrust of ignorance when it arrives at no conclusion.

But we do. Listen to unknowledgeable people—that's how most get along with folks: listening to share our thoughts as it relates to shared concerns and connections.

So be it, or as they say, such is life, or what it is, is what it is.

Psychology and the Bible

P sychology and the Bible.

> Trust in the Lord with all your heart, and do not lean on your own understanding.
> In all your ways acknowledge him, and he will make straight your paths. (Proverbs 3:5–6)

> Do not be conformed to this world, but be transformed by the renewal of your mind, that by testing you may discern what is the will of God, what is good and acceptable and perfect. (Romans 12:2)

> For unto us a Child is born, unto us a Son is given; And the government will be upon His shoulder. And His name will be called Wonderful, Counselor, Mighty God, Everlasting Father, Prince of Peace. (Isaiah 9:6)

> When Isaiah wrote his prediction of the coming of the "Wonderful Counselor" Isaiah 9:6, he was spurring Israel to remember their Messiah was indeed coming to establish His Kingdom. Isaiah 9:7.
> Isaiah was writing nearly 800 years before Christ.

This period of history was tumultuous as the Assyrians were on the march, taking people into captivity by droves.

Isaiah's prophecy gave the people of God a hope they so desperately needed.

We call it today a duel prophecy, both then and has come to pass.

How are you familiar with social psychology?

Its meaning is "the branch of psychology that deals with social interactions, including their origins and their effects on the individual."

Social psychologists examine factors that cause behaviors to unfold in a given way in the presence of others.

They study conditions under which certain behavior, actions, and feelings occur.

Social psychology is concerned with the way these feelings, thoughts, beliefs, intentions, and goals are cognitively constructed and how these mental representations, in turn, influence our interactions with others.

As often as we think, social phenomenon is that of foreign language as well, its differences of meaning.

Now study the contents of your Bibles, as it relates to society differences between our day and theirs.

What would you do in a moment to protect your life or integrity, family?

Besides your good works, how would you respond?

Which ones? The rich man inquired. Jesus replied, you shall not murder, you shall not commit adultery, you shall not steal, you shall not give false testimony. (Matthew 19:18)

The Bible says, "Then some soldiers asked him, 'And what should we do?' 'Do not take money by force or false accusation,' he said. 'Be content with your wages'" (Luke 3:14).

Question: how many people have eaten crumbs from the rich man's table in order to survive?

How many have lied on their time report for work?

> Those people worked only one hour, and yet you've paid them just as much as you paid us who worked all day in the scorching heat. (Matthew 20:12)

How can any call Halloween a good thing? It is about witches, ghosts, magic, and evil wicked things hanging around your doorstep; giving out candy; and the children would say "trick or treat!"

Or by some Christians who have reestablished Halloween by saying "Trunk or Treats," giving evil a better look, while Christmas is all about what is lovely and pure—to which some say, not a good thing. Hmmm!

Race

Paraphrase the message and meaning combined.

You've all been to the stadium and seen the athlete's race. Everyone runs; one wins. Run to win. All good athletes train hard. They do it for a gold medal that tarnishes and fades. You're after one that's gold eternally. I don't know about you, but I'm running hard for the finish line. I'm giving it everything I've got. No sloppy living for me! I'm staying alert and in top condition. I'm not going to get caught napping, telling everyone else all about it and then missing out myself. (1 Corinthians 9:24–27)

Recompense

Recompense is a much-needed effort today.

Jesus said, "O Jerusalem, Jerusalem, you that kill the prophets, and stone them which are sent to you, how often would I have gathered your people together, even as a hen gathers her chickens under her wings, and you would not!" (Matthew 23:37). Why?

Rejecting Christ

When a man rejects Christ, he already says implicitly where he is going (John 12:48), and when a man rejects the church and brings charges against it, well, you know who his father is (John 8:44).

Christians should work ever so hard to get people right for the police or political forces to take them in.

> Save others by snatching them from the fire; to others show mercy, mixed with fear-hating even the clothing stained by corrupted flesh. (Jude 1:23)

Listen: "Righteousness exalts a nation, again I say Righteousness exalts a nation, but sin condemns any people" (Proverbs 14:34).

> Treat everyone with respect:
> But, Love the brotherhood of believers, fear God, honor the king; and give honor to those who are in authority. (1 Peter 2:17, Romans 13:1)

Back in the days, God spoke to the fathers and the prophets (Hebrews 1:1ff).

Back in the days, God spoke to others in dreams.

Today, it is different. God speaks to us by his Son Jesus Christ (Matthew 17).

Suppose a man in a nice suit told you the truth (John 17:17) about what Jesus said, how would you respond to the Word?

Suppose Jesus came to you or the church and said, "Be baptized," should you believe him?

I think you would, so why is it difficult for some to believe the inspired word given from God today (2 Timothy 3:16)?

Now I'm asking you to read again John 12:48; 1 Corinthians 4:1–2; 1 Thessalonians 2:4; 2 Corinthians 4:1–2.

Things that matter should concern us today. Today is the day of your salvation. Take the Word as it is written; believe it and obey it.

When God favors you, and its people follow, why have you decided to find fault in God's favor? Or why have you decided to establish your own ways?

Example: When Samuel did arrive, he told Saul, "You have done a foolish thing," using the Hebrew term for people who act without regard for God.

Samuel warned that Saul's kingdom would not endure, meaning that his family would not establish a dynasty. He'd be succeeded on the throne by someone from a different family (1 Samuel 15).

> What do you think? If a man owns a hundred sheep, and one of them wanders away, will he not leave the ninety-nine on the hills and go to look for the one that wandered off? (Matthew 18:12)

Now are they quickly doing this or letting it go by so long that it really doesn't matter?

> He that rejecteth me, and receiveth not my words, hath one that judgeth him: the word that I have spoken, the same shall judge him in the last day. (John 12:48)

Get busy, not too late; go find the strays. They are backed in the world looking for opportunities. And give no opportunity to the devil (Ephesians 4:27).

Rejoice

Come, everyone! "Clap your hands! Shout to God with joyful praise!" Psalm 47:1.

Question: Is change too hard for you? Or do you want to be a finger pointer?

If so, "whom will you serve?" is an honest question that deserves an honest answer.

But I must tell you, finger-pointer society groups are lost. Because they refuse to listen to the Bible.

When they refuse to hear the Word of God, many will walk in rhythm with other lost souls.

Read Psalm 1:1ff and Matthew 7:1ff.

When you are married to Christ, and you decide to walk away from him, totally, you then commit spiritual fornication by living with the world, having no part with Jesus, leading into a divorce with Christ. For this reason, one is lost (2 Peter 2:20–22).

Here's a Bible answer to your question if you want to be against God's Word.

> For everything in the world-the lust of the flesh, the lust of the eyes, and the pride of life-comes not from the Father but from the world. (1 John 2:16)

Read Isaiah 59:1–2.

Get to know Jesus and stay in the Word (Ephesians 4:20–27).

Preaching is my life.

Although this is all I get, I'm satisfied.

Thanks, FB.

Repent

God has told the sinful world, in no uncertain terms, to repent (Mark 6:12; Luke 24:47; Acts 3:19, 17:30).

To repent means to change your mind from embracing wrong-doings. Come to Christ, let go of sin.

Those who refuse to repent and turn to Christ will suffer eternal consequences.

Therefore, you, my friends, will drive yourselves to an eternal destiny of no return.

> In a large house there are articles not only of gold and silver, but also of wood and clay; some are for special purposes and some for common use. (2 Timothy 2:20)

There are others whom another will follow and those of whom will lead.

Because of this, God has allowed those who may be timid or having physical problems unable to lead but made themselves a good vessel fitted for use.

Verse 19 says, "Nevertheless, God's firm foundation stands, bearing this seal: 'The Lord knows those who are His,' and, 'Everyone who calls on the name of the Lord must turn away from iniquity.'"

Notice verse 21: "So if anyone cleanses himself of what is unfit, he will be a vessel for honor: sanctified, useful to the Master, and prepared for every good work."

Sticky fingers become icky fingers when playing in the sandbox with your worldly friends (2 Corinthians 6:14).

Matters become worse when things are not seen by others that matter.

Then how can one return back to God? Repentance (Luke 13:3).

Give God your sincere heart in prayer and submit to him who cares for you and commit yourself to God; it is he that delivers.

Watch.

> Cast all your anxiety on him because he cares for you. (1 Peter 5:7)

> Do not be anxious about anything, but in everything by prayer and supplication with thanksgiving let your requests be made known to God. (Philippians 4:6–7)

> Then call on me when you are in trouble, and I will rescue you, and you will give me glory. (Psalm 50:15)

Watch your miracle come into existence.
God is faithful.

> But the Lord is faithful, and he will strengthen you and protect you from the evil one. (2 Thessalonians 3:3)

Out of the church came a blessing, into the world became a curse (2 Peter 2:20). Or out of the world came a curse, into the church a blessing.

When a person turns his/her life to God, it is a blessing.
Turning back to the world after your blessing is a curse.

> Do not be yoked together with unbelievers.
> For what do righteousness and wickedness have in common?

Or what fellowship can light have with
darkness? (2 Corinthians 6:14)

Who has spoken, and it came to be permanent?

David said, for he spoke, and it came to be;
he commanded, and it stood firm. (Psalm 33:9)

Within our hearts, we speak temporarily things except that
which has been allowed to become permanent.

Who has spoken, and it came to pass, unless
the Lord has ordained it? (Lamentations 3:37)

Allow change with people to whom you don't trust because of
their past sins repented of, for we are not to judge what God has
already forgiven.

Have you repented of your sins?

God allows us (you) to begin again.

Question: Are you made for heaven, or should I say, have you
prepared yourselves for heaven?

I mean, have you really been listening to Jesus?

Jesus said, "I am the way and the truth
and the life. No one comes to the Father except
through me." (John 14:6)

Spiritual adultery is that of Adam and Eve. Question: Did God
forsake us?

No!

God provided a way to save you through repentance and obedience today, right now.

Get rid of your super pride; that goes to destruction.

Read 1 John 2:16 and Proverbs 16:18.

Listen.

What shall we say then?

Are we (you) to continue in sin that grace may abound? By no means!

How can we (you) who died to sin still live in it? (Romans 6:1ff)

For if you live according to the flesh, you will die; but if by the Spirit you put to death the misdeeds of the body, you will live. (Romans 8:13)

Do you not know that all of us who have been baptized into Christ Jesus were baptized into his death?

We were buried therefore with him by baptism into death, in order that, just as Christ was raised from the dead by the glory of the Father, we too might walk in newness of life.

For if we have been united with him in a death like his, we shall certainly be united with him in a resurrection like his.

We know that our old self was crucified with him in order that the body of sin might be brought to nothing, so that we would no longer be enslaved to sin.

For one who has died has been set free from sin.

Now if we have died with Christ, we believe that we will also live with him. (Romans 6:2ff)

But God, who is rich in mercy, for his great love wherewith he loved us.

Even when we were dead in sins, hath quickened us together with Christ, by grace ye are saved.

For he hath raised us up together, and made us sit together in heavenly places in Christ Jesus. (Ephesians 2:4–6)

We know that Christ, being raised from the dead, will never die again; death no longer has dominion over him.

Question: Does this mean that we will not ever commit a sin again?

No!

For all have sinned and fall short of the glory of God. (Romans 3:23)

If we claim to be without sin, we deceive ourselves and the truth is not in us. (1 John 1:8)

Reputation

Do you have a purpose? If so, why is it taking you long to get there?

Have you ever been in a situation where others wanted to destroy you (Daniel 6)?

Reputation
Your name
Your church family
Your present family
Your job
Your friend
Etc.

> So, these administrators and satraps went as a group to the king and said: "May King Darius live forever!
>
> The royal administrators, prefects, satraps, advisers and governors have all agreed that the king should issue an edict and enforce the decree that anyone who prays to any god or human being during the next thirty days, except to you, Your Majesty, shall be thrown into the lions' den.
>
> Now, Your Majesty, issue the decree and put it in writing so that it cannot be altered—in accordance with the law of the Medes and Persians, which cannot be repealed."
>
> So, King Darius put the decree in writing.
>
> Now when Daniel learned that the decree had been published, he went home to his

upstairs room where the windows opened toward Jerusalem.

Three times a day he got down on his knees and prayed, giving thanks to his God, just as he had done before.

Then these men went as a group and found Daniel praying and asking God for help.

So, they went to the king and spoke to him about his royal decree:

"Did you not publish a decree that during the next thirty days anyone who prays to any god or human being except to you, Your Majesty, would be thrown into the lions' den?"

The king answered, 'The decree stands—in accordance with the law of the Medes and Persians, which cannot be repealed."

Then they said to the king, "Daniel, who is one of the exiles from Judah, pays no attention to you, Your Majesty, or to the decree you put in writing. He still prays three times a day."

When the king heard this, he was greatly distressed; he was determined to rescue Daniel and made every effort until sundown to save him.

Then the men went as a group to King Darius and said to him, "Remember, Your Majesty, that according to the law of the Medes and Persians no decree or edict that the king issues can be changed."

So, the king gave the order, and they brought Daniel and threw him into the lions' den. The king said to Daniel, "May your God, whom you serve continually, rescue you!"

A stone was brought and placed over the mouth of the den, and the king sealed it with his own signet ring and with the rings of his nobles, so that Daniel's situation might not be changed.

Then the king returned to his palace and spent the night without eating and without any entertainment being brought to him.

And he could not sleep.

At the first light of dawn, the king got up and hurried to the lions' den.

When he came near the den, he called to Daniel in an anguished voice, "Daniel, servant of the living God, has your God, whom you serve continually, been able to rescue you from the lions?"

Daniel answered, "May the king live forever! My God sent his angel, and he shut the mouths of the lions. They have not hurt me, because I was found innocent in his sight. Nor have I ever done any wrong before you, Your Majesty."

The king was overjoyed and gave orders to lift Daniel out of the den. And when Daniel was lifted from the den, no wound was found on him, because he had trusted in his God.

Read Psalm 57:5–6. What about Acts 24:5–6?

We have found this man to be a trouble-maker, stirring up riots among the Jews all over the world. He is a ringleader of the Nazarene sect 6 and even tried to desecrate the temple; so, we seized him.

Are people doing much harm to you because of your righteousness?

People will set traps against you to destroy your life.

Season all your grain offerings with salt. Do not leave the salt of the covenant of your God out of your grain offerings; add salt to all your offerings. (Leviticus 2:13)

The role of salt in the Bible is relevant to understanding Hebrew society during the Old Testament and New Testament periods.

The Bible contains numerous references to salt.

In various contexts, it is used metaphorically to signify permanence, loyalty, durability, fidelity, usefulness, value, and purification.

Respect

Malfeasance is a comprehensive term used in both civil and Criminal Law to describe any act that is wrongful.

It is not a distinct crime or tort but may be used generally to describe any act that is criminal or that is wrongful and gives rise to, or somehow contributes to, the injury of another person.

Definition of any public official who rips up public documents.

Describes an intentional conduct that is wrongful or unlawful, especially by officials or public employees called Malfeasance.

I speak the truth in love based upon my own submission.

After prayer and meditation, it is so.

Takes faith and belief to accomplish my trust in God.

Takes faith that mankind must live in and trust.

Amen.

God is my salvation and life.

LORD, our Lord, how majestic is your name in all the earth! (Psalm 8:9)

Remember Christians who forfeit truth.

For this reason, God sends them a powerful delusion so that they will believe the lie. (2 Thessalonians 2:11)

Well, those who are blinded by the gospel are not Christians but in danger of judgment (2 Corinthians 4:4).

The devil is busy evangelizing against the Word of God (1 John 4:1–6).

Matthew 12:32 makes it even more clear: "Whoever speaks a word against the Son of Man, it will be forgiven him. But whoever speaks against the Holy Spirit, it will not be forgiven him, either in this age or in the one to come."

The Holy Spirit gave us the Word of God from heaven by his chosen apostles (2 Peter 1:3, 19–21).

> For the prophecy came not in old time by the will of man: but holy men of God spake as they were moved by the Holy Spirit.

So, for men to reject the Word of God (John 12:48) means they have brought judgment upon themselves.

> If your enemy is hungry, give him food to eat, and if he is thirsty, give him water to drink.
> For in so doing, you will heap burning coals on his head, and the LORD will reward you.
> As the north wind brings forth rain, so a backbiting tongue brings angry looks. (Proverbs 25:21–23)

My friends, keep feeding them the Word of God, keep on doing good.

When man rejects the Word of God, he is the same as ashes in a fireplace (John 12:48).

Read Hebrews 9:27.

When you try to help someone, at times, repeated strong words shall be an exhortation to him.

> And others save with fear, pulling them out of the fire; hating even the garment spotted by the flesh. (Jude 1:23)

This is why it is said "Wake up, sleeper, rise from the dead, and Christ will shine on you." (Ephesians 5:14)

To define Romans 12:2 should indicate your trust to represent God in every way.

The Bible speaks.

> And be not conformed to this world: but be ye transformed by the renewing of your mind, that ye may prove what is that good, and acceptable, and perfect, will of God.
>
> You therefore must be perfect, as your heavenly Father is perfect. (Matthew 5:48)

Indicating "be complete in life and judgment toward all things."

> The best way to earn the respect of your peers is to show respect and kindness to everyone you meet. You should also show others that you are open-minded, trustworthy, and mature.

> Woe to those who call evil good and good evil, who put darkness for light and light for darkness, who put bitter for sweet and sweet for bitter! (Isaiah 5:20)

What does it mean in plain everyday language?

It simply means, don't say when sin comes it is good; and when God disciplines your life, don't say it is bad.

> No temptation has overtaken you except what is common to mankind.
>
> And God is faithful; he will not let you be tempted beyond what you can bear.

But when you are tempted, he will also provide a way out so that you can endure it. (1 Corinthians 10:13)

For we do not wrestle against flesh and blood, but against the rulers, against the authorities, against the cosmic powers over this present darkness, against the spiritual forces of evil in the heavenly places. (Ephesians 6:12)

Remember, most evils are not from within but are brought into our justification of our righteous behavior toward mankind.

"Then they will deliver you up to tribulation and put you to death, and you will be hated by all nations for my name's sake."
And then many will fall away and betray one another and hate one another.
And many false prophets will arise and lead many astray. And because lawlessness will be increased, the love of many will grow cold.
But the one who endures to the end will be saved. (Matthew 24:9–13)

A word fitly spoken is like apples of gold in settings of silver. (Proverbs 25:11)

When you speak truths, question is, how well will it be received?

There are some who reject truths by going along with popular opinion.

Not a way to keep in step with truth.

James 1:13–14 says, "When tempted, no one should say, 'God is tempting me.' For God cannot be tempted by evil, nor does He tempt anyone. That when Temptation comes, it comes from our own desires, which entice us and drag us away."

Come now, who teaches one evil, not God, but self to follow others into anger or rage against the righteous man of God.

Don't follow silly remarks, but righteous truths, and even if others don't follow truths, the truth will stand against evils.

Romans 5:16 says, "And the free gift is not like the result of that one man's sin. For the judgment following one trespass brought condemnation, but the free gift following many trespasses brought justification."

Reverence

Praise the Lord, practice your Christianity. Show reverence to the Lord.

In New Testament Christianity, reverence for God is demonstrated by our willingness to voluntarily die to self and obey his commands (Galatians 2:20, 5:13; James 2:12).

Jesus reminded us that we must properly reverence God. He taught the disciples to begin their prayers with "Our Father, who is in heaven, hallowed be your name" (Matthew 6:9–13).

Hallowed means "set apart as holy." We are to treat the name of God with reverence.

Reward

Don't be asunder by sin. (Break your life into pieces.)
Stay with the Word of God.
Nobody made me but the Lord.
How about you?

> I will praise thee; for I am fearfully and wonderfully made marvelous are thy works; and that my soul knoweth right well. (Psalm 139:14)

Who made Cain?
Get your hope in studying the Scriptures.
Read 1 Peter 1:3–9.

> This truth gives them confidence that they have eternal life, which God—who does not lie—promised them before the world began.
> In His own time, He has revealed His message in the proclamation entrusted to me by the command of God our Savior. (Titus 1:2–3)

Once upon a time, a high school teacher said to his student, "I don't understand what you are saying."

So, he quit school, went and got his GED at a local university, and made high honors. He took it back to his school years later and said, "Can you take a look at this?"

> Do not be deceived: "Bad company corrupts good morals." (1 Corinthians 15:33)

Teach mankind what they ought to know; the way of salvation leads to eternal life with God.

> Give to everyone what you owe them: Pay your taxes and government fees to those who collect them and give respect and honor to those who are in authority. (Romans 13:7)

The motivation of reward for Christian service is absolute and not to be forfeited.

It is true that the reward motive for Christian service is not the highest biblical motive, but it is a biblical one. As the highest, we are told to do all we do for God's glory.

Read 1 Corinthians 10:31 and Colossians 3:23–24.

We are to do all we can to be accepted by Christ, for the good of others, and out of gratitude and love for all God has done for us.

Even the fear of the Lord that is going to fall on the unsaved is a legitimate incentive for service in seeing the lost saved (2 Corinthians 5:11).

According to Paul, it is possible to build on the foundation, which is Christ, but to be building with "wood, hay, or straw," which cannot stand the test of fire, the builder will be saved but "only as one escaping through the flames" (1 Corinthians 3:11–15).

In other words, people can be busy with the Lord's work and still receive no reward.

They may be taking advantage of opportunities to labor for the Lord and yet not be engaged in endeavors that meet with God's approval because they have the wrong motives.

For example, if they seek the praise of others, they can have that praise but receive no reward from God later (Matthew 6:1–18).

Along with this forfeiture of reward will go a severe sense of shame and remorse (1 John 2:28) and a possible divine reprimand for wasted living as a Christian (Matthew 25:26–28).

Now the question: How do you feel about your full reward today?

Rich Man / Poor Man

Luke 16:19–31; this is what homeless looks like.

> There was a rich man who was dressed in purple and fine linen and lived in luxury every day.

A well-to-do man had all he needed, but...

> At his gate was laid a beggar named Lazarus, covered with sores, and longing to eat what fell from the rich man's table.

A poor homeless man went to his gate, wanted food and substance to get by. No government proposal to help the beggar, no food stamps, jobs, or healthcare insurance.

Listen, today we can direct any to get the help they need long-term. I'm not talking about someone needing a sandwich or general needs at one time, and I'm not speaking about seeing a person in need and you offer them a meal.

What I'm addressing here is admission to long-term help by using available resources that are to our concerns.

Today a lazy person gets by begging most of his life; it's a business.

We now see a needy person, we help them or direct them to resources available.

But we lend our support if an urgent need is called for.

If shoes, take them to Payless; if food, Food 4 Less; clothes, thrift store.

Or give them something to wear from out of your closet if they can fit your clothes.

There are many ways to help a needy person or child of God.

Use your scruples.

Amen.

God directs that person to you and finds your concerns.

> The Parable of the Good Samaritan
> On one occasion an expert in the law stood
> up to test Jesus. "Teacher," he asked, "what must
> I do to inherit eternal life?" (Luke 10:25–37)

When I was down on my luck, I prayed to God and was directed to the VA; and from that business, I gained my knowledge, wisdom, and understanding to resources available.

Asking the church may not be your best bet because there are certain ones who'd rather pay for rental or water and garage rather than help a child of God, depending on who you're friends with.

But hear me, not all cases, just a few who haven't grown to understand the mission of God, period.

However, such will be accountable to their decisions.

Use your available resources.

Notice the rich man and his brothers knew God, but they were not following a lead from the old law.

The first part of Proverbs 14:31 says, "He who oppresses the poor shows contempt for their Maker."

Showing contempt, interrupting them.

1. Correcting them.
2. Criticizing them.
3. Finishing their sentences.
4. Making fun of them.
5. Communicating nonverbal negatives.
6. Redoing what they have done.

We all use at times colloquial terms in our everyday conversations.

The definition of *colloquial* refers to words or expressions used in ordinary language by common people.

An example of colloquial is casual conversation where some slang terms are used and where no attempt is made at being formal.

Righteousness

Having traditional family values means walking in truth and practices in advocacy among those who are without (Galatians 6:1–10).

If you have failed in your life, begin again; you have value and self-worth.

Don't put off your clothes of righteousness because of the first Adam; the second Adam came as a life-giving spirit.

That's Jesus, who puts life back into your body; "you were dead in your trespasses and sins" but now alive in Christ (Ephesians 2:1).

> Although you are fully aware of this, I want to remind you that after Jesus had delivered His people out of the land of Egypt, He destroyed those who did not believe.
>
> And the angels who did not stay within their own domain, but abandoned their proper dwelling, He keeps under darkness, in eternal chains for judgment on that great day.
>
> In like manner, Sodom and Gomorrah and the cities around them, who indulged in sexual immorality and pursued strange flesh, are on display as an example of those who sustain the punishment of eternal fire. (Jude 1:5–7)

Who were these angels that unclothed themselves?
People who put off the righteousness of God to serve sin.

> Knowing this, that our old self is crucified with him, that the body of sin might be

destroyed, that henceforth we should not serve sin. (Romans 6:6)

Understand the meaning of 2 Corinthians 5:17—very important.

Be awake to righteousness or death in sins (Ephesians 5:14).

Go to your private area or your private spot and shout, "Hallelujah, my God is alive."

Go to your secret spot.

Read Matthew 19:16–22 and Mark 10:17–27.

Careful what you ask of Jesus, because he just might test your heart.

Examine yourselves to see whether you are
in the faith; test yourselves. Do you not realize
that Christ Jesus is in you-unless, of course, you
fail the test? (2 Corinthians 13:5)

Today, we want salvation/freedom from our common trusts, but we overlook the simple things that matter to our salvation.

Why do that?

Life is short; your promise awaits, and if you forfeit your claim for earthly good, my friends, that's your reward.

Keep heaven in mind; the Word is sanctified and true (John 17:17).

Did not Jesus foresee the future? Could the wealthy man buy new stuff?

Don't let Jesus catch you in your selfish thoughts.

You can know that you are saved—heaven-bound without objection (Romans 8:1).

Run the Race

Christians are defined by the Word of God (John 14:15). The non-Christian is defined by the Word.

> For everything in the world—the lust of the
> flesh, the lust of the eyes, and the pride of life—
> comes not from the Father but from the world.
> (1 John 2:16)

People are changing all the time; nobody likes to be given bad choices.

We like results to be seen and appreciated.

Otherwise, keep going.

General thoughts of men as those who bond themselves by everyday philosophy: men find their places in the church by taking a seat until they are asked to do something; it is a bad philosophy to take hold of.

The reasonable thing to do is ask, "What shall I do?"

Remember the controller is God.

> And we know that all things work together
> for good to them that love God, to them who are
> the called according to his purpose. (Romans 8:28)

Things cannot work together for the good of God if you expect someone to ask you to do something.

Remember this:

> If anyone, then, knows the good they ought to
> do and doesn't do it, it is sin for them. (James 4:17)

And if you do volunteer to give your sincere service, no one is expected to deny you of your service.

Baptized believers are commanded to work.

> Dear friends, you always followed my instructions when I was with you.
>
> And now that I am away, it is even more important.
>
> Work hard to show the results of your salvation, obeying God with deep reverence and fear. (Philippians 2:12)

Who is it that can tell you not to obey?

No one! For you are doing exactly what God commands you to do.

> Therefore, since we are surrounded by such a great cloud of witnesses, let us throw off everything that hinders and the sin that so easily entangles.
>
> And let us run with perseverance the race marked out for us, fixing our eyes on Jesus, the author and perfecter of our faith. (Hebrews 12:1)

Fixing our eyes on who?

Jesus.

Listen now.

> For the joy set before him he endured the cross, scorning its shame, and sat down at the right hand of the throne of God.
>
> Consider him who endured such opposition from sinners, so that you will not grow weary and lose heart.

Listen to your Bible.

> Because strait is the gate, and narrow is the way, which leadeth unto life, and few there be that find it. (Matthew 7:14)

No child should be left behind (Ephesians 4:15).
Let us look at some clear definitions of characters.
A psychological difference on demand.
For example.

> In a psychological experiment, a demand characteristic is a subtle cue that makes participants aware of what the experimenter expects to find or how participants are expected to behave.
> Demand characteristics can change the outcome of an experiment because participants will often alter their behavior to conform to expectations.

Like a gathering of saints who stand for Jesus, but not hearers.
Common cause could set in the minds of those to know that working together for the same common cause matters.
Does it matter to some?
Discipleship first begins at home.
(If your actions begin at church, and to be seen of men, you are lacking in discipleship.)
Always begin at home, first.
Then working with others in a much broader role.
Watch.
Read 2 Corinthians 6:6.
Working together with God, we share alike.
We don't put anything in anyone's way.
So, no one can find fault with our work for God.
Instead, we make it clear that we serve God in every way.

We serve him by standing firm in troubles, hard times, and suffering.

We don't give up. We serve God. We work hard for him.

My friends, if you decide to hear only and not be obedient to the Word, you have not followed alone; for the Bible says, "Do not merely listen to the word, and so deceive yourselves. Do what it says" (James 1:22).

Who will turn the water off?

"Not me" is never an option; everyone must have an awareness of circumstances surrounding them.

How do you live?

Listen, believer.

> For though we walk in the flesh, we do not war according to the flesh. For the weapons of our warfare are not carnal (worldly), but mighty in God for pulling down strongholds. (What we do together). (2 Corinthians 10:3–7)

How?

> By casting down arguments and every high thing that exalts itself against the knowledge of God, bringing every thought into captivity to the obedience of Christ, and being ready to punish all disobedience when your obedience is fulfilled.

One cannot submit to God if you are thinking like an addict for the world.

Question: How full is your obedience?

Well, if it is not fulfilled in Christ, then what percentage are you living?

You, my friend, must be 100 percent in Christ or no percentage at all.

A man cannot live or think like the world while trying to live like Christians.

Either you're in or you are out.

Romans 8:5–8 says, "Those who live according to the flesh set their minds on the things of the flesh; but those who live according to the Spirit set their minds on the things of the Spirit. For to be carnally minded is death; but to be spiritually minded is life and peace. Because the carnal mind is enmity against God: for it is not subject to the law of God, neither indeed can be."

So, then they that are in the flesh cannot please God.

Bearing Fruit

> Jesus said, I have other sheep that are not of this fold. I must bring them in as well, and they will listen to My voice. Then there will be one flock and one shepherd. (John 10:16)

What does it mean?

Simply delivering the Word of God as commanded by us to do.

To get results—succeed, meet with success, be successful, be effective, be profitable—work, go as planned (Mark 16:15–16).

The Bible says, "For a good tree bringeth not forth corrupt fruit; neither doth a corrupt tree bring forth good fruit. For every tree is known by his own fruit. For of thorns men do not gather figs, nor of a bramble bush gather they grapes" (Luke 6:43–44).

I'm still running the race, not giving up.

> For I am persuaded, that neither death, nor life, nor angels, nor principalities, nor powers, nor things present, nor things to come, Nor height, nor depth, nor any other creature, shall be able to separate us from the love of God, which is in Christ Jesus our Lord. (Romans 8:38–39)

> Therefore, as we have opportunity, let us do good to all people, especially to those who belong to the family of believers. (Galatians 6:10)

We will pass from this life so quickly, it's not a matter of whether we desire to stay (Hebrews 9:27).

Furthermore, "while we look not at the things which are seen, but at the things which are not seen: for the things which are seen are temporal; but the things which are not seen are eternal" (2 Corinthians 4:18).

Sacrifice

> God presented Him as an atoning sacrifice
> through faith in His blood, in order to demon-
> strate His righteousness, because in His forbear-
> ance He had passed over the sins committed
> beforehand. (Romans 3:25)

Must guilty man remain under wrath? Is the wound forever incurable?

No. Blessed be God, there is another way laid open for us.

This is the righteousness of God; righteousness of his ordaining and providing and accepting.

How?

It is by that faith that has Jesus Christ for its object; an anointed Saviour, so Jesus Christ signifies.

But why?

Justifying faith respects Christ as a Savior in all his three anointed offices—as prophet, priest, and king; trusting in him, accepting him, and cleaving to him: in all these, Jews and Gentiles are alike welcome to God through Christ.

The work God had to do to save his created man.

Thank God for Jesus (John 1:1ff).

And the blood of the bullock offered on the great Day of Atonement was to be sprinkled "upon the mercy-seat," and "before the mercy-seat," "seven times" (Leviticus 16:14–15).

This sprinkling or offering of blood was called making "an atonement for the holy place because of the uncleanness of the children of Israel" etc. (Leviticus 16:16).

It was from this mercy seat that God pronounced pardon or expressed himself as reconciled to his people.

Now the blood of animals cannot take away the sins of mankind today.

> For it is not possible that the blood of bulls and of goats should take away sins. (Hebrews 10:4)

Why?

Jesus's blood takes away our sins.

My take on "the cake and eat it too."

Race should not be an issue, but folks in ignorance will make it so.

"We live on a placid island of ignorance in the midst of black seas of infinity," and it was not made from the revelation of God.

In times past: "And the priest shall make an atonement for the soul that sinneth ignorantly, when he sinneth by ignorance before the LORD, to make an atonement for him; and it shall be forgiven him" (Numbers 15:28).

Jesus is our atoning sacrifice.

Ask God, repent of your sins, and it shall be forgiven.

Those of the world will act like the world.

Haters of what is good and equal to others.

Does segregation still exist?

Among the ignorant of course.

They live in a country of their own apart from civility.

The question is, how can we reshape our constituents while we reshape our own country?

There has to be a draining of the swamp first.

The country needs to set forth a new improved constitution rather than pick apart old borders in order to bring order.

When all men shall be treated equally by the law.

America needs to show uniformity of strength. Other countries need to see present examples of Americans by ridding themselves of all bad past examples of humanity.

Others shall follow its lead.

Sacrifice of Jesus

W atch Hebrews 10:10–12.

Our sins are washed away, and we are made clean because Christ gave his own body as a gift to God.

He did this once for all time.

All Jewish religious leaders stand every day killing animals and giving gifts on the altar.

They give the same gifts over and over again.

These gifts cannot take away sins.

But Christ gave himself once for sins, and that is good forever. After that, he sat down at the right side of God.

Salvation

Children, find your salvation (Acts 4:12) and your saving grace (Ephesians 2:8) by being obedient to the Word of Christ (John 12:48)

> Salvation is found in no one else, for there is no other name under heaven given to mankind by which we must be saved. (Acts 4:12)

Read Luke 19:10 and Acts 1:14.

Although mankind was not at the resurrection of Jesus, but to convert one today (Acts 2:38), you must see the resurrection of Jesus (Acts 1:11).

The mind's eye must be able to see the Feast of Weeks, normally called Pentecost (Acts 1:1ff); then many shall understand the mission of Christ.

Salvation.

> Then He said to them, "My soul is consumed with sorrow to the point of death." In telling his apostles, "Stay here and keep watch with Me."
>
> Going a little farther, He fell facedown and prayed, "My Father, if it is possible, let this cup pass from Me. Yet not as I will, but as You will." (Matthew 26:38–39)

We have a lot to be thankful for.
Read Luke 8:11.

Salvation is a property of God, not man's. A biblical taste, and our societies are in line with laws as defined.

What does slavery mean (1 Timothy 6:1)?

"Slaves, obey your earthly master."

> Slaves obey your earthly masters in everything; and do it, not only when their eye is on you and to curry their favor, but with sincerity of heart. (Ephesians 6:5; 1 Peter 2:18)

Slavery is not slavery in our supposed work ethic today.

They are called bosses or supervisors or foreman, perhaps a president; but by laws that are inactive, they are to treat such as it should with all respect.

The workplace has rules and regulations that do not require mankind to be a slave, but coworkers within a workplace where one serves, there those particular supervisors being the head over you.

Listen to your Bible.

> If then you have been raised with Christ, seek the things that are above, where Christ is, seated at the right hand of God. Set your minds on things that are above, not on things that are on earth. (Colossians 3:1–25)

> However, Paul was also aware of the "real-world," but not omniscience as God, but in his day age or generation and conditions in which Christians lived.

> Christianity was a spiritual transformation that sought to change people from within. It was not a political movement aimed at overthrowing existing governments or worldly institutions by force.

It is in my opinion that potential movements of politics is at our doorstep today. Some churches are playing politics in areas of leadership and to whom they are willing to listen to or who they want in front of them to preach—as in nepotism. Simply not the way God set this thing up.

As Jesus had told Pilate during his trial, although he had a kingdom, it was not of this world (John 18:33–38).

The Pharisees wanted him out anyways in spite of what miracles he performed.

Jesus was not satisfied with slavery or politics.

> He who walks in integrity walks securely,
> but he who perverts his ways will be found out.
> (Proverbs 10:9)

Savior

Holiday season is the best time of the year.

People sharing and caring, loving to give their time and appreciation unto others, even if they don't know them, and best of all, speaking about Christ, who was born to save us from our sins.

How wonderful it is to speak about Jesus all the time, not just at holidays

Among other things, Jesus is the reason for our learning God, and we thank him daily.

> For God did not send his Son into the world to condemn the world, but to save the world through him. (John 3:17)

Seek the Lord

And the Lord answered me, and said, Write the vision, and make it plain upon tables, that he may run that readeth it.

For the vision is yet for an appointed time, but at the end it shall speak, and not lie though it tarry, wait for it; because it will surely come, it will not tarry.

Behold, his soul which is lifted up is not upright in him: but the just shall live by his faith. (Habakkuk 2:2–4)

Seek ye the Lord, all ye meek of the earth, which have wrought his judgment; seek righteousness, seek meekness: it may be ye shall be hid in the day of the Lord's anger. (Zephaniah 2:3)

Be silent before the Sovereign Lord,
for the day of the Lord is near.
The Lord has prepared a sacrifice;
he has consecrated those he has invited.
On the day of the Lord's sacrifice
I will punish the officials
and the king's sons
and all those clad
in foreign clothes.

On that day I will punish
all who avoid stepping on the threshold, [c]
who fill the temple of their gods
with violence and deceit. (Zephaniah 1:7–9)

Separation from God

Who shall separate us from the love of Christ?

Shall tribulation, or distress, or persecution, or famine, or nakedness, or peril, or sword?

As it is written, For thy sake we are killed all day long; we are accounted as sheep for the slaughter.

Nay, in all these things we are more than conquerors through him that loved us.

For I am persuaded, that neither death, nor life, nor angels, nor principalities, nor powers, nor things present, nor things to come, Nor height, nor depth, nor any other creature, shall be able to separate us from the love of God, which is in Christ Jesus our Lord. (Romans 8:35–39)

What has separated you?

As Noah preached in his day, so I now preach to you.

Go to God, obey his word.

Some allow spouses to separate themselves from the love of God.

Men and women, don't let brothers and sisters be separated.

Listen, you are stronger than you think.

So humble yourselves before God. Resist the devil, and he will flee from you. (James 4:7)

Withstand the action or effect. Stand up for yourself.

When you do, the devil will leave you.

But do not invite him back when things get better for your life. Remember your Bible.

> When an evil spirit leaves a person, it goes into the desert, seeking rest but finding none.
>
> Then it says, "I will return to the person I came from."
>
> So, it returns and finds its former home empty, swept, and in order.
>
> Then the spirit finds seven other spirits more evil than itself, and they all enter the person and live there.
>
> And so that person is worse off than before.
>
> That will be the experience of this evil generation. (Matthew 12:43–45)

Don't be a dry-clean Christian.

Come to God with a pure heart.

Say goodbye to witches.

Say goodbye to evil workers.

Say goodbye to wrongdoings.

Go in prayer to Jesus.

You know what you were taught (Matthew 6:33; 1 Peter 5:7; Philippians 4:6–7).

The Holy Spirit told you the word of God.

Read it again.

Get away from things that violate your conscience.

Don't dine with evil workers for advice (Psalm 1:1ff).

God loves you, and so do we (Galatians 6:1ff).

I'm not an old conventional commentary writer.

I see the Word of God as defined by sources other than yourselves.

There are many things by which we can educate ourselves and God's people—in a way other than buying countless copies of commentaries.

References and research are nice, but do not copy other material as if it's your own (1 Peter 2:21).

> You yourselves are our letter, written on our hearts, known and read by everyone. (2 Corinthians 3:2)

Live Jesus (1 Peter 2:21), teach the Word (Mark 16:15; 1 Peter 3:15; John 17:17; Proverbs 30:5–6).

Sermons

What's the big idea?

Sermons are built upon guided principles and general thoughts.

Reading the newspaper. Reading a magazine. Reading a book.

Go to the library, a collective idea method to making delivery and good decisions.

Real-life events by walking in the mall.

Community things.

Seeing a movie.

All the while you are guided by principles and general thoughts.

Make your idea in word picture.

I'm very disappointed when a delivery of sermon has to take too many questions rather than one; thus, the whole of idea is taken up by time, leaving only the point barely to remember.

Make your point, ask your question, amplify your concerns, reinstate your purpose, sit down.

I would suggest that anyone who is to be put public should deliver a message before elders in the church alone.

Short ten to fifteen messages.

This is a trustworthy way to ensure that good conversation has the idea for the church.

Otherwise, more to learn before publishing your mind.

By using current events in your preaching fills the present needs of God's people to perform a better service in him who has called us to purpose in life (Romans 1:17, 15:4).

Howbeit that the sum of us need to support one another in their practices in ministry?

Have kindly affection for one another with brotherly love, in honor preferring one another (Romans 12:10).

It seems as if but a little of people don't really recognize our concerns while on FB.

Servant of God

Forever, O LORD, your word is settled in heaven. (Psalm 119:89)

He sent redemption unto his people: he hath commanded his covenant forever: holy and reverend is his name. (Psalm 111:9)

What is man? A servant and not to be called "Reverend."

Never ever call a man something that God has not approved or appointed in his place.

Never call man "Reverend."

An honest man is blessed in the sight of God. His light shines through the lens of the gospel of God.

For God has given him skills above all else who claim popularity among men.

Pride of men goes to an end.

Serve God

All the work of God is supposed to be put into action by personal contact. Some of which would be by letter. How important is that?

Nobody can be Jesus; it is the Jesus in you, wherefore your body is here to minister you. The body is formed; God made your body to serve him.

Your services to God are when you leave the assembly to go minister to anyone who listens to the Word of God.

Therefore, your eyes, feet, hands, and brain are in your body to minister for Jesus.

You were perfectly made for that purpose, not to worry about another but only yourself. It is a motivating power and a mutual program (1 Corinthians 12:12–18).

Now go do your work. You cannot be arrogant in the body; it can't be at war with one another (Romans 12:3ff), cannot be in disunity. There must be loyalty to the head, Jesus. Is loyalty to each one of you in the body?

Stand strong and sure-footed in the Word of God; "as for me and my house, we shall serve the Lord."

My friends, honor the King, replace bondage with eternal life.

Honor all people, love the brotherhood,
fear God, honor the king. (1 Peter 2:17)

Verse 16 says, "Live in freedom, but do not use your freedom as a cover-up for evil; live as servants of God."

When you join the military, you will go into boot camp; there is a lot of stuff that you're gonna learn. You will have to grasp the information they give you; otherwise, you will not make it in regular service—they will dismiss you in boot camp send you back to where you come from.

Now if you're going to serve, then serve rightfully. They will recommend that you to go to other schools, of your choice, or recommend a school based upon the test results given.

Great place to serve.

All you who want to be soldiers out there, join the military, make it a life to serve for your countrymen; it is a privilege to serve. Given to its citizens.

> No one serving as a soldier gets entangled in civilian affairs, but rather tries to please his commanding officer. (2 Timothy 2:4)

Jesus wants you to do as Paul advised; fight the good fight of faith, take hold of eternal life.

Sociology psychology philosophy teaches us to jive in our day and age as if it were in the days of Jesus and the prophets.

No one lived under a "one-thought society" before the Bible was written today, and even that doesn't jive too well in the religious circle.

Although most will not compromise the Word of God except those of different faiths.

Where there is no psychology, there is no philosophy.

Except for general conversation.

Structure is a must.

Legalism is not a way to start your ministry for those who graduated.

Relax, allow the work to come to you.

Church knows who you are; most people don't mind if you preach a reasonably good sermon for about twenty minutes and sit down.

Others have their part in serving.

Lastly, don't always be seen; allow the work to come to you, and at a reasonable time, share partnership with assigned efforts, then build other things as needed.

But, don't take over; be proactive and build others the same.

If you cannot do simple things, this may not be the profession for you.

Your friends will not help.

But your family will support your efforts in serving.

What made America great in the past doesn't seem to work anymore.

Sharing Jesus

There is much more to be thankful for: Jesus Christ and his crucifixion.

What joy. He is the reason I love my family.

A quick reminder: When we believe joy is achieved, the gospel is sharing Jesus Christ.

We can't all be preachers, but we all can be reachers.

For this reason, man cannot be guilty of treason before the highest court in heaven.

Remember, a prophetic message from God, dual in nature.

> A river of fire was flowing, coming out from before him.
> Thousands upon thousands attended him; ten thousand times ten thousand stood before him.
> The court was seated, and the books were opened. (Daniel 7:10)

It is not too late to begin again.

Talk to Jesus, get into practice by obeying the gospel of God.

> Though I am free of obligation to anyone, I make myself a slave to everyone, to win as many as possible. (1 Corinthians 9:19)

Get to know the Word of God. Obedience is better than sacrifice.

Do it today.

Family is everything; in times of holidays, joy, and peace, it's a place where it fulfills our hearts. A warm feeling of happy memories to share.

Except those who have scattered too far away and are not swayed to return back (a city cannot survive without its people).

Why? Selfishness, covetousness moves others away from the nucleus, and where others have made bad choices in life and are too embarrassed to want to recover.

For this reason, not depending upon Jesus, they refuse to be delivered.

Such a one or more tend to be left behind.

A life without family is a lonely city without people.

What can you do?

If reckless lives desire to serve others who are bound to dysfunctional traits, such a decision desires to have a life being alone.

Have mercy.

No way to think.

Shining Light

Always prove an argument with an intellectual concept.

The property of an argument is arranged (or should be) in a correct grammatically defined order.

Sloppiness is prohibited and proves derangement.

The battle of correctness will succeed, always.

You are my friends, a shining light on a hill for Jesus.

Brightly beam our Father's mercy.

Amen.

Behind the story of Herod, "the Great," or Herod, "the Impious."

> King Herod was known to the Romans as "the Great," but in the eyes of the people over whom he ruled he was always known as "the Impious," despite his costly restoration of the Temple in Jerusalem. Herod was a Roman citizen, Governor of Galilee by 47 BC, and then King of Judea from 37 to 4 BC.
>
> He was one of the major figures in politics of Palestine in the early years of the Roman Empire.
>
> In 7 BC he strangled to death two of his sons, Aristobulus and Alexander, drawing a comment from Roman Emperor Augustus (27 BC–14 AD) that it was safer to be one of Herod's pigs than one of his sons.
>
> Another son was later born to Herod and, for his safety, his mother dispatched him to

the care of her family in Ariminum, a city near Ravenna in northern Italy.

He was Prince Joseph, the Joseph of Arimathea in the Gospels, and he later became the unseen power behind his father's throne.

Are there more Herods out there in the world, who have taken up a bit more of the original Herod's acts?

Having a working body by the Word of God and not from a nepotistic idea.

Making the church work the way it was intended to be.

Megachurch is all right; the church at Pentecostal was about three thousand plus who were saved.

Missionaries came out of that group; teachers were made, preachers and deacons, among the greater honor given to God, except that of Ananias and Sapphira.

The Word is spread, souls are saved, yet mankind wants to have a small group, and not sharing the responsibility among others today.

Example: In an automobile (I'm sure most have or a bicycle, skateboard, etc.), all parts must work together; otherwise, you will call upon a mechanic.

Let's say that you are the mechanic in the business of church administration.

What will you do, how would you help all parts to work together for the administration of the church?

Paul said, "Now I want you to know that if you are led by God's Spirit, you will say that Jesus is Lord, and you will never curse Jesus" (1 Corinthians 12:3).

Listen.

> There are different kinds of spiritual gifts, but they all come from the same Spirit.
> There are different ways to serve the same Lord, and we can each do different things.
> Yet the same God works in all of us and helps us in everything we do.

> The Spirit has given each of us a special way of serving others.
>
> Some of us can speak with wisdom, while others can speak with knowledge, but these gifts come from the same Spirit. (1 Corinthians 12:4–8)

(Some of us, not to say the same person, does the same things all the time.) Are you getting this!

When you—a preacher, a teacher, or any member—do not submit to the Word of God, you have blasphemed against it in an operative or implicit way.

Foolishness does not belong to any leader who is selfishly driven. The Bible says it explicitly, and not to taken as an experiment. Listen your Bibles.

> From whom the whole body fitly joined together and compacted by that which every joint supplieth, according to the effectual working in the measure of every part, maketh increase of the body unto the edifying of itself in love. (Ephesians 4:16)

To know things about your automobile, if one part is not working in your engine, it will affect other parts.

The function must come together for things to have a smooth transition.

A crippled engine makes noise and has no complete continuity. Paul speaks.

> Though I speak with the tongues of men and of angels, and have not charity, I am become as sounding brass, or a tinkling cymbal.
>
> And though I have the gift of prophecy, and understand all mysteries, and all knowledge; and

though I have all faith, so that I could remove mountains, and have not charity, I am nothing.

And though I bestow all my goods to feed the poor, and though I give my body to be burned, and have not charity, it profiteth me nothing. (1 Corinthians 13:1–3)

First Corinthians 3:13 indicates all work will be shown for what it is, because the day will bring it to light.

It will be revealed with fire, and the fire will test the quality of each person's work.

Echo chambers of negativity is an effect or effected to be by some.

"Don't let the green grass fool ya."

A song back in the days.

This today may be an important message to you.

When you have members who put down God's members in the house of God, so shall the sum of its members; my friends, it is time for change.

Why?

Because influences are not of God but the agents of falling angels against God; and after one has been taught the way of righteousness and turn his back against the written word, he will eventually cause damages to the whole body.

Simply get rid of the lump.

First Peter 4:17 says, "For the time is come that judgment must begin at the house of God: and if it first begin at us, what shall the end be of them that obey not the gospel of God?"

What else?

Many people don't take backbiting and gossip seriously.

Some quickly recognize stealing, anger, and jealousy as sins, but often don't consider that it is also a sin to gossip and backbite.

Listen to your Bibles.

But shun profane and idle babblings, for they will increase to more ungodliness. And

their message will spread like cancer. (2 Timothy
2:16–17)

Now listen.

Folks in the church will often speak a good word but talk down on other members behind their backs.

The echo chamber becomes extremely important to backbiters. Satan is all about division.

He enjoys any opportunity he gets to break down brotherhood and unity; it is incredible what gossip and backbiting can tear down.

> A whisperer separates the best of friends.
> (Proverbs 16:28)

Sin

God has no time in criticizing you when you have wronged yourself.

Therefore, to anyone who knows the right thing to do and does not do it, to himself, it is sin (James 4:17). If you die in your sin, you have placed judgment upon yourself (Hebrews 9:27).

Apart from the righteousness of God, it is your shame.

It is deeply a shame.

> It would have been better for them not to have known the way of righteousness, than to have known it and then to turn their backs on the sacred command that was passed on to them. (2 Peter 2:21)

Why? Because you decided to crucify Christ all over and out him to open shame, to which you have no feelings of his mission to save you, so what matters to you is nothing.

What a shame.

God has commanded righteousness in your favor, but if you have turned your back against the grace of God to serve your own selfish desires, my friends, you judge your own life.

Read Luke 16:19–31.

Touch somebody today and tell them "I love you."

Don't drag your feet in serving God.

Listen to your Bibles.

> Stand firm then, with the belt of truth fastened around your waist, with the breastplate of righteousness arrayed, and with your feet fitted with the readiness of the gospel of peace.

In addition to all this, take up the shield of faith, with which you can extinguish all the flaming arrows of the evil one. (Ephesians 6:14–16)

How beautiful upon the mountains are the feet of him that bringeth good tidings, that publisheth peace; that bringeth good tidings of good, that publisheth salvation; that saith unto Zion, Thy God reigneth! (Isaiah 52:7)

The sins of some are obvious, reaching the place of judgment ahead of them; the sins of others trail behind them. (1 Timothy 5:24)

This is simply called a dent within the characters of sinners' population.

He who sins is of the devil, for the devil has sinned from the beginning. For this purpose, the Son of God was manifested, that He might destroy the works of the devil. (1 John 3:8)

So how can you hate your brother?
By committing sins and disassociating himself from God.

Anyone who claims to be in the light but hates a brother or sister is still in the darkness.
Anyone who loves their brother and sister lives in the light, and there is nothing in them to make them stumble. (1 John 2:9–10)

Listen to your Bible.

If we say we have no sin, we deceive ourselves, and the truth is not in us. (1 John 1:8)

> If we say we have fellowship with Him yet walk in the darkness, we lie and do not practice the truth. (v. 6)

> But if we walk in the light as He is in the light, we have fellowship with one another, and the blood of Jesus His Son cleanses us from all sin. (v. 7)

The decision is ours to make.

Don't give opportunity to the devil (Ephesians 4:27).

Temptations come when a condemned fool mocks your past sins.

Don't fret about that; God will judge everyone of corrupt minds.

Live and forget about inconsistencies of those accusers at large against God's elect.

> To those who by perseverance in good works seek glory and honor and immortality (God will give) everlasting life. (Romans 2:7)

Redemption is important and not impossible.

I came from a discussion because certain brethren could not defend their position on what inherent sin is or where it came from.

I wish such would go read 1 Peter 3:15, then return to the table of reasoning.

They said a child is not born in sin.

My position is that a child has no knowledge of sin until he is convicted.

Now if our brethren were to know anything about debates, then don't state your proposition if you cannot defend your own mind.

Children are naturally born with similar things associated with sin but have no knowledge of its existence. Therefore, they cannot be called a transgressor.

Such as covetousness and "tantrum, temper tantrum, or hissy fit is an emotional outburst, usually associated with those in emotional distress, that is typically characterized by stubbornness, crying, screaming, violence, defiance, angry ranting, a resistance to attempts at pacification, and, in some cases, hitting, and other physically violent behavior. Physical control may be lost; the person may be unable to remain still; and even if the "goal" of the person is met, they may not be calmed."

Now, my friends, if you think by reading other common commenters you find your answers other than the word picture from your own Bibles, you have to know that David from Psalm 58 and 51 is not talking in figurative language to his son or his own people of God.

> The Bible teaches that we are all born sinners with sinful, selfish natures. Unless we are born again by the Spirit of God, we will never see the kingdom of God. John 3:3.
>
> Furthermore, we are born with a sinful nature, and we inherited it from Adam.
>
> "Sin entered the world through one man, and death through sin, and in this way, death came to all people" Romans 5:12.
>
> Every one of us was affected by Adam's sin; there are no exceptions. "One trespass resulted in condemnation for all people" verse 18. (Christian Marcel)

So a message to those brethren: when is a child lost?

Until you say he is lost? When is that?

I say that any infant child born at such ages without understanding is not subject to transgressions under the law.

I'm in support of our people, but I will not condone their walks of life where sin is a lifestyle.

It doesn't matter how famous one has become.

Sin is a transgression of the law of Christ.

Righteous change is indeed necessary until the day of your redemption.

Otherwise, what am I glad for (2 Corinthians 7:14)?

> Whosoever commits sin transgress' also the law: for sin is the transgression of the law.
> And ye know that he was manifested to take away our sins; and in him is no sin.
> Whosoever is born of God doth not commit sin; for his seed remaineth in him: and he cannot sin, because he is born of God. (1 John 3:4, 5, and 9)

Nothing wrong with being famous for singing, dancing, or other extraordinary talent or gifts.

But if it leads to sin, don't do it.

Sin is not in every profession, talent, or gifts one has.

Especially knowing your Bible.

Not necessarily mastering it, but to know the will of God.

Not all are teachers, preachers, or evangelists, but we all can be servants.

First Corinthians 12 explains it all.

Read it.

Now listen any of you who have forgotten God.

One cannot do all kinds of sins in their lives; then when some bad thing happens in your life, you ask God for deliverance.

Not going to happen.

Perhaps someone else might have helped you get over your sin, but it wasn't God in heaven.

Some have said,

> "The LORD isn't looking," they say, "and besides, the God of Israel doesn't care." (Psalm 94:7)

Get it right, or God will turn away from you (Isaiah 59:1–2).

> The LORD is far from the wicked, but he hears the prayer of the righteous. (Proverbs 15:29)

He heareth the prayer of the righteous. For
they desire above all things to do His will, and
so their petitions to this effect are heard by Him.

Many are taught good table manners at home, use your skills.
Basic skills are unlimited in our active participating lives.
Best efforts are growing concerns in a regular basis.
There is sin leading to death, and that would be an unrepentant
sin.

There is a sin not leading to death; that would be a repented sin.

You cannot go on, for example, hating a brother or sister, gossiping, showing no change in behavior or practices from which a
heart has no godly sorrow (2 Corinthians 7:10).

We must remember Galatians 6:1 in response to any denominational problem so that we see an opportunity to set straight expectations that we are called to do (2 Corinthians 2:15).

People who are guided by the Spirit can make judgments, but
they cannot be judged by others (who are not spiritual).

We, belonging to Christ, do the things that are spiritual.

Sin Not

When someone throws rocks into your yard too many times, and it gets your full attention, and you act upon it, don't get mad, my friends, from the acts of criticism from others, be Christlike and humble.

Above all, be upset with the rock thrower and not the action of the criticism.

> Be ye angry, and sin not: let not the sun go down upon your wrath. (Ephesians 4:26)

> Do not take revenge, my dear friends, but leave room for God's wrath, for it is written: "It is mine to avenge; I will repay," says the Lord. (Romans 12:19)

Sing

In your private lives, sing joyfully unto God, for he is the father of all and maker of all that lives.

> Sing joyfully to the Lord, you righteous;
> it is fitting for the upright to praise him.
> Praise the Lord with the harp;
> make music to him on the ten-stringed lyre.
> Sing to him a new song;
> play skillfully, and shout for joy.
> For the word of the Lord is right and true;
> he is faithful in all he does.
> The Lord loves righteousness and justice;
> the earth is full of his unfailing love. (Psalm
>   33:1–5)

Read Romans 15:4.

Jesus never taught using instruments of music when He walked the earth.

Jesus taught about behavior practices. And the law (Matthew 5:17).

The Holy Spirit told us we should sing and make melody in our hearts to the Lord (Ephesians 5:19).

It was written by one of the apostles who were chosen to carry the truth.

It was Paul.

> For the prophecy came not in old time by
> the will of man: but holy men of God spake as

they were moved by the Holy Ghost. (2 Peter 1:21)

Now this is the comforter Jesus said that was coming who will teach us in all truth (John 14:16).

Anything else is blaspheming against the Holy Spirit. That was not authorized by the Holy Spirit.

The unpardonable sin is blasphemy against the Holy Spirit.

Blasphemy includes ridicule and attributing the works of the Holy Spirit to the devil.

Remember this?

> The situation was that the Pharisees were eyewitnesses to Jesus' miracles, but they attributed the work of the Holy Spirit to the presence of a demon (Mark 3:22–30).

Stop listening to unproven things that are not supported by evidences; rather, listen to facts that are supported by evidences.

The Word of God.

When you attend church on Sunday, be sure to tell God in prayer that you love him.

While at church in the presence of many witnesses.

Refer to Romans 12:10.

> In honour preferring one another; saints should think honourably of one another, and entertain an honourable esteem of each other; yea, should esteem each other better thou themselves; and not indulge evil surmises, and groundless jealousies of one another, which is contrary to that love that thinks no evil.

We all share in honor toward one another, but where a gift shall apply, work is needed.

> If one part suffers, every part suffers with it;
> if one part is honored, every part rejoices with it.
> (1 Corinthians 12:26)

Have you ever thought about how the Scriptures make plain sense for all our every need?

Let me give you an example.

Just one.

I got a pneumonia shot in my arm the other day, and after I got it, my arm started to hurt, then my whole body started feeling pain, because of the pain in my arm. I felt bad for a little while, didn't eat much, lay down much of the time. My arm was really sore.

Just one shot affected my whole body; every joint suffered, felt sore.

Sometime later after taking Tylenol for a couple of days, things began to get better.

This simple example should teach us how things work in the body of Christ.

At times, the body of Christ gets a little sore and needs others to care.

So in Christ, we, though many, form one body, and each member belongs to all the others (Romans 12:5).

Romans 12:15 says this: "Rejoice with them that do rejoice, and weep with them that weep."

> I have labored and toiled and have often gone without sleep; I have known hunger and thirst and have often gone without food; I have been cold and naked.
>
> Beside those things that are without, that which cometh upon me daily, the care of all the churches. (2 Corinthians 11:27, 28)

> Bear ye one another's burdens, and so fulfil
> the law of Christ. (Galatians 6:2)

Some people want to live like hypocrites and walk like Christians on Sunday.

> In brief, Diotrephes was a self-seeking trou-
> blemaker in an unnamed local church in the first
> century.
> We know nothing of his background, other
> than he was "probably a Gentile."

In my strict opinion, having a Gentile name does not necessarily mean his name warrants but a common name, as of today.

His name means "nurtured by Jupiter." It was also a Zeus name to which both Jewish and Gentiles use, meaning Jupiter (Latin: *Iuppiter*) is the king of the gods in Roman mythology.

He was the god of the sky and thunder.

He is known as Zeus in Greek mythology.

John wrote to his friend Gaius.

The passage mentioning Diotrephes: "I wrote to the church, but Diotrephes, who loves to be first, will not welcome us." (Was Diotrephes a Jew or Gentile?)

> So, when I come, I will call attention to
> what he is doing, spreading malicious nonsense
> about us.

Is John given a note about Diotrephes's attitude?

> Not satisfied with that, he even refuses to
> welcome other believers.
> He also stops those who want to do so and
> puts them out of the church. (3 John 1:9–10)

For what reason?

In these two verses; we have the following statements made about Diotrephes: "loves to be first."

It is to my knowledge, possible that Diotrephes was Jewish and didn't want to have fellowship with pagans.

Not yet proven but emphasizes how important this is today.

Diotrephes is in almost every work today.

Research shows but little evidence in his history.

However, the actions of most Jewish behaviors continue.

Read Romans 9:1–24, 2:21.

Wherever Althea and I attend church, it is important to us.

Being united with our brethren.

Bless the Lord at all times.

Memorize these verses, keep them near to thy heart.

> I will bless the Lord at all times: his praise shall continually be in my mouth.
>
> My soul shall make her boast in the Lord: the humble shall hear thereof and be glad.
>
> O magnify the Lord with me and let us exalt his name together.
>
> I sought the Lord, and he heard me, and delivered me from all my fears. (Psalm 34:1–4)

Read Acts 17:11.

> The Greek word used in Acts is (eugen/este/roi) eugenesteroi, which comes from eugenes, from which we derive the personal name "Eugene."
>
> Originally, it meant "wellborn" and implied nobility.
>
> Later, it described those of a generous spirit, who are open-minded toward truth, not prejudiced, hostile or suspicious of others, but give others a fair hearing.

The Bereans are considered as noble because they listened to the preaching of the gospel with open hearts as they pursued God and His whole truth.

Greek meaning is where it starts.
Pay attention to the endings.

Singing

Okay, let's talk about singing.

First of all, humming is not singing; no one hums into a microphone. Sometimes it is known that one may sing in the shower or hallways—even carpenters sing.

Why don't you?

Songs that you sing should be married to the music and rhythm for it to sound pleasant.

Speak out with it (Ephesians 5:19); teach it (Colossians 3:16); write it in your heart (Hebrews 13:15).

Practice it at home.

Remember, homework is good.

Record a song using the microphone of the voice recorder application on your smartphone or laptop and hear yourself.

This will tell you how far you've improved and what you have to work on.

If you can't do it yourself, get help with your tone and range.

Why have man change the Word of God concerning singing, and why are they using mechanical instruments of music, whereas less people are singing, to which they develop choirs to entertain their congregation, plus change the hymns to contemporary-style music?

Why?

Read Ephesians 5:19.

> Let the word of Christ dwell in you richly
> in all wisdom; teaching and admonishing one
> another in psalms and hymns and spiritual songs,

singing with grace in your hearts to the Lord.
(Colossians 3:16)

The scriptures say nothing about a choir and additional groups apart from congregation commands to sing alone.

Sing means sing, not playing drums, guitars, piano, bass guitars.

What has man done?

Don't fall into a trap to overlook God's commands to sing.

Never.

Change back.

People will do anything to entertain themselves in the Lord's house and call it a necessity.

However, God is not reduced to their level of knowledge.

Rather our Creator is greater than us.

Jesus said, "Why do you call me, 'Lord, Lord,' and do not do what I say?" (Luke 6:46).

Sometimes things are hard to trust, particularly when your thoughts are managed in your subconscious.

Who else knows the mind of man except God and himself?

The liberal soul shall be made fat: and
he that watereth shall be watered also himself.
(Proverbs 11:25)

Remember your home, because your days are without understanding.

Thanks to mothers.

Examples include singing.

We know the words so well that we can sing them without thinking about them, and we do.

If we were pressed to actually think about some of what we sing and explain the meaning of the words, we may be at a loss.

James wrote, "My brethren, these things ought not be so" (James 3:10b). Like Paul, we ought to "sing with the understanding" of what we are singing (1 Corinthians 14:15).

How can we effectively "teach and admonish one another" if we do not understand what we are saying through our singing to one another (Colossians 3:16)?

So how do we develop the understanding we need?

We can begin by examining the context and listening.

Did you hear your mother?

Remember what she said.

Honor your freedom that you have in Christ.

Thank you, Mother.

Sinner

My friends, I can pick up the same Bible, the Word of God in written form, unaltered, and read it the same as others who study (2 Timothy 2:15); so how can you who don't study can come to a different conclusion other than what has been written?

Answer: you cannot, because there is a self-sufficient understanding by others who don't believe and trust.

Look now again.

You can't make yourself a man or woman if you weren't created that way.

If a child acts soft like a girl, then you have made that choice for that child by fixing their hair to look like a girl and buying him clothes, psychologically driven by your desires to have a girl in your Paradox defects.

This is not the way you train up a child in the Lord.

Creating belongs to God and fixed so that his creation is by divine authority.

Now if you change divine design authority, given by God, and you desire your daughter to do manly things by dressing her up to be a boy, to perform the same, you have changed the design God has made in that child's life.

A girl is designed to become a woman and not a man, and vice versa.

Men are not women.

So, keep the order the same as God has created.

Now listen.

Thus, she will probably not have children or the man to have children.

But if she or he adopts a child by other means, it is not designed the way that God has for the family.

Two women and one acting like a man so that a child will call her daddy is a lie. Vice versa for men too.

Parents who change the pattern set from God have offered a lie (John 8:44) to the whole world to accept.

My friends, you are not God or the Creator of mankind, so in order to do the will of God, it must be the design the way God has made it to be.

You remember how gays and lesbians and queers marched in a parade in San Francisco to prove equal rights with normal people who don't share their mental health issues.

Nothing but the devil's people doing the work of Satan, whose church location is in San Francisco.

Started 1979.

Who wears colored hair, with exotic looks, makeup in abnormal fashion, tattoos, nasty attire and call themselves normal people?

These devices they use are of the devil, whose misdeeds don't fit in normal, everyday lives of our citizens.

Look, normal people are not deranged.

The devil wants to look like himself, and perhaps some are wanting to look just like the devil.

Playing in the fires of hell.

Stay there, and you willingly will get there (John 8:44).

> History reveals that, the First Satanic Church is an organization founded by Karla LaVey on October 31, 1997 in San Francisco, California, that is dedicated to LaVeyan Satanism as codified by Anton LaVey in The Satanic Bible.

My friends, find Jesus.

Listen to salvation; it brought deliverance and comfort to all who will believe and trust.

Are you with me?

Read Matthew 11:28, Titus 2:11, John 6:47, and John 3:15.

Sins

Look now.

Gays, lesbians, homosexuals, and queers.

If you believe in the written word of God, the same Word as all who reads, it is wrong to live and practice such acts as you do.

And if you don't change your ways from unrighteousness, you are going to be burned in the fires of hell.

God in heaven says so.

You who have left the Word of God to suit your own lifestyle, you are blind guides, fools, and hypocrites who are worse than those who never knew God (2 Peter 2:20).

Listen.

> But as for the cowardly, the faithless, the detestable, as for murderers, the sexually immoral, sorcerers, idolaters, and all liars, their portion will be in the lake that burns with fire and sulfur, which is the second death. (Revelation 21:8)

Wait, there's more to read.

> Do you not know that the wicked will not inherit the kingdom of God?
> Do not be deceived:
> Neither the sexually immoral, nor idolaters, nor adulterers, nor men who submit to or perform homosexual acts. (1 Corinthians 6:9)

> The acts of the flesh are obvious: sexual immorality, impurity, and debauchery. (Galatians 5:19)

Now go read it, repent, and get saved; change your lifestyle.

The man and the woman are partners in exercising dominion over God's creation.

Anything else is not of God.

> For this reason, God gave them over to dishonorable passions.
>
> Even their women exchanged natural relations for unnatural ones.
>
> Likewise, the men abandoned natural relations with women and burned with lust for one another.
>
> Men committed indecent acts with other men and received in themselves the due penalty for their error.
>
> Furthermore, since they did not see fit to acknowledge God, He gave them up to a depraved mind, to do what ought not to be done. (Romans 1:26–28)

Now, if you serve the God in heaven, one cannot build a different way against God.

Unless you serve a god from hell, the devil.

Jesus says the Father's son spoke these words: "I am he that lives, and was dead; and, behold, I am alive for ever more, amen; and have the keys of hell and of death" (Revelation 1:18)

Read Hebrews 1:2ff.

Listen, one last thing.

If you are going to hell, then don't expect to change (John 12:48).

As for me and my house, we shall serve the Lord God in heaven.

Soldier for God

The mind is strengthened when you read and understand more of the Word of God (Ephesians 4:23).

Let the Spirit renew your thoughts and attitudes.

> Do not be conformed to this world but be transformed by the renewing of your mind. Then you will be able to discern what is the good, pleasing, and perfect will of God. (Romans 12:2)

Are you with me?

Know how far you want to go in the Word of God.

Know it and tell it wherever you go.

Be a strong soldier for God.

Just do it.

How much do you love Jesus to care to know more of his divine purpose on earth?

Jesus was God in the flesh (John 1:14).

Now he's not in the flesh, no longer, only for a time to redeem mankind.

> The Son is the radiance of God's glory and the exact representation of his being, sustaining all things by his powerful word.
>
> After he had provided purification for sins, he sat down at the right hand of the Majesty in heaven. (Hebrews 1:3)

> Who gave himself for us, that he might redeem us from all iniquity, and purify unto himself a peculiar people, zealous of good works? (Titus 2:14)

In prophecy, Jesus said,

> My life is poured out like water, and all My bones are out of joint.
> My heart is like wax, melting within Me.
> My strength has dried up like sunbaked clay.
> My tongue sticks to the roof of My mouth.
> You have laid Me in the dust and left Me for dead. My enemies surround Me like a pack of dogs; an evil gang closes in on Me.
> They have pierced My hands and feet. (Psalm 22:14–16)

But Christ has rescued us from the curse pronounced by the law. When he was hung on the cross, he took upon himself the curse for our wrongdoing. For it is written in the Scriptures, "Cursed is everyone who is hung on a tree" (Galatians 3:13).

Listen carefully: Jesus can appear at any time or place as we wish.

God can present himself as he was willing after his resurrection to prove to the unbeliever that it was he that was crucified.

There are many reliable proofs.

> After that, he was seen by more than 500 of his followers at one time, most of whom are still alive, though some have died. (1 Corinthians 15:6)

> "Why are you troubled," Jesus asked, "and why do doubts arise in your hearts?
> Look at My hands and My feet. It is I Myself.

Touch Me and see—for a spirit does not have flesh and bones, as you see I have." And when He had said this, He showed them His hands and feet. (Luke 24:38–40)

God can appear in different forms.
Why?
Because he can.
I think we all agree that angels can appear looking like human beings.

Do not forget to entertain strangers, for by so doing some have unwittingly entertained angels. (Hebrews 13:2)

So, the question comes: "Does God appear in various forms?"
He appeared in another form to two of them as they walked and went into the country (Mark 16:12).

Now when she [Mary Magdalene] had said this, she turned around and saw Jesus standing there, and did not know that it was Jesus. (John 20:14)

Here are some ways God chose to appear (as written in Scripture).

I. As the angel of the Lord
   A. To Hagar

Then the Angel of the LORD said to her, "I will multiply your descendants exceedingly, so that they shall not be counted for multitude." (Genesis 16:10; also see Genesis 16:7–11, 21:17)

B. To Jacob

Then the Angel of God spoke to me [Jacob] in a dream, saying, "Jacob." And I said, "Here I am." (Genesis 31:11)

C. To Moses

And the Angel of the LORD appeared to him [Moses] in a flame of fire flame midst of a bush.

So, he looked, and behold, the bush was burning with fire, but the bush was not consumed. (Exodus 3:2)

D. To the Camp of Israel

And the Angel of God, who went before the camp of Israel, moved and went behind them; and the pillar of cloud went from before them and stood behind them. (Exodus 14:19)

E. Other Examples

1. Balaam and the donkey (Numbers 22:22–27, 31–35)
2. All the children of Israel (Judges 2:1, 4)
3. Gideon (Judges 6:11–12, 20–22)
4. Manoah and his wife (Judges 13:3, 6, 9, 13, 15–18, 20–21)
5. Zechariah 1:11–12; 3:1, 5–6; 12:8

Songs

I've got the love of Jesus Christ my savior down in my heart.

I've got the wonderful love of my blessed redeemer way down in the depths of my heart.

And if the devil doesn't like it, he can sit on a tack, ouch,

sit on a tack,

ouch sits on a tack.

I've got the love of Jesus, love of Jesus down in my heart.

Can you sing "I Really Love the Lord"?

I will sing the wondrous story.
Of the Christ who died for me
Sing it with the saints in glory,
Gathered by the Crystal Sea!

"Blessed assurance, Jesus is mine."

Who will follow Jesus, who will make reply?
I am on the Lord's side, Master here am I.

Speech

Some music is all right to listen to, as long as it isn't in dirty languages.

Just like speech.

> Let your conversation be always full of grace, seasoned with salt, so that you may know how to answer everyone. (Colossians 4:6)

> Allow perseverance to finish its work, so that you may be mature and complete, not lacking anything. (James 1:4)

> All of us who are mature should embrace this point of view. And if you think differently about some issue, God will reveal this to you as well. (Philippians 3:15)

Stay strong in the Lord, forgetting nothing.

> Finally, be strong in the Lord and in his mighty power. (Ephesians 6:10)

> I press on toward the goal to win the prize for which God has called me heavenward in Christ Jesus. (v. 14)

Spirit of God

There are some who will never be spoken of because they are but a hot mess.

Unspiritual in mind and character (1 John 4:1).

Codependence and interdependence.

Without being selfish works together, rather than withhold your grace in a relationship.

Family members at times tend to withhold their rights to dinner rather than share the bill.

If then Jesus teaches us how to rediscover ourselves, why the old man under the new beginning?

Such man is needed to change.

Listen, some folks are referring to the church belonging to Christ as a cult (Matthew 16:18).

Where on earth did they get such idea? Only one answer: the devil!

Study your Bible (2 Timothy 2:15) and be ye filled with the spirit of God (Ephesians 5:18).

Remember the devil is trouble (John 8:44).

But being filled with the spirit of God means, basically, having great joy in God.

And since the Bible teaches that "the joy of the Lord is our strength" (Nehemiah 8:10), it also means there will be power in this joy for overcoming besetting sins and for boldness in being a witness.

Having an astute mind—that means "having or showing shrewdness and an ability to notice and understand things clearly: mentally sharp or clever."

God's word is not earthly but heavenly (Matthew 24:35).

Jesus says this.

> So is my word that goes out from my mouth: It will not return to me empty, but will accomplish what I desire and achieve the purpose for which I sent it. (Isaiah 55:11)

Don't talk to anyone who says that the Holy Spirit does not dwell in you or influences your heart.

Why?

Because such a person is not of God.

Remember that.

It took years for people to study and learn that commentaries were wrong in their thinking because others were disputing denominational folks, and they were laughing at those who were telling folks in their groups the Holy Spirit did not.

Watch your sources.

The Bible is absolutely clear.

Jesus said in the first century as I so now say, "Do not suppose that I have come to bring peace to the earth. I did not come to bring peace, but a sword" (Matthew 10:34).

> Take the helmet of salvation and the sword of the Spirit, which is the word of God. (Ephesians 6:17)

Stop, look, and listen to your heart in what it is saying.

> And I will give them a heart to know me, that I am the LORD: and they shall be my people, and I will be their God: for they shall return unto me with their whole heart. (Jeremiah 24:7 KJV)

Yes, the Lord speaks to our hearts today.

The Greek word translated here "counselor" means "one who is called alongside" and has the idea of someone who encourages and exhorts. The Holy Spirit takes up permanent residence in the hearts of believers (Romans 8:9; 1 Corinthians 6:19–20, 12:13).

> But you are not controlled by your sinful nature. You are controlled by the Spirit if you have the Spirit of God living in you. And remember that those who do not have the Spirit of Christ living in them do not belong to him at all. (Romans 8:9)

> Do you not know that your bodies are temples of the Holy Spirit, who is in you, whom you have received from God? You are not your own; you were bought at a price. Therefore, honor God with your bodies. (1 Corinthians 6:19–20)

Spiritual Partnership

Matthew 10:33 is often repeated.

> But whoever disowns me before others, I
> will disown before my Father in heaven.

Sad to say that many people are obvious to deny Christ.

If Jesus asks of you to acknowledge him, how many would raise their hands for Jesus?

Don't let the world, who favors other religious entities, frighten you from Jesus.

> His neighbors and those who had formerly
> seen him begging asked, "Isn't this the same man
> who used to sit and beg?"
>
> Some claimed that he was.
>
> Others said, "No, he only looks like him."
>
> But he himself insisted, "I am the man."
>
> "How then were your eyes opened?" they
> asked.
>
> He replied, "The man they call Jesus made
> some mud and put it on my eyes. He told me to
> go to Siloam and wash. So, I went and washed,
> and then I could see."
>
> "Where is this man?" they asked him.
>
> "I don't know," he said. (John 9:8–12)
>
> His parents said this because they were afraid
> of the Jewish leaders, who already had decided

that anyone who acknowledged that Jesus was the Messiah would be put out of the synagogue.

That was why his parents said, "He is of age; ask him." (vv. 22–23)

Some folks are afraid to testify for Jesus.

Will you today?

Ever man or woman should be proud of what they have and how they arrived at their own conclusion.

Separation of church and state; the government writes sin and good in the same law.

Allowing both to exist on the same books.

Not so with God—there are two books.

What's your story?

How did you meet God?

When and where?

Time and place.

Were you lying on your bed thinking about why you haven't been attending church? Or who God really was and how to meet him?

I mean, what's your story?

Can you think about how you met him but then turned loose of his hands?

What's your story?

Everyone has a quick story about how they came to know God but might have decided not to pursue him; perhaps they were afraid or didn't want to give up on how there were living. A religion or relationship with God is too much, and then you blame God's people for not following him.

Did you think that God is fashioning his people and that he is the potter and you are the clay?

Well, if you haven't been that far in your thinking, God makes us, and that might take some time.

Get to know God; focus your attention on him and not on everything else (Romans 12).

Stand Firm

Listen, you who believe in worldly lifestyles.
For such are haters of God and his creation as defined.
Don't get caught in your sins.
Listen.

> Backbiters, haters of God, despiteful, proud, boasters, inventors of evil things, disobedient to parents, (those who disregard godliness that is taught in homes)
> Without understanding, covenant breakers, without natural affection, implacable, unmerciful:
> Who knowing the judgment of God, that they which commit such things are worthy of death, not only do the same, but have pleasure in them that do them? (Romans 1:30–32)

Other things that matter.

> He that deviseth to do evil shall be called a mischievous person. (Proverbs 24:8)

> For I fear, lest, when I come, I shall not find you such as I would, and that I shall be found unto you such as ye would not: lest there be debates, envying's, wraths, strife's, backbiting's, whisperings, swellings, tumults. (2 Corinthians 12:20)

For men shall be lovers of their own selves, covetous, boasters, proud, blasphemers, disobedient to parents, unthankful, unholy (who never wanted instructions from the Lord [Ephesians 6:1]). (2 Timothy 3:2)

Anyone who has family members who despise the work you do are full of themselves, don't go to church, but show up once or twice to be seen, who lie to others about your love for God (Job 1ff).

Simply because they want to be recognized by their foolishness and self-desires; such who do are undeserving and has no part in the kingdom of God, because they practice unrighteous behaviors and without understanding.

World servers and not God serving.

Turn away your ears from such who are but blasphemers of God's creation (Isaiah 44:18).

Study

If you want to be in church, get there; all that's required is that you obey the Word of God.

But if you run to some other place that doesn't teach you what you should know.

That's called a wrong place.

Listen, if you read or study for yourself the Word of God, and you or your preacher or teacher omits what you should know, what they or you have decided on doesn't matter.

Are you listening (John 12:48)?

The Bible says.

> For the time will come when they will not endure sound doctrine; but after their own lusts shall they heap to themselves teachers, having itching ears;
> And they shall turn away their ears from the truth and shall be turned unto fables. (2 Timothy 4:3–4)

Be sure that you are in the right place.

Acts 4:12, says, "Salvation is found in no one else, for there is no other name under heaven given to mankind by which we must be saved."

Peter is right: only one place, not many.

> Because strait is the gate, and narrow is the way, which leadeth unto life, and few there be that find it. (Matthew 7:14)

> Enter ye in at the strait gate: for wide is
> the gate, and broad is the way, that leadeth to
> destruction, and many there be which go in there
> at. (v. 13)

There are some who prefer to go to a group where they can feel something.

Or perhaps run and jump up and down.

Some even take their clothes off while sitting in a chair.

They like noises and hollering and speaking as if they know a different language, then call it in an unknown tongue.

Ask yourself a question: Did Jesus ever walk this earth practicing noises, unknown languages, or hollering?

The answer is no.

Apostle Paul corrected people at Corinth who stepped out of line defending their own way of doing.

Today we see folks copying same things after Paul corrected their acts (1 Corinthians 12, 13, 14).

They were completely wrong.

This is called mockery.

> Be not deceived; God is not mocked: for
> whatsoever a man soweth, that shall he also reap.
> (Galatians 6:7)

My friends, do it God's way and don't allow yourself to follow them that know not.

Best to consider 2 Timothy 2:15.

Don't let the devil tell you that you can't be faithful to the Lord because of all the stuff going on in the world today.

Remember this: John 8:44.

Don't forget Jesus made a promise to you (John 14:1–3).

How about you?

Instructors don't let people of ignorance lead you to quit your jobs.

Because there are three more buses that will ambush you if you quit.

Stand firm in the Word and always be ready to know or not know how to answer every man.

Whatever you do, if you don't know the answer, go study the question before giving an answer.

Never leave an open door. Get back to the question for answering; otherwise, you didn't intend to see an answer to their question anyways. Being proactive is possible when in the habit thereof.

Write the questions down, make note of it; furthermore, don't pretend to know what one does not know.

Keep it real.

What does the law of liberty in the Bible mean (James 1:25)?

It is very important that we leave commentaries to mouths alone in some cases (you might pick up the wrong writings) but to study the Word of God in its written form and not to give things by which others have systematically placed in a form to persuade your mind (some writers are good and follow the Bible in what it says).

Remember, not everyone is a "Do you understand what thou readeth?" person.

History and psychology goes without question, where philosophy questions thoughts that have been taught without findings.

Where the sum total has placed findings to be left alone, and with an introduction of a normalcy of systematic writings put before us, man follows what looks good, sounds good by prolific writers of times past who are not considered our forefathers. But rather writers in generational circles and times to their full understanding and research.

Today the church is much largely structured in doctrine, and proofs and findings are widely accepted and considered.

When mankind back themselves into a wall, such become tinted and out of care and decency to the work order of the Scriptures.

We have become the importance of decency.

Explain: That is decency of behavior that is good, moral, and acceptable in society.

Behavior that conforms to acceptable standards of morality or respectability, things required for a reasonable standard in life—that is our purpose and practices, principles of Christ today.

Today, in matters of doctrinal purposes, we must not allow those who have not increased in their studies and research to stunt our growth, but to their limited knowledge.

When coming up into Christ or growing up into him, I suggest that we surround ourselves with positive, optimistic thinkers.

Even outside the body of Christ, we find them; they are everywhere.

We believe that negative events are caused by external factors and that they are isolated, exceptions to the rule.

Optimistic thinking is more than a type of positive thinking; it is characterized by the belief that the future is full of hope and opportunities to be successful.

Now inside the body of Christ, most if not all should be positive in thinking.

Those who were before us spoke of those who still speak today who have labored long ago.

> Therefore, since we are surrounded by such a huge crowd of witnesses to the life of faith, let us strip off every weight that slows us down, especially the sin that so easily trips us up. And let us run with endurance the race God has set before us. (Hebrews 12:1)

Be Christlike.
Words seasoned with salt.

Submit

Don't allow the world to throw a rock into your marital pond.

Stay away from tricksters.

Listen to the Lord.

Life lessons are learned from past deceptions.

Don't let the devil turn your mind away from God.

You can be the best you can be, and that would be best (Romans 12:1–5).

Stay in your own lane for Jesus.

Jesus will make a good vessel for his use (1 Timothy 2:21).

Copying others is a form of hypocrisy, just be followers of Jesus (1 Peter 2:21), following the doctrine of God to your best efforts.

> For by the grace given me I say to every one of you:
>
> Do not think of yourself more highly than you ought, but rather think of yourself with sober judgment, in accordance with the faith God has distributed to each of you.
>
> For just as each of us has one body with many members, and these members do not all have the same function, so, in Christ we, though many, form one body, and each member belongs to all the others. (Romans 12:3–5)

Stand on your feet for Jesus.

> Therefore, put on the "full armor" of God, so that when the day of evil comes, you may be

able to stand your ground, and after you have
done everything, to stand. (Ephesians 6:13)

We crawl, we walk, and then we run.
Running the race for Jesus.

> Since we are surrounded by such a great
> cloud of witnesses (those were people listed in
> the hall of faith [Heb 11:1ff]), let us throw off
> everything that hinders and the sin that so easily
> entangles.
> And let us run with perseverance the race
> marked out for us. (Hebrews 12:1)

Listen, are you running? Let folks see you.
Are you an athlete for Jesus who is surrounded by witnesses to
this day?
Get in the race to win your crown of life (James 1:12).

> The "race," then, is the Christian life. It's a
> marathon, not a sprint, and we are called to stay
> the course and remain faithful to the end.

Paul used this same imagery near the end of his life: "I have
fought the good fight, I have finished the race, I have kept the faith"
(2 Timothy 4:7).

Teaching

Now as Gentiles are concerned, God brought the Gentiles in by the same blessings as the Jews (Acts 19).

Matthew, being a Jew, thought like most Jewish people thought.

For example, Peter (Galatians 2:11–13).

The Epistle to the Galatians, chapter 2.

Peter had traveled to Antioch, and there was a dispute between him and Paul.

Galatians 2:11–13 says:

> When Peter came to Antioch, I opposed him to his face, because he was clearly in the wrong.
>
> Before certain men came from James, he used to eat with the Gentiles; but when they were come, he withdrew and separated himself, fearing them which were of the circumcision.
>
> And the other Jews dissembled likewise with him; insomuch that Barnabas also was carried away with their dissimulation. (v. 13)
>
> But when I saw that they walked not uprightly according to the truth of the gospel, I said unto Peter before them all, If thou, being a Jew, livest after the manner of Gentiles, and not as do the Jews, why compellest thou the Gentiles to live as do the Jews? (v. 14)

How will you weigh this today? Between the different races of people. Well, you can't, because many are saved by the gospel; therefore, you cannot call out folks as viewed between races of people.

When reading your Bibles, ask yourself who is the author of the book talking to.

And why is he addressing the few, (if many) a concern of some particulars?

And how was the outcome?

Now listen. Romans 15:4 teaches us the things written before was for our learning.

One can learn how appointed men handle situations when either asked a question or was given a rebuke and then a reproach.

At times there could be some repeated behaviors we might be faced with.

But not so much as those who lived in that particular generation or time.

Some things are necessary for us today.

I'm personally tough in my opinion because I love the Lord and his people.

Test Yourselves

If you want to change the quality of your life, you must change the way you think.

The psalmist prayed, "Test me and know my anxious thoughts" (Psalm 139:23).

Now test yourselves as David did.

> Examine yourselves to see whether you are in the faith; test yourselves.
>
> Do you not realize that Christ Jesus is in you—unless, of course, you fail the test? (2 Corinthians 13:5)

My friends, God will help you become aware of what's going on.

Your mind can become a risk to your eternal destiny; don't let it be a risk but rather a privilege to your salvation (1 Corinthians 10:13).

God will not only show you how to remove wrong thoughts, but also how to replace them with the positive powerful thoughts by setting your mind on "what the Spirit desires."

> Those who live according to the flesh have their minds set on what the flesh desires; but those who live in accordance with the Spirit have their minds set on what the Spirit desires. (Romans 8:5)

Where do you want to live?

Have you thought about it?

Remember, 1 John 2:16 says, "For everything in the world-the lust of the flesh, the lust of the eyes, and the pride of life-comes not from—the Father but from the world."

Now where do you want to live? Meaning eternity (2 Corinthians 4:18).

Thankfulness

O give thanks unto the Lord; for he is good; for his mercy endures forever. (1 Chronicles 16:34)

Rejoice evermore.
Pray without ceasing. In everything give thanks: for this is the will of God in Christ Jesus concerning you. (1 Thessalonians 5:16–18)

Are you with me?

Thank God for everything.

Amen.

To live, be among the living, be alive (not lifeless, not dead).

Show joy and appreciation (Ephesians 2:1ff).

There is no "guess what's!"

Everything has a purpose, state your plan.

Otherwise!

People will use assumptions in a joke, where most lies are imposed (thrust).

State your purpose. Get on with it. Why the teaser?

There many things to be thankful for.

Good health. Family. God.

Good foods, olive garden.

Good friends. Church. Education.

I came to know God from my mother, when I was lying on the grass in Kentucky, looking up at the sky, and said, "What's up there?"

Mom said, "That's the sky." In continuing our conversation, she informed me that God is up there somewhere.

Of course, I didn't know anything about heaven back then.

That day, the sky was blue and beautiful; no clouds were in sight, as I can remember.

As I grew up, I asked my dad the same question; of course he gave the same attention to the question, saying, "God is up there."

I found myself going to church, Sunday school, learning who God is and those wonderful stories about God.

I wanted to know who this person was and his people.

Seems so magical, and there were so many questions I had.

I learned to appreciate those wonderful stories written about God.

Gave me hope and something to look forward to someday.

What is your story?

Training

Sometimes our beliefs may run a little bit short of what God intended them to be—in that if you give in to the slightest notion to move things differently than what the Word says, God gives an answer.

Read John 12:48.

And when you believe your thoughts above God's words, it makes it much harder for you to catch on when the truth has been told.

See the point.

Don't allow yourself to be locked out of eternity with God by locking yourself in eternal darkness away from the presence of God.

Read Hebrews 9:27.

You must believe the Word of God and be doers of it.

Test yourself, what will your answer be (2 Corinthians 13:5)?

Wil you change or not change?

Which?

Folks should change their minds to serve the master of Creation who spoke everything into existence.

Otherwise, no obedience, no life with God.

Psychology at its best.

> We surround ourselves with information that matches our beliefs.
>
> Plus, we tend to like people who think like us.
>
> Think about it, if we agree with someone's beliefs, we're more likely to be friends with them.
>
> While this makes sense, it means that we subconsciously begin to ignore or dismiss any-

thing that threatens "our world" and "how we may view" since we surround ourselves with people and information that confirm what we already think.

This is called confirmation bias.

If you've ever heard of the frequency illusion, this is very similar.

The frequency illusion occurs when you buy a new car, and suddenly you see the same car everywhere.

Or when a pregnant woman suddenly notices other pregnant women all over the place.

It's a passive experience, where our brains seek out information that's related to us, but we believe there's been an actual increase in the frequency of those occurrences.

Can it be changed?

No, there is a downside to this.

At times, maybe gear up just to wiggle into the minds of those whom we have the most concern, not necessarily to agree but to get what we want.

We want information.

We want to be accepted.

We want freedom, and to be in the in crowd controlled by freedom itself.

Thoughts created by self.

Trust

In a body, there is a manifested person.

The person who lives in that body is you.

Jesus lives in his body, the church.

Where is your trust worthiness, in yourself or in God?

Now the second question: where are you putting your trustworthiness, in something else or in God?

Think on these things.

Read 1 Corinthians 12:12–18.

Remember, teachers, the simple things people are lacking—the technicalities they feed on.

How sadly a few missed the point.

We used to sing the songs that build our soul; these days, songs are sung to just give you praise but not remind you of your obligation to God that matters.

One cannot build a house if you don't know the basics; how will you know which tools to use to build a house?

I saw a man pick up a blueprint but didn't know what the symbols mean, so he put it down and asked a skilled person to help him build the house.

Not so, my friends, it's supposed to be the skilled person who asks you, not the other way around; God's infinite wisdom knows those who can build a house.

Watch.

> So, Bezalel, Oholiab and every skilled person to whom the LORD has given skill and ability to know how to carry out all the work of con-

structing the sanctuary are to do the work just as the LORD has commanded. (Exodus 36:1ff)

Just recently I saw a lot of skilled persons build a Costco building near me; not one was unskilled.

No one was just sitting around finding things to do.

No one just hung around trying to escape the work, nor hid away from work.

Why?

Because it was a timely project that had to be done by a certain time.

And it was timely built; everything was put in place from the inside and out—perfect as it was planned.

Now, how would God help us to succeed?

By doing what was asked of you.

Remember the ark. Well, that ark is you.

Build it and take your family home to the promised land.

Who is your family?

Anyone who listens and obeys the will of God.

If you think your teacher is tough, wait 'til you get a boss.

He doesn't have tenure.

Bless your family.

Trust in God

> This is how love is made complete among us so that we will have confidence on the day of judgment:
> In this world we are like Jesus. (1 John 4:17)

My friends, consider your confidence in the Lord, in that you genuinely believe in the Lord, obey his word; steadfastly trust and allow faith to condition your heart.

It's so easy to become disappointed because we don't see life going the way we want it to, and we do not see the big picture that God is working through everything to produce in us a character like Jesus Christ.

We lose confidence in trusting God and begin to trust in ourselves and what we can accomplish.

Pride and arrogance take over quick, and we find ourselves forgetting the goodness and grace of God.

Then before we know it, something happens or goes wrong that we cannot control, and we blame God.

The Bible says there are some things we should not have confidence in. For example: "Have no confidence in the flesh" (Philippians 3:3).

Proverbs 14:16 says that a righteous man departs from evil, but a fool rages in his confidence. In other words, to arrogantly assume that sin has no consequences is a foolish confidence.

If we're going to be confident in something, let's view what it should be.

Psalm 118:8, 9 tells us what it should be: "It is better to trust in the Lord than to put confidence in man. It is better to trust in the Lord than to put confidence in princes."

Those who trust in government, finances, other people, or themselves will be disappointed in the end.

On the other hand, those who put their confidence in God will never be ashamed (Romans 10:11).

Unbelievers

There is a body of skeptics within our societies that cannot make up their minds to follow the righteousness of God, so another course is set forth in their chosen destiny.

> With every wicked deception directed against those who are perishing, because they refused the love of the truth that would have saved them.
> For this reason, God will send them a powerful delusion so that they will believe the lie, in order that judgment will come upon all who have disbelieved the truth and delighted in wickedness. (2 Thessalonians 2:10–12)

Then there is a body of eternal security.

They believe that "once saved, always saved."

Perseverance of the saints is a Christian teaching that asserts that once a person is truly "born of God" or "regenerated" by the indwelling of the Holy Spirit, nothing in heaven or earth "shall be able to separate from the love of God," resulting in a reversal of the converted condition.

False doctrine, false assumptions.

I have friends who believe the Bible but do not walk in faith.

> For it is by faith that we walk and not by sight. (2 Corinthians 5:7)

Show no acceptance to be living with sins.

In the past God overlooked such ignorance, but now he commands all people everywhere to repent. (Acts 17:30)

Be perfect, therefore, as your heavenly Father is perfect. (Matthew 5:48)

Therefore, beloved, since we have these promises, let us cleanse ourselves from everything that defiles body and spirit, perfecting holiness in the fear of God. (2 Corinthians 7:1)

Uncertainty

I have noticed that in talking with some, I see a problem in general conversation.

People who can't keep their mind on one particular thing will switch from one conversation then switch back, then go back and switch to something else, then switch back to their original thought—in general, in a five-minute conversation; they may have some serious issues with their neurological system.

But most will not bother to tell them.

Usually when there is a pattern of behavioral practices, it goes unnoticed to them.

Could be a practice from being around others.

Or a foothill practice.

People will get on your nerves that provoke you to turn away.

Have you welcomed Jesus into your life, are you partly to blame for standing away from Christ?

Your philosophy doesn't count.

Your ignorance is a bliss.

The phrase "ignorance is bliss" means that a lack of knowledge equals an absence of concern.

Such ignorant behavior says, "What I don't know can't hurt me." Ignorant people are not ensured to salvation and don't want to seek truth.

Plain and simple.

> Let them alone; they are blind guides. And if the blind lead the blind, both will fall into a pit. (Matthew 15:14)

How to spot uncertainty in people.

> Here are some signs that someone might be lying
> to you:
> People who are lying tend to change their head
> position quickly.
> Looking away often.
> Their breathing may also change.
> Eyes change.
> They tend to stand very still.
> Folding arms.
> They may repeat words or phrases.
> Saying same things over and over again.
> They may provide too much information.
> Want to get it off their mind very quickly.
> They "might" touch or cover their mouth.
> Or rub their nose, scratch their head, looking
> away.

All liars shall or will or must be burned up at judgment.

> But to the cowardly and unbelieving
> and having become abominable
> and murderers
> and the sexually immoral
> and sorcerers
> and idolaters
> and all liars, their portion is in the lake burning
> with fire and brimstone, which is the second
> death. (Revelation 21:8)

This is why being born again is so important to our salvation (John 3).

On the other hand, lies are imposed in an argument when an "argument from ignorance" is used, "also known as appeal to ignorance, a fallacy in informal logic. It asserts that a proposition is true because it has not yet been proven false."

It is probably a supposition (means uncertain).

Lies are built in an unknown language of the builders who continually use a different way to think about what they are doing.

Such will not come to define its conclusion from their first premise. Their argument is scattered and has no value to validity, making it invaded.

Many times, such will draw from their previous premise over and over again, but establishing a deserted place introduces no life.

Statements.

Unclean

W oe to her that is filthy and polluted, to the oppressing city!"

She obeyed not the voice; she received not correction; she trusted not in the LORD; she drew not near to her God.

Her princes within her are roaring lions; her judges are evening wolves; they gnaw not the bones till the morrow.

Her prophets are light and treacherous persons: her priests have polluted the sanctuary; they have done violence to the law. (Zephaniah 3:1–4)

But we are all as an unclean thing, and all our righteousness are as filthy rags; and we all do fade as a leaf; and our iniquities, like the wind, have taken us away. (Isaiah 64:6)

Unity

Behold, how good and how pleasant it is for brethren to dwell together in unity!

It is like the precious ointment upon the head. (Psalm 133:1–2)

When brethren don't, it never was of God, but of man.

For he seeth that wise men die, likewise the fool and the brutish person perish, and leave their wealth to others. (Psalm 49:10–13)

For he knoweth vain men: he seeth wickedness also; will he not then consider it? (Job 11:11, 12)

Vacation Plans

One should make every effort and opportunity that when you travel, come to know your distance brethren in Christ.

I've noticed that some brethren go on vacation on the Lord's day in distant locations and have not made contact with others.

Exhorting and reporting is the thing to do on the time God has given you.

Such a people will glorify themselves and not even think about going to church or meeting brethren and taking pictures. Yet such habits are to take pictures and make a photo album of buildings and other structures.

Give thanks to God in everything.

Vision

Visions are given to last more than two thousand years.

God is the author of visions for the purposes of growing his people for a home prepared in heaven (John 14:1ff).

> However, as it is written: "What no eye has seen, what no ear has heard, and what no human mind has conceived"—the things God has prepared for those who love him. (1 Corinthians 2:9)

Get in the vision.

Read Proverbs 11:30.

When you come to know your vision in your life, share your vision that God gave you. Stretch yourself to accomplish your goal. You don't own it; God gave you a vision for his particular purpose.

> Now to each one of us grace has been given according to the measure of the gift of Christ.
>
> This is why it says:
>
> "When He ascended on high, He led captives away, and gave gifts to men."
>
> What does "He ascended" mean, except that He also descended to the lower parts of the earth? (That might fulfill all things according to his will.) (Ephesians 4:7–9)

> He who descended is the one who also ascended far above all the heavens, that he might fill all things. (v. 10)

Watching your plan go into action is like having a written story just as God had planned it.

Nobody can tell your story like those who watch you operate within limited time, then your vision will become strategically strong by having the right motivation. Putting the right people in the direction following the goal.

Then you must give all glory and praise to God, by whom all blessings flow.

Amen.

Challenges are goals and objectives to meet.

Goal-scoring is your challenge, as in football or soccer or basketball etc.

Getting your aim by placing others in a direction to make it work.

Why?

Because it's a goal.

My short story, but within content of some groups (church folks): an offer was made to use tools that made a change.

Making it a goal because they didn't have one.

Because of certain groups, you may offer your tools, but they may not always accept your offer; how funny that when you teach tools or give folks tools in groups that could make a massive change for them, later they reject it, resulting in failure to them.

It's easy to stay in your comfort zone and not do anything but die in it.

I learned quickly that some people don't operate under goals. No vision. Nothing but assumptions and meeting alone.

> My people are destroyed for lack of knowledge: because thou hast rejected knowledge, I will also reject thee, that thou shalt be no priest to me: seeing thou hast forgotten the law of thy God, I will also forget thy children. (Hosea 4:6)

One time my plan was accepted by some, and quickly without question, their work increased to much larger results.

Later, the pulpit preacher of that particular group decided in his own fate, resulting in failure.

When he saw an increase, he told others, "I'm the preacher here, I call the shots."

Folks left; the group got smaller too than its original size: from 125-plus to thirteen or so, then back to ten in a short period of time.

Why? He looked back and not forward.

The force of vision left him.

Why?

He wasn't in the plan and didn't have a vision or a gift—no goals but a pride performer. Resulting in failure. Just like Judas Iscariot.

My friends, God gives gifts to men to restart their lives by sending his wisdom in human form. Sometimes you may recognize it, then sometimes you may be skeptical to what change may be.

That's okay, at least you will give God's angels or messengers a platform to speak a word to better build up the work in his kingdom.

The church on earth.

Remember.

Listen, folks, if you fail to plan, then you plan to fail.

Seeing at times some people from religious groups assign to others to think and plan for them; they can't think or plan themselves.

Having no tools means failure; this is why it's important to have tools to accomplish your goals—that is, the right kind of tools.

Long-term goals.

Seeing a vision unified by the group and working toward it.

By not having a goal means that you have a resolution that oftentimes fails to work; but by a few months, then without tabling their so-called goals, they called it goals, but it's their resolution.

Usually things of this sort will not last or are dismissed, and no one seems to care later.

Remember that feeding your goal is important; it needs food, or starvation will set in and take over your vision.

But grow in the grace and knowledge of our
Lord and Savior Jesus Christ. To him be glory
both now and forever! Amen. (2 Peter 3:18)

Always keep in mind Galatians 6:7.

> Be not deceived; God is not mocked: for whatsoever a man soweth, that shall he also reap.

Walk Steadfast

> The highway of the upright is to depart from evil: he that keepeth his way preserveth his soul. (Proverbs 16:17)

If you are in a dark place in your life and you want to be delivered, listen to the Word of God.

He will save you.

Listen carefully.

> You're blessed when you stay on course,
> walking steadily on the road revealed by God.
> You're blessed when you follow his directions,
> doing your best to find him.
> That's right—you don't go off on your own;
> you walk straight along the road he set.
> You, God, prescribed the right way to live;
> now you expect us to live it.
> Oh, that my steps might be steady,
> keeping to the course you set;
> Then I'd never have any regrets
> in comparing my life with your counsel.
> I thank you for speaking straight from your heart;
> I learn the pattern of your righteous ways.
> I'm going to do what you tell me to do;
> don't ever walk off and leave me. (Psalm 119:1–8)
> Let love be without dissimulation. Abhor that which is evil; cleave to that which is good. (Romans 12:9)

Read Psalm 1:1ff.

Don't drink out of the same cup your enemies drink from.

Excuse yourself from the table of evildoers.

God bless the world we live in and especially our country, that by every man might be saved by the gospel of Christ.

> The highway of the upright is to depart from evil: he that keepeth his way preserveth his soul. (Proverbs 16:17)

> Then Nebuchadnezzar spake, and said, Blessed be the God of Shadrach, Meshach, and Abednego, who hath sent his angel, and delivered his servants that trusted in him, and have changed the king's word, and yielded their bodies, that they might not serve nor worship any god, except their own God. (Daniel 3:28)

> I beseech you therefore, brethren, by the mercies of God, that ye present your bodies a living sacrifice, holy, acceptable unto God, which is your reasonable service. (Romans 12:1)

To beseech is to urge, beg, or advise everyone to do the right things in your chosen vessel given by God and being present in representing God in your body the best in your life (Revelation 4:11).

Now listen.

> Do not turn to the right or the left; keep your foot from evil. (Proverbs 4:27)

> The highway of the upright is to depart from evil: he that keepeth his way preserveth his soul. (Proverbs 16:17)

Praise the LORD! I will give thanks to the LORD with my whole heart, in the company of the upright, in the congregation.

He sent redemption unto his people: he hath commanded his covenant forever: holy and reverend is his name. (Psalm 111:1, 9)

Remember that no man can occupy the office of reverend, to which, beloved, it belongs to God.

Read Acts 4:12.

That no finite person, man or woman, on earth has given an everlasting covenant to any people in this life nor in the life to come.

God is holy and is effective. Double positive.

For any of your concerns, stop calling men or women "Reverend."

That name alone belongs to God.

War

The House and Senate fights are ongoing because of evils and tricky issues in bad places.

> For our struggle is not against flesh and blood, but against the rulers, against the authorities, against the powers of this dark world and against the spiritual forces of evil in the heavenly realms. (Ephesians 6:12)

Without any restrictions to reasoning, men fail to come to terms of its purpose.

Christians don't get into wars with those who are outside the gate.

For we stay within the promises of God; knowing the terror of God, we persuade men.

> Since, then, we know what it is to fear the Lord, we try to persuade others. What we are is plain to God, and I hope it is also plain to your conscience. (2 Corinthians 5:11)

But if Christians are subjected to such, remember James 4:1–4.

> From whence come wars and fighting's among you? come they not hence, even of your lusts that war in your members?

You lust, and have not: you kill, and desire to have, and cannot obtain you fight and war, yet you have not, because you ask not.

You ask, and receive not, because you ask amiss, that ye may consume it upon your lusts.

You bunch of adulterers and adulteresses, know you not that the friendship of the world is enmity with God? whosoever therefore will be a friend of the world is the enemy of God.

For I know the thoughts that I think toward you, says the Lord, thoughts of peace and not of evil, to give you a future and a hope. (Jeremiah 29:11)

Change is necessary to survive a nation.

Go to the church of the Lord and not a church of politics, where hate is formed against the Word of God.

Christians, that is the sum of us, will speak to keep God's people from being subjected to sins that are followed by judgment.

Warrior

Don't run, stand for truth, let the power of God give you mighty strength.

> David said to the Philistine, "You come against me with sword and spear and javelin, but I come against you in the name of the Lord Almighty, the God of the armies of Israel, whom you have defied.
>
> This day the Lord will deliver you into my hands, and I'll strike you down and cut off your head.
>
> This very day I will give the carcasses of the Philistine army to the birds and the wild animals, and the whole world will know that there is a God in Israel.
>
> All those gathered here will know that it is not by sword or spear that the Lord saves; for the battle is the Lord's, and he will give all of you into our hands. (1 Samuel 17:45–47)

It takes a warrior to stand and fight.
Otherwise, another may opt out from the gate.
Read John 6:66–68.
Want God to speak to you? Read the book.
This last dispensation comes in written form.
God speaks in the Word.
Folks are still living by the faith of osmosis, rather than the faith that was once delivered.

Today, a compiled book called the Bible, one has trouble reading it and knowing what God intends for us to do.

Listen.

> Beloved, although I was very eager to write to you about our common salvation, I found it necessary to write appealing to you to contend for the faith that was once for all delivered to the saints. (Jude 1:3)

Notice
The faith.
Not some or many faiths, but one.
If then one, why so many?

It is mankind who has established more than one faith, making it a choice you can make.

Not so, the Bible emphatically explicitly says one faith (Ephesians 4:1ff).

What God Hates

The Lord hates anyone who is arrogant; he will never let them escape punishment.

> Better to eat a dry crust of bread with peace
> of mind than have a banquet in a house full of
> trouble. (Proverbs 17:1)

Wisdom

Wisdom is the ability to discern and judge which aspects of that knowledge are true, right, lasting, and applicable to your life. It's the ability to apply that knowledge to the greater scheme of life. It's also deeper; knowing the meaning or reason; about knowing why something is, and what it means to your life.

Sometimes that could be hard for non-Christians to grasp.

Wisdom is pure, unearthly, and manages the Word of God in life (1 Corinthians 15:58).

Putting God back in America is the thing to keep; silencing evildoers can be accomplished by standing together as one.

President has led examples on how other countries can clean up their own messes in house.

For those who haven't grown in knowledge and truth, wisdom is far to reach for them.

Get wisdom, get understanding: forget it not; neither decline from the words of my mouth.

Forsake her not, and she shall preserve thee: love her, and she shall keep thee.

Wisdom is the principal thing; therefore, get wisdom: and with all thy getting get understanding.

Exalt her, and she shall promote thee: she shall bring thee to honour, when thou dost embrace her.

She shall give to thine head an ornament of grace: a crown of glory shall she deliver to thee. (Proverbs 4:5–9)

Wisdom is an honor to keep close to your mind.

It shall protect you and keep you from falling.

We work for money, we keep our bill in consideration, how then can any man keep themselves from not learning the commands of life?

Wisdom is worth finding.

Application is applied knowledge.

A useful tool to have.

Wise/Foolish

We tell the truth (John 17:17).

> A fool is quick-tempered, but a wise person
> stays calm when insulted. (Proverbs 12:16)

Wise Interpretation

Why do you allow others to interpret misleading information?
Read it.
Study it.
Meditate upon it.
The idea methodology of some of our denominational friends
is explicitly explained.

> Exegesis and eisegesis are two conflicting
> approaches in Bible study.
> Exegesis is the exposition or explanation of
> a text based on a careful, objective analysis.
> The word exegesis literally means "to lead
> out of."
> That means that the interpreter is led to his
> conclusions by following the text.

Here's what they do, denominational churches.

> The opposite approach to Scripture is eise-
> gesis, which is the interpretation of a passage
> based on a subjective, non-analytical reading.
> The word eisegesis literally means "to lead
> into," which means the interpreter injects his
> own ideas into the text, making it mean whatever
> he wants.

For examples.
They believe in women preachers, deacons, and bishops.

They believe the Lord's Supper is to be taken once a month.

They believe "once saved, always saved," no matter what you do, that God will not leave you or forsake you. They believe in entertainment—music instruments while they worship.

They believe in gay wedding and entertainment.

They do not believe in the Bible commands—as it exists today as it was when it was first written.

They believe in not talking to us, when the Bible speaks about sins.

They believe that baptism is not essential for salvation.

And the list comes from interventionism from its convention's headquarters.

Witness

T here's a train bound for glory; don't you want to go?

All you need is faith and obedience—that's the ticket.

Just one ticket (Ephesians 4:5).

Have you noticed that if you are too good to some people, they interpret as weird?

Strange how many are still in captivity.

Its strategies probably will never change.

Then some of which have misused the scriptures.

> Woe unto you, when all men shall speak well of you! for so did their fathers to the false prophets. (Luke 6:26)

The project to their thinking is their cohabitation in the sense that some are keeping company with the wrong people in wrong places.

Read Psalm 1:1ff.

> But now I have written to you not to keep company with anyone named a brother, who is sexually immoral, or covetous, or an idolater, or a reviler, or a drunkard, or an extortioner—not even to eat with such a person. (1 Corinthians 5:11)

Yes, all these things listed are important to know.

What happens is the sum total have lost their will in their lives by copying others or seeking others and by living a lifestyle not associated with God.

Then if we are not a friend of the world as they, the sum total will see us as weird.

Of course, they know that you are religious, but they will distance themselves from you or either pull you away from your convictions, to their lifestyles.

Since we step out on faith, we don't step away from faith by copying the world's actions and their sin faiths.

Whereas ours is one faith, the world has many faiths of sins.

Our actions are active in God, so we smile, invite, and welcome the other sheep to come to the better side of life.

> Jesus said, I have other sheep that are not of this sheep pen. I must bring them also.
> They too will listen to my voice, and there shall be one flock and one shepherd. (John 10:16)

This means there are those who are almost there but really haven't made up their minds as yet.

Mark 16:1–16

So, we work for Jesus.

As our preacher said Sunday night, "I say to all of you, make your light shine brighter. Don't let your light go dim. Adjust the switch in your life. Turn the light up."

Who were all the prophets who testified, and what did Luke mean or Peter by saying,

> All the prophets testify about Him that everyone who believes in Him receives forgiveness of sins through His name. (Acts 10:43)

Was Peter as Luke recorded, meaning the sum total of all prophets or the totality of prophets listed in the OT?

To best grab a handle on this, I would favor the following: "To him give all the prophets witness." See Isaiah 9:6, Isaiah 52:7, Isaiah 53:5, Isaiah 53:6, Isaiah 59:20, Jeremiah 31:34, Daniel 9:24, Micah 7:18, and Zechariah 13:1. As Jesus Christ was the sum and substance of the law given unto us.

> And you know that God anointed Jesus of Nazareth with the Holy Spirit and with power. Then Jesus went around doing good and healing all who were oppressed by the devil, for God was with him. (Acts 10:38)

> And we apostles are witnesses of all he did throughout Judea and in Jerusalem.
> They (certain ones of the Jews) put him to death by hanging him on a cross, Him God raised up the third day, and showed him openly;
> He was not seen by all the people, but by witnesses whom God had already chosen—by us who ate and drank with him after he rose from the dead. (vv. 39–41)

Proof that God has control of all things.

> And he ordered us (Apostles) to preach everywhere and to testify that Jesus is the one appointed by God to be the judge of all—the living and the dead. (vv. 42)

If Jesus was a real person, why do others say he was not?

> Dear friends, do not believe every spirit, but test the spirits to see whether they are from God, because many false prophets have gone out into the world. (1 John 4:1)

Remember this:

> Then the prophet replied, "I too am a prophet like you, and an angel spoke to me by the word of the LORD, saying, 'Bring him back with you to your house, so that he may eat bread and drink water.'"
>
> The old prophet was lying to him, etc. (1 Kings 13:18)

> "The prophets are prophesying lies in My name," the LORD replied. "I did not send them or appoint them or speak to them.
>
> They are prophesying to you a false vision, a worthless divination, the futility and delusion of their own minds. (Jeremiah 14:14)

> This is what the LORD of Hosts says: "Do not listen to the words of the prophets who prophesy to you. They are filling you with false hopes. They speak visions from their own minds, not from the mouth of the LORD. (Jeremiah 23:16)

> For this is what the LORD of Hosts, the God of Israel, says: Do not be deceived by the prophets and diviners among you, and do not listen to the dreams you elicit from them. (Jeremiah 29:8)

> Beware of false prophets. They come to you in sheep's clothing, but inwardly they are ravenous wolves. (Matthew 7:15)

We are to study and examine the Word of God to show ourselves approved, as a workman who is not ashamed (2 Timothy 2:15, Acts 17).

Women

Let's see.

Women are not designed to crawl around on their stomachs like men do in army training or combat.

That's the world's view apart from the exact command of God.

> For thousands of years of military wisdom and noble instincts that reasoning would have been unintelligible. Of course, there are women of valor.
>
> But for a male commander-in-chief to say that since they are willing to die in combat, therefore we should arm them for it, is a non-sequitur, and a shame on the president's manhood.

Some women want to disregard what they are supposed to do. After the sin of both humans.

The echoes of this ultimate manhood in Christ are found throughout the Bible as men take the initiative to protect their women.

And when Barak insists that Deborah go with him to battle, she makes it clear that this will be to his shame: "I will surely go with you. Nevertheless, the road on which you are going will not lead to your glory" (Judges 4:9).

Jael would get the glory.

She put a tent peg through the skull of the enemy commander (Judges 4:21, 5:24–26).

She was a woman of great valor.

And all the more so because she was not a soldier.

> The Lord God said to the woman,
> "I will increase your pain when you give birth.
> You will be in great pain when you have children.
> You will long for your husband.
> And he will rule over you."
> The Lord God said to Adam,
> "You listened to your wife's suggestion. You ate
> fruit from the tree I warned you about. I
> said, 'You must not eat its fruit.'
> "So, I am putting a curse on the ground because
> of what you did.
> All the days of your life you will have to work
> hard.
> It will be painful for you to get food from the
> ground.
> You will eat plants from the field,
> even though the ground produces thorns and
> prickly weeds.
> You will have to work hard and sweat a lot
> to produce the food, you eat.
> You were made out of the ground.
> You will return to it when you die.
> You are dust,
> and you will return to dust."

The woman is designed for the home.
Her body is formed to have children.
She can work in helping her husband (unless she doesn't have one), but not to become a man.
Women who dress and behave like men have lost their station.
God created man and woman, that is, male and female.
Impersonators are not a creation of God and cannot be mocked.
Man is always man, and woman is always a woman.

One could look like a female or a male, but those parts put into by God's created system is fixed; that will not change.

Parents are man and woman.

Not two she's and two he's living together as man and wife.

If you don't know what this means, read Romans 1:25–27.

Listen now.

> Know ye not that your bodies are the members of Christ? shall I then take the members of Christ, and make them the members of an harlot? God forbid.
>
> What? know ye not that he which is joined to an harlot is one body? for two, saith he, shall be one flesh.
>
> But he that is joined unto the Lord is one spirit.
>
> Flee fornication. Every sin that a man doeth is without the body; but he that committeth fornication sinneth against his own body.
>
> What? know ye not that your body is the temple of the Holy Ghost, which is in you, which ye have of God, and ye are not your own?
>
> For ye are bought with a price: therefore, glorify God in your body, and in your spirit, which are God's. (1 Corinthians 6:15–20)

Hard saying, difficult to explain.

Never call a woman a weaker vessel (1 Peter 3:7).

Peter uses exaggerated statement, commonly called hyperbole.

God did not create any woman weaker, then man.

Nor did he think man had a weaker side when he caused a deep sleep to fall upon man while he created a woman out of man.

What Peter emphasizes here: she was deceived by Satan in the beginning (1 Peter 3:7).

Question: Would a man marry an idiot?

Or has she become an idiot after marrying her?

God didn't create such a partnership.

No no no.

God gave specific commands not to eat of the forbidden fruit (Genesis 3:3); she ate and gave to her husband. He ate. Right!

Now, is he weak as well?

No.

Notice what Peter is saying.

The whole of any conjugal conversation is all the responsibility and duties incumbent on men in a married state.

Yes, the wife plays a big part in marriage.

She is not only the helper, but she was given to man from God and blesses him in their marriage.

Notice, my friends: by this, it is not necessarily meant that she is of feebler capacity or of inferior mental endowments, but she is more tender and delicate—more subject to infirmities and weaknesses; and some might be less capable of enduring fatigue and toil or less adapted to the rough and stormy scenes of life.

> So, take a new grip with your tired hands and
> strengthen your weak knees. (Hebrews 12:12)

She is not weak.

Today, Christian women are subject to their husbands and do everything to keep their home a beautiful place.

She is not weak.

What has happened before time does not necessarily happen in our Christian walk today.

Historically speaking, we are confident that Peter died under the reign of Nero. The story goes that he was crucified upside down.

This would be around AD 67–68 or before.

I see where people would decorate their houses with spooky stuff all over the place, as if Halloween was a Christmas story.

Not so.

Yet it shows that evil looks have a place in our generation.

No need to advocate more.

Let's talk a little more about soul salvation.

The Word

There are world floods before us today.
Christ's message never changes.
Preach Christ, save lives.

> Save others by snatching them out of the fire; to others show mercy with fear, hating even the garment stained by the flesh. (Jude 1:23)

Remember Mark 16:15–16.

The truth is, while many Churches of Christ don't mention Christmas at church, that does not mean you can't say it or celebrate it at home.

And many have.

The Word of God

Psalm 13:3 suggests that those who are bound together without God rather than the guidance of God fall short of God's providence. God moves where others can't see.

> Please listen, LORD God, and answer my prayers.
> Make my eyes sparkle again, or else I will fall into the sleep of death.

> Wake up, thou that sleepest, and arise up from among the dead, and the Christ shall shine upon thee. (Ephesians 5:14)

> God says, "You are not going to believe what I am about to tell you,
> Habakkuk, but I am already at work to deliver you and punish the sinners around you." (Habakkuk 1:5–11)

Answer: we must understand what God's work is. Psalm 74:12 says, "God is…working salvation in the midst of the earth."

Words

Don't curse, use words that count.

Words that encourage rather than describe yourself as ignorant (unlearned).

Do as it is written (2 Timothy 3:16).

> Do not let any unwholesome talk come out of your mouths, but only what is helpful for building others up according to their needs, that it may benefit those who listen. (Ephesians 4:29)

> Everything you say should be kind and well thought out so that you know how to answer everyone. (Colossians 4:6)

Remember this one thing.
God is not mocked (Galatians 6:7).

> Do not be deceived: God is not mocked, for whatever one sows, that will he also reap.

> Mocking God means disrespecting, dishonoring, denying or ignoring His existence.
> It is a serious offense committed by those who David describes as wicked because there is "no fear of God before "their "eyes" (Psalm 36:1).

> But God is not mocked for long and eventually there will be consequences for such behavior.

In the Bible mockery is a behavior and attitude shown by the fool Psalm 74:22, the wicked Psalm 1:1, the enemy Psalm 74:10, the hater of knowledge Proverbs 1:22; 13:1, the proud Psalm 119:51; Isaiah 37:17, and the unteachable, Proverbs 15:12.

The mocker's heart is cold and, in his foolishness, and wickedness, he makes a conscious decision to turn his back on God and pursue evil. Mockers lack humility, wisdom, and goodness in spiritual matters. (Christian Marcel)

What the Bible speaks of is of great importance for your salvation.

Do what it says.

Elders are without excuse.

Citizens in the church are without excuse.

Not a joking matter.

Either you're in or out of the church in the heavenly world.

Go to the Word for answers; don't distance yourself from God.

Work for the Lord

GET UP AND START MOVING.

Have you ever got tired of your responsibilities to Christ?

And ask yourselves why you have waited so long and just gave up? Hmm.

I tell you, it is not Jesus, for he gives you strength to carry on; perhaps you find no joy in saving souls, working for Jesus.

So then when a man fails to plan, he plans to fail.

Don't waste your eternal life on the foolishness of this world.

Life is short.

Forfeiting your claim on eternal life is just devastating.

Stay heaven bound.

You must do the work of God.

Read Matthew 28:18–18 and Revelation 4:11.

A mess is a mess before our public view and a disgrace to our growing economy and democracy.

If the far left wanted resolution, why put up a fight to gain power?

Power comes with a growing age of reasoning and results, but not to compromise your office of reasoning.

Work of God

The sea, the work of God, spoken in action.

> When Jesus woke up, he rebuked the wind and said to the waves, "Silence! Be still!" Suddenly the wind stopped, and there was a great calm. (Mark 4:39)

> Who stills the roaring of the seas, The roaring of their waves, And the tumult of the peoples? (Psalm 65:7)

> You rule the swelling of the sea; When its waves rise, you still them. (Psalm 89:9)

> He caused the storm to be still, so that the waves of the sea were hushed. (Psalm 107:29)

Work Together

W hen we have successful leaders in the military, we all support each other's mission.

Team participation is what it is all about.

We all count in making the military work.

I've never found or even heard of a Navy ship that didn't work together in war.

We are qualified in everything that calls for our participation.

A house divided against itself cannot stand (Matthew 12:25).

I believe this government cannot endure permanently if it disrespects the other parties. There must be respect of the constitution and its integrity.

I do not expect the Union to be dissolved; I do not expect the house to fall, but I do expect it will cease to be divided.

Works

If a man steps out of the doctrine of Christ, he will find it not easy to be accepted by others in the denominational realm of religion because they would want to know why he did it.

And if it doesn't satisfy their culture, he is rejected.

So, my friends, don't step out into a world of make-believe.

Such will go nowhere but left alone.

> But seek first his kingdom and his righteousness, and all these things will be given to you as well. (Matthew 6:33)

That means you will come to know all things that are written that have satisfied God.

Read John 12:48.

Never sit on your doorstep doing nothing when there's work to do for God.

Read Mark 16:15–16 and Proverbs 11:30.

> I must work the works of him that sent me, while it is day: the night cometh, when no man can work. (John 9:4 beloved King James Version)

They say a person needs just three things to be truly happy in this world: someone to love, something to do, and something to hope for.

If a man goes hunting, should he pet his prey before destroying it?

How shall he feed his stomach if he shows compassion upon his prey?

Discipline thyself, esteem others the same.
Enjoy your life.

> Nothing is better for man than to eat and drink and enjoy his work.
> I have also seen that this is from the hand of God.
> For apart from Him, who can eat and who can find enjoyment?
> To the man who is pleasing in His sight, He gives wisdom and knowledge and joy, but to the sinner He assigns the task of gathering and accumulating that which he will hand over to one who pleases God.
> This too is futile and a pursuit of the wind. (Ecclesiastes 2:24–26)

For you of little concerns.

Fix everything that has been left broken in your work.

Doing nothing should be off the table.

Get proactive and have a mission to finish your goals.

Brethren, step up.

Not sit up.

Amen!

Build, paint, add more classrooms; change your order of style about things.

Same ole stuff over the years that had not increased are not worth to continue, where things are not going anywhere.

Rebuild, rethink, revive.

If the church is going to be autonomous apart from other denominations, then prove yourself not to model yourself after another.

Build your own work, serve God, build.

Keeping up with other manufacturers is dining from another table.

Carefully using Paul's inspiring words of wisdom, to borrow from this account carefully.

> By the grace God has given me, I laid a foundation as a wise builder, and someone else is building on it. But each one should build with care. (1 Corinthians 3:10)

> The LORD says, "The women of Zion are haughty, walking along with outstretched necks, flirting with their eyes, strutting along with swaying hips, with ornaments jingling on their ankles." (Isaiah 3:16)

When the sum of you know this, then why are you thus looking, longing to test God?

Read 1 John 2:16.

In fact, this is the cause of every sin in the world today.

Man testing God.

It is time for all men to come to the aid of their habitation and manage it rightfully in the sight of God.

Not to worry about past time but present time (Philippians 3:13).

Listen to your Bible.

> LORD, I know that people's lives are not their own; it is not for them to direct their steps. (Jeremiah 10:23)

> But blessed is the one who trusts in the LORD, whose confidence is in him. (Jeremiah 17:7)

> He will be like a tree planted by the waters that sends out its roots toward the stream.
> It does not fear when the heat comes, and its leaves are always green.

It will not worry in a year of drought or
cease to produce fruit. (v. 8)

We are the engine behind the gospel (Mark 16:15–16). Your electrical skills are needed (Romans 12:10).

Innovation is suggested in your work already, keep your upgrade (Exodus 35:35).

Why have your own house denied and then suggested sitting in castles while your feet are dirty?

Don't you know that others follow your history in life?

Set your foundation to be fitted to walk upon before your broader perspective.

What does this mean?

A mental view, a cognitive orientation, a way of seeing a situation or a scene; the more truth we bring into our lives, the more we reduce our ignorance and enrich our lives overall, creating ourselves anew.

Worship

Listen, at your place of worship, there might be some people who will refuse to conform to the image of Christ.

Why?

Because they get wet instead of being baptized for their remission of sins.

Some of which chose to walk alongside with Jesus but don't get into Christ (John 6:66).

How to get into Christ requires that you study your Bible.

Read 2 Corinthians 5:17, Romans 6:3, 2 Timothy 2:15, 2 Timothy 3:16.

Don't take your eyes off God.

Stop fighting party politics. The devil is trying to destroy the people of God. Rather, set your foundation with the Lord God of heaven.

Read Colossians 3:1–3.

Listen.

> Worship the Lord your God, and his blessing will be on your food and water. I will take away sickness from among you. (Exodus 23:25)

> If, (a thing to consider) my people, who are called by my name, will humble themselves and pray and seek my face and turn from their wicked ways, then I will hear from heaven, and I will forgive their sin and will heal their land. (2 Chronicles 7:14)

A quick release in a matter of seconds.

Perpetual and a reasonable thought of concern.

You don't have to put a ton of your energy into a thing that has but little respect for you.

But one advice given: you can pray for them.

Listen to your Bible.

> Therefore, I exhort first of all that supplications, prayers, intercessions, and giving of thanks be made for all men, for kings and all who are in authority, that we may lead a quiet and peaceable life in all godliness and reverence.
>
> For this is good and acceptable in the sight of God our Savior. (1 Timothy 2:1–3)

The Lord bless you
and keep you;
the Lord make his face shine on you
and be gracious to you;
the Lord turn his face toward you
and give you peace. (Numbers 6:24–26)

> For I know the plans I have for you, declares the Lord, plans to prosper you and not to harm you, plans to give you hope and a future. (Jeremiah 29:11)

But blessed is the one who trusts in the Lord,
whose confidence is in him.
They will be like a tree planted by the water
that sends out its roots by the stream.
It does not fear when heat comes;
its leaves are always green.
It has no worries in a year of drought
and never fails to bear fruit. (Jeremiah 17:7–8)

Have you put the totality of your trust in the Lord today?
Think about it, do it, believe all the way to the end.
Salvation promised (James 4:14).
Read 2 Corinthians 4:18.
Eternal life gained (1 Corinthians 2:9).

Your Appearance

For "the grace of God" that brought salvation to all men teaches us many good things (Titus 2:11).

To the man who sees himself in the mirror, are you looking at Jesus in you?

> Now we see but a dim reflection as in a mirror; then we shall see face to face. Now I know in part; then I shall know fully, even as I am fully known. (1 Corinthians 13:12)

Why? Because when you grow, you change. Christians look beyond into the eternal side (1 Peter 3:18 and 2 Peter 3:18).

> But as it is written, Eye hath not seen, nor ear heard, neither have entered into the heart of man, the things which God hath prepared for them that love him. (1 Corinthians 2:9)

> And after observing himself goes away and immediately forgets what he looks like. (James 1:24)

Why have you changed your appearance (Romans 12)?

Your Value

Listen, ye who graduate, take your degree and make someone great.

Don't take that paper and hang it on the wall to try and make yourself great; that's not how you change the world.

One is already great from your astute academic studies.

Staying in school all your life teaches you nothing.

Folks donating laptops, shoes, and computers, giving you money and equipment has ceased.

How can you learn anything without experience?

You must cross the bridge to learn how to fail then win in your life. There is going to be a blessing and a lesson.

Don't fool yourself into thinking that you will not fail or that you will not experience failures.

Get over it.

Be a stronghold in someone's life and teach others, and make the greatest possible productive life of success you can in the lives of others.

Build a bridge, take someone else across the bridge.

Folks need to taste life.

Teachers who taught you have made you great, and you are, so now go teach others to be great, not successful.

Don't worry about that.

Let God control your life.

Success will either come or go, depending upon circumstances surrounding you.

Your days of freebies are over.

Show your greatness by building others to become great.

Teach.

Your greatest is in your imagination.

But don't tell your imagination to the wrong people.

If you allow others to destroy your imagination, you just set fire to your dream.

Your meaning in life gives you purpose and sets the direction of how you want to live your life. Without meaning, you will spend the rest of your life wandering through life aimlessly with no direction, focus, or purpose.

Haven't you seen persons who pass on opportunities just to wiggle out of challenging opportunities?

They pass up the door to enter another door of nowhere.

Why?

Because the door they are looking at is dressed up to look like a career opportunity, but isn't the right door.

Wasting your life blaming others for putting up false doors, but they're not to blame; that was your decision to correctly make good decisions for your own greatness.

Challenge yourself to greatness, don't worry about something else, focus on you.

Covetousness is a failed opportunity for you to develop your skills in your life.

Just be you.

Remember, when you help someone other than members from your own family, you will have an opportunity in making that person great.

Launch out; your opportunity has changed.

Remember the Gospel is God's power to save.

Read Romans 1:16.

Talk to other important people and find a clue, discover how they got where they are at now.

They all had struggles in life, and they came out of them to greatness.

It's never too late, and don't give up trying.

To find your place in society, a place where you can teach another greatness.

Time is scrutinized, time is now, time is short.

You are valuable to God, so let your gifts be known.

Dining with minds of deception is a lack of trust in partnership with God.

When you have partnership with God, you trust in him fully.

Negativity has no partnership with royalty.

Leave junk food alone.

Your answer is with God.

Remember that.

Also, people tend to lose their partnership with each other in a relationship by listening to folks who have neither a partnership nor a pattern of responsibility perfect with God.

Such people are arching for negativity.

My answer to that is, leave them alone.

They are guided by deception.

What this means by principle: if folks don't appear to be in partnership, they are onlookers.

Therefore, their actions are in question.

Their laughter is your failure.

As for me, I'm looking for opportunities to bridge, not for losses.

When the devil is looking for help, he then tends to run over to Christians (weak) and begs for mercy; and when you give it, he smiles.

From that point, he began using you for all purpose.

Leave him alone (John 8:44).

Give no opportunity to the devil (Ephesians 4:27).

> Be alert and of sober mind. Your enemy the
> devil prowls around like a roaring lion looking
> for someone to devour. (1 Peter 5:8)

Don't help a devilish liar.

Read John 8:44.

Look, leaders, tell more your group how important this is.

As for me, I am sober to all possibilities.

Your Work

Do you know the way to finish the course? Keep looking to Jesus.

I've been preaching the Gospel over years, and God knows I have my faults and sins.

He also knows I repent and aim to get right with him each and every day.

I'm far from perfect, but I can testify that God has kept me on course.

He has kept me preaching the Gospel.

Finishing the course God has planned for us is never easy.

It cannot be easy, but we can be steadfast, unmovable, always abounding in the work of the Lord (1 Corinthians 15:58).

It takes discipline and hard work.

It takes picking ourselves up, dusting ourselves off, and starting over when you fall.

One of these days, you are going to have to look back on your life; and I hope you will be able to say that you fought as a warrior and finished as an athlete.

Good Christian warriors.

Point: "Let us lay aside every weight, and the sin which doth so easily beset us, and let us run with patience the race that is set before us, looking unto Jesus the author and finisher of our faith" (Hebrews 12:1b–2a).

Keep on looking, keep on doing for Jesus.

But don't look back (Luke 9:62).

About the Author

J. Marcel Shipe

Attended—Nashville Bible School 1990, Bible and Greek Language

South East Biblical Institute (formally called) East Tennessee School of Preaching and Mission

Studies in Bible, Missions, Ethics, and Greek Language, 1990–1993 Diploma

Johnson Bible College 1994–1995, Biblical Studies, Speech and Communications, Marriage & Family and Philosophy.

Taught Bible classes in Tennessee and California

Former Director of Lectureship Committees in Fresno CA

Educational Director

Ingram Content Group UK Ltd.
Milton Keynes UK
UKHW010657250423
420747UK00001B/7